ROBERT BURNS – A LIFE

Robert Burns—
A Life

HUGH DOUGLAS

READERS UNION
Group of Book Clubs
Newton Abbot 1977

Contents

Illustrations

between pages 64 and 65

ACKNOWLEDGEMENTS

Scottish National Portrait Gallery nos. 1, 2, 3, 4, 5, 12, 13, 14, 15, 16, 17, 19, & 29.; Radio Times Hulton no. 6; Edinburgh Booksellers' Association no. 18; R. Bankes Esq. no. 21; The Dick Institute, Kilmarnock no. 9

To the memory of my Father

For Mother,
Amelia and Margaret
and all who remember
Monkwood Mains

Envy, if thy jaundiced eye,
Through this window chance to spy,
To thy sorrow thou shalt find,
All that's generous, all that's kind,
Friendship, virtue, every grace,
Dwelling in this happy place.

Foreword

My father was a farmer upon the Carrick border O
And carefully he bred me, in decency and order O
He bade me act a manly part, though I had ne'er a farthing O
For without an honest manly heart, no man is worth regarding, O.

I have that in common with Robert Burns, and it formed a starting-point for thinking about the man who represents Scotland and the Scot more than any other. Life on a tenant farm close to the River Doon in my childhood in the 1930s may have been gentler than that which William Burnes and his family knew in the 1760s, yet its quality was very much the same.

Both were times of rapid change and insecurity and of long, hard hours of ill-rewarded work. There was little time to stop to admire the folding Ayrshire hills, for to us, as to Burns, this was earth which needed much persuasion to give up its harvest. It is land which has seen joy and contentment but much suffering too, for it knew the fiery youth of William Wallace and Robert the Bruce, the feuding Kennedies and the dour, unyielding Covenanters. This was the place that made all of them: it made Burns, it made me.

For many years I have felt that, grateful as we ought to be to the fine scholars who have worked on Burns and his writings in this century, we have reached a point at which the poet has come under so many microscopes that we tend to see only the details of his life, much magnified, and to lose sight of Robert Burns, the man and the poet. It is time to rediscover him and to place him in the context of his time and in relation to the people whom he knew.

It is hard for a man to spend his life in the public eye: it is hard to pass eternity there – yet that is the fate of Robert Burns. Since Dr James Currie produced the first Life of Burns in 1800, only four years after the poet's death, there has been an endless succession of writings, some factual, some embroidered, but many parading the author's opinions rather than the poet's life and works. Scottish people, and now the world, have made their own assessment of Burns without these opinions of others. It is so now, and it was so in the early days when George Thomson, Robert Heron and Currie were writing about his excesses, for the first Burns club was formed only five years after the poet's death – at Greenock, a town which he visited briefly if at all.

Today this affection for Burns has grown into a cult, a kind of worship, which, for many Burnsians, permits no whisper of criticism. And that is a pity, for Burns was neither a man nor a poet in pure black and white. His was a life of a hundred shades of grey, and his poetry ranged from the hastily tossed-off, topical piece to gems in the Scottish tongue. There can be no heights without hollows, no greatness without lesser moments, and the truth about Burns lies somewhere between the Victorian's sore sinner and the idolator's demigod. In short, Burns was a human being who, if he lived his life over again, would order it very differently – and the result would be very much the same!

In this search for Robert Burns I have read those authors who have devoted years of scholarship to the poet. I am grateful to many libraries, but especially to the National Library of Scotland; the British Library; the London Library; the Carnegie Library, Ayr; the Mitchell Library, Glasgow; Edinburgh Public Library and the Dick Institute, Kilmarnock. On visits to places connected with Burns in Ayrshire and Dumfriesshire over many years I have met with unfailing courtesy and interest in the poet – how much less fortunate was John Keats who complained of the landlord at the cottage at Alloway when he visited it: "The dull dog made me write a dull sonnet." The late Mr John Gray of Ayr took an interest in my project, and the Tam O' Shanter Museum, Ayr, lent me copies of the *Burns Chronicle*, which made research work easier. Mr James Hunter of the Dick Institute,

Kilmarnock, and my good friend, Mr James T. Gray of Maybole, have both been generous with assistance and advice – my thanks to both.

My family and friends have given much encouragement, especially my mother, who has been her usual generous self in acting as a link between me and many people in Ayrshire. My wife, Sheelagh, and Jean Land have read the manuscript and proofs and given much sound advice. I am grateful to all of them for their part in the progress of *Robert Burns – A Life*.

Hugh Douglas

1

A Well-Inclined Lad

The Burnes family were good east coast lowlanders from that part of Scotland with which our generation has become familiar through Lewis Grassic Gibbon's trilogy of North-east Scotland, *A Scots Quair*. Segget lay in the valley of the Bervie water in the district of Kincardineshire called the Mearns, a land of small upland farms, straggling villages and sober kirks stretching inland and south from Stonehaven. It was hard country which made granite men like William Burnes, father of the poet Robert Burns. (The name was pronounced Burns, and the poet was the first of the family to omit the 'e'.)

Gibbon's description of the Burnes family and their life has all the starkness of the Mearns in time past. Of the poet's grandfather, another Robert, he wrote: "His folk had ups and downs of all flesh till the father of Robert Burns grew up, and grew sick of the place, and went off to Ayr, and there the poet Robert was born, him that lay with nearly as many women as Solomon did, though not all at one time."

What a devastatingly bleak assessment. There is no evidence to suggest that William left home because he was sick of the place: he moved because his family were poverty-stricken and he had to find his own living, and the account of his departure which he gave to his sons is full of deep regret, neither rancour nor revulsion stirring him as he described how he and his brother looked back towards their beloved Mearns for the last time.

Up to 1700 the tenor of life in the Mearns had been tolerably even, for the North-east missed the sharp agonies of Covenanting times when the killing was confined to the South and South-west. A great many Mearns folk were Episcopalians who had no quarrel with the king over his desire to have bishops grace the Kirk, but even the Presbyterian religion thereabouts was not tinged with the zeal of the south-western Scots who had died for their faith rather than change it.

Grandfather Robert Burnes grew to manhood in the early years of the eighteenth century and earned a living as a gardener in the service of George Keith, the Earl Marischal. Keith had served Queen Anne well, but on her death he joined the Jacobite cause of the exiled Old Pretender. We do not know whether Burnes followed the Earl at the outbreak of the '15 Rising or not, although his grandson has suggested that he did. This is unlikely, however, since Burnes, a Presbyterian, would have been opposed both to the Stuarts and to the Catholic religion which they would have imposed on him. Whether Burnes joined the Jacobites or not is of little consequence. He suffered with them. When the Earl Marischal fled to the Continent following the collapse of the rising he was attainted and his estates were forfeited to the crown. As a result, Burnes lost his livelihood.

But life went on. Robert married Isabella Keith of Criggie in Dunottar parish, and at last in 1720 he managed to take over the tenancy of Clochnahill farm just a mile north of Fiddes Castle. The Burneses already had two sons, James, born in 1717, and Robert, born in 1719. On 11th November 1721 a third son, William, was added to the family, to be followed by Margaret (1723), Elspet (1725), Jean (1727), George (1729), Isabel (1730) and Mary (1732).

For a time Robert and Isabella Burnes fared well enough on the bare soil of Clochnahill, but they were eternally short of capital to buy equipment, stock, fertilizers and seed, so that in time bankruptcy loomed over them, and Robert was forced to raise a loan and take over two small farms to try to make ends meet. Hunger seldom left their doorstep until a severe winter in 1740, coupled with persistent low prices, brought the family to the brink of starvation. Then the '45 Rising, which brought chaos, terror and depression, left behind it a new order with which Robert Burnes just could not cope. He was finally forced to abandon Clochnahill and move to Denside at Dunottar to live on the charity of his daughter Elspet and her well-doing husband, John Caird. Young James Burnes left home to live in Montrose where he was a wright and eventually became a member of the town council. A little later the other surviving sons, Robert and William (George had died young), also had to leave to make their own way in the world. It was a hard decision and it hurt the old man and his sons equally.

William, a gardener like his father, was a tall young man with a serious, expressive face and a lively mind. He was deeply religious and could talk on Kirk topics with fluency and knowledge. If he had a fault it was that he was inclined to show dour assertive pride, amounting to what the Scots called *essertness*. Was it possible that on occasions this led him to wrong judgments? If not, why should his son, Robert, qualify his assessment of his father as better able than most to understand men with a dark hint: "But stubborn, ungainly integrity, and headlong ungovernable irascibility, are disqualifying circumstances: consequently, I was born a very poor man's son." Did William Burnes's pride or ill temper cost him some chance in life which might have made the lot of all the family easier?

In his pocket when he left home William took a certificate, signed by three Kincardineshire landowners, to testify that he was "the son of an honest Farmer in this neighbourhood, and is a very well-inclined lad himself". It was a wise precaution in those days shortly after Prince Charles Edward's defeat, for any young man from the north was bound to be looked on with suspicion. William walked to Edinburgh while his brother struck west to settle at Titwood in north Ayrshire, where he worked in the lime quarries at Lochridge near Stewarton in summer and, when his rheumatism came on in winter, taught the sons of local farmers. In time "poor Uncle Robert" became too crippled even for that and lived out a pathetic and empty life until his death in 1789.

In Edinburgh, William found work on private estates and then on laying out what is now the Meadows, that gentle, sloping oasis of green to the south of the old grey town. After two years he headed west, possibly drawn by his brother's reports of the great agricultural improvements being carried out by the Earl of Loudon, the Earl of Eglinton and other Ayrshire landowners. First, he worked for one of these improvers, Alexander Fairlie of Fairlie, the man credited with developing the Fairlie system of crop rotation, which was an important part of the new agriculture. Two years later Burnes moved south to Alloway to become gardener to John Crawford of Doonside.

This was a time of great change around Ayr. New estates were being established by prosperous professional men, returned colonial merchants and administrators and the first princes of the infant Industrial Revolution. It was an area where there was plenty of scope for William Burnes's gardening skill.

Immediately before Burnes's arrival, the town of Ayr had experienced terrible financial difficulties. The disastrous failure of Scotland's great colonial venture at Darien in Panama had struck hard at its pocket at the beginning of the century, and recovery in the 1730s was checked by the Jacobite Rising. By 1750 the burgesses were £8500 in debt and were faced with a number of pressing problems, including the threatened collapse of the only bridge spanning the River Ayr. To meet its financial needs the council decided to sell off the ancient barony of Alloway to the land-hungry merchants.

Alloway was divided into parcels of land, varying in size, and put up for auction on Wednesday 5th June 1754. John Crawford, who was to be Burnes's employer, bought Alloway Cottage field, Clochranhill, Dumfries Park and part of Doonholm for £1792. The other pieces were bought by Dr William Fergusson, provost of Ayr, who was also to be William's employer and landlord.

William Burnes was a hard worker and highly regarded by his employer. He even found time for some freelance activity: when a new road was planned to replace the old winding one which ran to the Auld Brig O' Doon, he tendered for the contract and won it. From these earnings he managed to save a little money for himself and to send back to his parents in Kincardineshire.

When William Burnes arrived, Ayrshire was a place of rough, dark, lowering heath, broken only occasionally by a reedy meadow and a few strips of cultivated land. Bleak hills, lochs and bogs abounded as the names of the Burnes farms testify – *Mount* Oliphant, *Loch*lie and *Moss*giel. Here and there this depressing landscape was broken by straggling woodland and crossed by rough roads which did not so much lead from town to town as pick an erratic path from farm to farm. The few hedges were seldom cut, most ditches were choked with weeds, and the country, to quote a phrase which recurs in contemporary descriptions, was "in a state of nature".

Under the old, unimproved system of farming there was a small cultivated patch, a cluster of cottages – hovels would be a better word – which housed a group of farmers and their families, with an area of ground enclosed by a dry stone dyke close to the house for a garden or kailyard. Close by lay the infield or croft, not enclosed, and cultivated by all the farmers, each working several riggs or strips of his own. The riggs were ploughed yearly, fertilized with all the dung from the midden which stood close to the house door and sown with oats or other grain. Patches of land a little farther off, known as the outfield, were also ploughed but received no fertilizer, other than the droppings of the cattle which grazed there at other times of year. The outfield was cropped until its soil was exhausted and was then abandoned and another opened up.

The remaining land round the farms was rough pasture for grazing black cattle and a few sheep – hungry, ill-fed beasts which had to be herded diligently to prevent them from straying on to the crops. Occasionally the cattle were tethered or held in by temporary fencing, but generally they grazed as a herd in the care of a lad who had a difficult task to keep the poor starved brutes from the growing crops.

Money hardly entered into the eighteenth-century farmer's calculations. Rent was paid in kind or half-labour, and implements were bought jointly by landlord and tenant, who in return handed over a share of his crops to the landowner. Farms were almost completely self-sufficient. The family diet consisted of milk, butter and cheese from their own dairy and oatmeal from the infield crop, brightened only by a little kail from the garden. In autumn a cow might be killed off or bought in for slaughter and shared among the farmers, but otherwise meat was seldom seen. The winters were long and hungry for both men and cattle, and by spring the farmers were often almost too weak to tackle the ploughing and the cattle unable to stagger out to the grass. Occasionally in winter the poor had to bleed their cattle, mixing the blood with a little oatmeal for nourishment. A failed crop meant death or flight to Ireland or some other more fortunate part of the country.

A small crop of hemp or flax was usually grown, and this, together with wool from the sheep, was spun by the womenfolk to make material for clothes.

In comparison with many of the farmers, William Burnes enjoyed a good life, in paid employment and highly esteemed. Yet the very fact that he built the Alloway road shows that he had some yearning for independence. He began to work for a new employer, Provost Fergusson, at Doonholm but set his heart on running his own few acres and having a family around him.

Tradition has it that in 1756 William Burnes went to one of the fairs held at the foot of the steep High Street of Maybole and there met dark-eyed Agnes Brown, a farmer's daughter ten years his junior. Agnes's father farmed at Craigenton, on the estates of the Earl of Cassillis, near Kirkoswald, but his daughter was not living there at the time she met Burnes. Though Agnes was only ten when her mother had died, she had looked after her father and five brothers and sisters. When her father remarried two years later, Agnes was no longer needed at home, and so she moved into Maybole to live with her grandmother and later to keep house for her father's brother, William Brown. Agnes's grandfather was a baker and, as was common in those days, also had a small piece of land which he cultivated with the help of William Nelson. Nelson courted Agnes for seven years and then became friendly with another girl, who bore him a child. It was at this point that Agnes and William met and their courtship began.

As the exact date of the meeting is not known it is impossible to say whether William had already arranged to feu (taken on perpetual lease) seven acres of land at Alloway for use as a market-garden or whether he did so with marriage in prospect. The land was leased from Dr Alexander Campbell, a physician from Ayr, on 22nd June 1756, and on the eastern boundary Burnes began to build his house.

The cottage still stands at Alloway, restored as closely as possible to its original state. It is a typical farmhouse of the time – a long, low cottage built of rough stones cleared and collected from the land and held together with mortar compounded from clay and cut straw. The roof was of strong cupples, called syles, with crossbeams and brushwood laid over it and covered with sods of turf into which oat straw was fixed.

The house had two apartments, the living-room or in-seat and the spence. The in-seat had a fireplace built into the gable end of the building, an improvement on many houses which had the fire set in the middle of the floor with a hole in the roof to take away the smoke. Burnes's house had glazed windows too, instead of the draughty boarded apertures which were all that many farmers could afford.

Beyond the in-seat lay the second apartment, the spence, where there were beds, spinning-wheels, meal-chest, sowan-tub and a cask for collecting urine, known as the wash-tub. A closed-in bed was set into a kind of cupboard between the two apartments. The cottage was dark and cramped, but it was certainly more comfortable than many farmhouses in the neighbourbood. An integral part of the building was the stable, byre and barn, which had two entrances, one from the living quarters and one from the road – another improvement, for in many farmhouses, humans and animals shared a single doorway.

The year 1757 must have been a busy one for William Burnes, carrying on a full-time job on Dr Fergusson's estate, building his house and still finding time to walk to Maybole to court Agnes Brown. By late autumn the house was ready and William named it New Gardens. On 15th December he married and took his bride to live there.

William continued to work for Provost Fergusson, and in his spare time he cultivated a portion of his land, while the remainder grazed a cow which his wife, in true Ayrshire farming tradition, tended and milked, turning the milk into butter and cheese. She was well practised in dairy work and in home-making for she had been doing both since childhood.

Writers about Robert Burns tend to emphasize the influence of his father and to pass over the mother's part in the making of the poet. In fact, while Burns's father did much to provide the education which gave him the tools of his trade as a poet, it was from Agnes Brown that the creative spark was inherited. What was she like then, this Carrick farmer's daughter, who was mother of Scotland's greatest poet? Her daughter, Isabella, has left a description which rings vividly true:

She was rather under the average height; inclined to plumpness, but neat, shapely, and full of energy; having a beautiful pink-and-white complexion, a fine square forehead, pale red hair, but dark eyebrows and dark eyes often ablaze with a temper difficult to control. Her disposition was naturally cheerful; her manner, easy and collected; her address, simple and unpresuming; and her judgment uncommonly sound and good. She possessed a fine musical ear, and sang well.

There was much to admire in Agnes Brown's character and capabilities, and her husband made no secret of appreciating these fine qualities. He was an excellent husband, attentive to his wife and in due course to his children as well.

New Gardens was a happy home, where the children enjoyed their mother's sweet singing as she went about her work and where books and conversation were an essential part of life. Robert recalled his childhood:

There, lanely, by the ingle cheek,[1]   [1fireside
I sat and ey'd the spewing reek,
That fill'd, wi' hoast-provoking smeek[2]   [2choking smoke
  The auld clay biggin;
And heard the restless rattons[3] squeak   [3laths of roof
  About the riggin.

But this is taking us ahead of the story. In 1757 no small boy sat by the fireside at New Gardens; it was during the summer of the following year that Agnes found she was pregnant and set about preparing for the arrival of her first child, a boy born on 25th January 1759. Although he was not a stern Calvinist who believed that a baby who died unbaptized was condemned to eternal damnation, William was a good kirkman and he trudged into Ayr on the following day to bring back the minister of the Auld Kirk, Dr William Dalrymple, to baptize the child. "Dalrymple mild" named the boy Robert after his paternal grandfather in Kincardineshire and on his return to

Ayr entered the name in the parish register as "Robert Burns", dropping the 'e' in favour of the customary Ayrshire spelling of the name.

When he was twenty-eight years old Robert looked back on his entry into the world and the impact he was to make on it. The lively song "There was a Lad" shows much shrewd insight into his own character as well as bubbling exuberance and confidence in his own abilities. It demonstrates that no one knew Robert Burns better than he did himself.

There was a lad was born in Kyle,
But what na day o' what na style,
I doubt it's hardly worth the while
    To be sae nice wi' Robin.

Robin was a rovin' Boy,
    Rantin' rovin', rantin' rovin';
Robin was a rovin' Boy,
    Rantin', rovin' Robin.

Our monarch's hindmost year but ane
Was five-and-twenty days begun,*
'Twas then a blast o' Janwar' Win'
Blew hansel[1] in on Robin.   [1first gift

The "blast o' Janwar' Win'" which blew at the time when he was born must have been strong, for it displaced the carefully built gable of the cottage, and Agnes and her baby had to seek shelter in a neighbour's house until it was rebuilt.

In the poem a gossiping neighbour-woman read his palm and predicted the future for "rantin', rovin' Robin".

The Gossip keekit in his loof,[1]   [1looked at his palm
Quo' scho wha lives will see the proof,
This waly[2] boy will be nae coof,[3]   [2fine 3dolt
    I think we'll ca' him Robin.

He'll hae misfortunes great and sma',
But ay a heart aboon them a';

*25th January 1759, the year before the death of George II

He'll be a credit till us a',
   We'll a' be proud o' Robin.

But sure as three times three mak nine,
I see by ilka score and line,
This chap will dearly like our kin',
   So leeze me[4] on thee, Robin.   [4Term of endearment

Guid faith quo' scho I doubt you Stir,
Ye'll gar the lasses lie aspar;[5]   [5legs apart
But twenty fauts ye may hae waur –
   So blessin's on thee, Robin.

In 1787, when he wrote this, his first book of poems had already blown his fame through both country and capital like the "Janwar' Win'"; he had shown clearly that he was "nae coof"; he had made more than one lass lie "aspar" for him. It was a remarkably true self-assessment of the man all Scotland was to come to know before the century was out.

2

The First Fair Charmers

In the eight and a half years they lived at Alloway, William and Agnes Burnes were blessed with three more children, Gilbert, born in 1761, Agnes (1762) and Annabella (1764). John Murdoch, who taught Robert and Gilbert, confirms the happiness within the house: "In this mean cottage, of which I myself was at times an inhabitant, I really believe there dwelt a larger portion of content, than in any Palace of Europe. The 'Cotter's Saturday Night' will give some idea of the temper and manners that prevailed there."

The poem, clearly influenced by the English poet Gray, is largely autobiographical, relating the working and home life of the Burnes family at Alloway and at their two later homes, Mount Oliphant and Lochlie.

> November chill blaws loud wi' angry sugh;
>   The short'ning winter-day is near a close;
> The miry beasts retreating frae the pleugh;
>   The black'ning trains o' craws to their repose:
> The toil-worn Cotter frae his labor goes,
>   This night his weekly moil is at an end,
> Collects his spades, his mattocks and his hoes,
>   Hoping the morn in ease and rest to spend,
> And weary, o'er the muir, his course does homeward bend.

At home, the cotter's wife and younger children wait to welcome him, "expectant wee things", just as Burns must have waited at the door for his own father and just as his younger brothers and sisters welcomed him in due course. Then the older members of the family who are fee-ed out as servants to other farmers come in:

With joy unfeign'd, brothers and sisters meet,
   And each for other's weelfare kindly spiers:
The social hours, swift-wing'd, unnotic'd, fleet;
   Each tells the uncos[1] that he sees or hears.   [1news
The Parents partial eye their hopeful years;
   Anticipation forward points the view;
The mother wi' her needle and her sheers
   Gars auld claes look amaist as weel's the new;
The Father mixes a', wi' admonition due.

A lad drops in, faintly disguising the fact that he has come to court one of the daughters, and shares the supper of porridge, milk and cheese; then prayers follow:

The chearfu' Supper done, wi' serious face,
   They, round the ingle, form a circle wide;
The Sire turns o'er, the patriarchal grace,
   The big ha'-Bible,[1] ance his Father's pride: [1family Bible
His bonnet rev'rently is laid aside,
   His lyart haffets[3] wearing thin and bare;   [2grizzled locks
Those strains that once did sweet in Zion glide;
   His wales[3] a portion with judicious care;   [3chooses
'And let us worship God!' he says with solemn air.

Religion played an important part in the life of the Burnes family, though not in an oppressive way. William was a devout man and compiled a manual of religion for his children, but it did not touch on the narrow doctrines of predestination and damnation which were at that time dividing the Kirk. In other matters he was stern but not always severe. If Murdoch is to be believed he was tender and affectionate and led his children in the path of virtue rather than drove them towards it. He taught them by precept instead of threat, seldom beat them and from the earliest days worked to train their minds, "This," says Murdoch, "had a very good effect on the boys, who began to talk and reason like men much sooner than their neighbours."

Their father's influence was important; so too was their mother's, but in a different way. She could not have been aware that she was passing on to the children all the wealth of Ayrshire folksong – riches in which Robert was to find a lifelong passion and a mission to save Scottish folksong from the fate to which so much of the nation's heritage was being consigned in his generation. Agnes did not pause to consider whether the songs were good or bad or even suitable for small ears: she just sang.

> Kissing is the key o' love,
> An' clappin' is the lock,
> An' makin' o's the best thing
> That e'er a young thing got.

One of Robert's favourites was "The Life and Age of Man", which Agnes had from her old uncle in Maybole. This, with its doleful chorus "Ah, man was made to mourn", made so deep an impression on the boy's mind that he used it years later as the basis of a song, inspired by those dark thoughts which chased like ghosts through his mind in the periods of depression and sickness which he was to know so often.

> O death! the poor man's dearest friend,
>   The kindest and the best!
> Welcome the hour, my aged limbs
>   Are laid with thee at rest!
> The Great, the Wealthy fear thy blow,
>   From pomp and pleasure torn;
> But Oh! a blest relief to those
>   That weary-laden mourn!

As well as Agnes Burnes's folksongs the young Robert heard folktales from visitors such as old Betty Davidson, who stayed with them for long periods and talked by the fire's light of "devils, ghosts, fairies, brownies, witches, warlocks, spunkies, kelpies, elf-candles, dead-lights, wraiths, apparitions, cantraips, enchanted towers, giants, dragons and other trumpery". These were etched so deeply into Robert's mind that even the knowledge and common sense of manhood could not eradicate them. He admitted that he often kept a sharp lookout when walking or riding at night, and it was from these tales that "Tam O' Shanter" was to spring.

As soon as Robert was five he was sent off to a school at Alloway Mill, run by a man named Campbell, but this closed when the teacher left to become master of Ayr workhouse. For a while William Burnes taught Robert and his second son, Gilbert, the rudiments of reading and writing, but his time was limited and someone had to be found to take over the work.

Four neighbours were persuaded to join with Burnes in hiring a schoolmaster, and in March 1765, William went to Ayr to consult David Tennant, master of the English School in the town. Tennant had a candidate to offer for the job – John Murdoch, an eighteen-year-old youth then attending the school to improve his handwriting. Murdoch was young, but he was competent, and he would not require high payment.

Murdoch was summoned to bring his handwriting book to Simpson's tavern by the Auld Brig, so that Burnes might examine both the man and his work: having pronounced them satisfactory, he engaged the young teacher to start at Alloway in May. Murdoch's five employers were to accommodate him by turns and guaranteed to make up his salary if the quarterly payments from the pupils should fall short of an agreed figure.

John Murdoch has been criticized as a dull pedant who did the boys little good, and he certainly reached out for the pompous or involved phrase in preference to the simple one. The house in which he lived with the Burnes family he described as "a tabernacle of clay", "a mud edifice", "this mean cottage", "a humble dwelling", and "the argillaceous fabric". Of course, he was young and inexperienced, but he formed a deep affection for the family and did much to provide Robert with the sort of books and background which helped the boy to educate himself. John Murdoch's influence, like that of any teacher who cares for his pupil, cannot be dismissed as worthless.

At first Murdoch preferred Gilbert, the douce, amenable younger brother, to the contemplative, self-willed Robert, who had to be beaten at times, and Robert confessed later that he was "a good deal noted for a retentive memory and a stubborn, sturdy something" in his disposition. Robert was given to forming his own opinions, and his views were not always universally accepted or popular. When Murdoch was teaching him, Robert was already a rebel with an emerging social conscience.

I recall, and 'tis about the earliest thing I do remember, when I was quite a boy, one day at church, being enraged at seeing a young creature, one of the maids of his house, rise from the mouth of the pew to give way to a bloated son of Wealth and Dullness, who waddled surlily past her. – Indeed, the girl was very pretty; and he was an ugly, stupid, purse-proud, money-loving, old monster, as you can imagine.

Robert missed no detail of the people around him, and on visits to Ayr he enjoyed watching characters of the town, among them Charlie Caldwell, a drunken carrier, who, on reaching "the region of rapture", would say to his woman companion, "Margret, ye're a glory to God and the delight of my soul." Acute observation was backed by a good memory, so Robert and Gilbert soon mastered the rudiments of grammar and poetry. They could recite verse uncommonly well and analyse it far more skilfully than older boys in the class. From Mason's collection of prose and verse, the first book in which he encountered poetry, Robert was able, years later, to quote a couplet from Addison:

For though in dreadful whirls we hung
  High on the broken wave;

By that time he himself was high on the wave, which was about to break.

Strangely, for boys who showed aptitude for poetry, Murdoch complained that Robert and Gilbert both found great difficulty distinguishing one tune from another. "Robert's ear ... was remarkably dull, and his voice untuneable," Murdoch recorded.

Robert's later passion for Scottish song indicates that it may have been his teacher's ability to inspire him that was lacking, not his ear. Or perhaps it was nothing more than Murdoch's assessment that was wrong, as it certainly was when he claimed that the plodding Gilbert always appeared to possess a more lively imagination than his brother. Robert's withdrawn nature seems to have misled Murdoch, who was quite incapable of penetrating the true depths of his elder pupil's personality.

By the time Robert reached the age of ten Murdoch must

have begun to realize the boy's potential. He was reading and writing well, and "was absolutely a critic in substantives and principles". The bond which had existed from the first between Murdoch and William Burnes now grew between him and Robert. Murdoch lent the boy books which opened the doors to treasure-hoards far beyond the textbooks from which they worked daily. *The Life of Hannibal* was the first book Robert remembered reading apart from textbooks, and it so stirred him that he said he strutted "in raptures up and down after the recruiting drum and bagpipe, and wished myself tall enough to be a soldier".

The History of Sir William Wallace, lent by the blacksmith who shod his father's horses, had a different effect, pouring "a Scottish prejudice in my veins, which will boil along there until the flood-gates of life shut in eternal rest".

William Burnes was still ambitious. He did not want to be a cotter, nor yet a gardener, whose sons and daughters would be hired out to farms. "Had he continued in that station [gardener at Doonholm]." Robert wrote later, "I must have marched off to be one of the little underlings about a farmhouse, but it was his dearest wish and prayer to have it in his power to keep his children under his own eye, till they could discern between good and evil."

The mid-1760s seemed propitious to advancement: life in Scotland generally was improving following the Seven Years' War, which left Britain dominant in world affairs. Trade was booming, the Industrial Revolution was just beginning and farm improvements were rushing ahead.

On Dr Fergusson's estate, William Burnes was helping to enclose Mount Oliphant, one of the moorland farms which Fergusson was carving from his share of Alloway barony. Burnes asked for the tenancy and was offered a twelve-year lease with an option to break it after six years. For the first half, the rent was to be £40 a year, rising to £45 if Burnes chose to stay on. It would be difficult financially, he knew, but he was confident he could manage and took over the farm at Martinmas 1765, moving his family in on the following Whit Sunday.

From the start ill luck hounded Burnes. He could not dispose of the cottage and land at Alloway and so had to borrow capital from "his gen'rous master" to buy stock. On the eve of quitting the cottage, Burnes granted a bond on it to Fergusson as security. This loan helped in the short term, but in the long run it was to cause him terrible heartburning.

Mount Oliphant's soil had been in no way improved. It lay on an exposed slope facing towards the Firth of Clyde, the first to receive the rain borne in on the prevailing westerly winds, and there is a note of bitterness in Gilbert's memory of the farm: it was almost the poorest soil under the plough that he ever knew — so bad that after thirty years of cultivation, further improvements and an enormous rise in Scottish land values, the farm was let at £5 a year less than the rent paid by his father in 1766. The generous gesture by Burnes's master was soon exposed as a hard bargain. Gilbert recalled these years:

My father, soon came into difficulties which were increased by the loss of several of his cattle by accidents and disease. To the buffetings of misfortune, we could only oppose hard labour and the most rigid economy. We lived very sparingly. For several years butcher's meat was a stranger in the house, while all the members of the family exerted themselves to the utmost of their strength, and rather beyond it, in the labours of the farm. My brother at the age of thirteen, assisted in threshing the crop of corn, and at fifteen was the principal labourer of the farm, for we had no hired servant, male or female.

Mount Oliphant threw up the immediate disadvantage of loneliness too. It lay off the beaten track and was surrounded by strips of land cultivated by retired shopkeepers from Ayr or (worse still) by those still in business in the town who visited their holdings only occasionally. Gilbert remembered: "We rarely saw anybody but the members of our own family. There were no boys of our own age, or near it, in the neighbourhood … My father was for some time almost the only companion we had."

For a time the brothers continued to attend John Murdoch's school at Alloway each day; but it was a long, wearisome walk, and soon they were needed to help at home, so they were withdrawn and their father undertook to teach them in the evenings himself. Without William Burnes's driving force the school at Alloway soon closed, and Murdoch moved away from the district. His departure was a blow to every member of the Burnes family, for he had been one of their few regular visitors and a good friend. He walked up to Mount Oliphant to spend a last evening with them, bringing a small grammar book and a copy of *Titus Andronicus* as a farewell present. During the evening they gathered round to listen to him read the play. "We were all attention for some time," said Gilbert, "till presently the whole party was dissolved in tears. A female in the play (I have but a confused recollection of it) had her hands chopt off, and her tongue cut out, and then was insultingly desired to call for water to wash her hands. At this, in an agony of distress, we with one voice desired that he would read no more. My father observed that if we would not hear it out, it would be needless to leave the play with us. Robert replied that if it was left he would burn it. My father was going to chide him for this ungrateful return to his tutor's kindness, but Murdoch interposed, declared that he liked to see so much sensibility ..."

Burnes tactfully said no more, but when Murdoch set out for home, he left behind a translation of a French play, *The School for Love*, instead of the Shakespeare.

Entertainment such as that came seldom enough: life remained unremittingly hard as more children were added to the family – William in 1767, John in 1769 and Isabella in 1771. As the sad little inscriptions in churchyards of the period testify, this was a time when undernourishment and disease claimed many young lives. Yet William and Agnes Burnes must have done their work well, for every one of their children survived early childhood with all its hazards. Only John died young, at sixteen years of age, though William fell victim of an epidemic in London in 1790.

Twentieth-century farming in Ayrshire is hard but bears no comparison with conditions two centuries ago. It seems astonishing that Burnes managed to find time to teach his children. He talked to them like adults on every subject and watched their progress carefully. In 1772 he was far from satisfied with the handwriting of Robert and Gilbert, so he sent them for a term to the parish school at Dalrymple, a mile and a half away on the Maybole road. It was summer and a busy time on the farm, so the two attended week about. This tuition gave them both a rather similar, neat hand.

Books came into the house from many sources, and Burnes tapped all of them for his children. From travelling chapmen "the excellent new songs" could be bought cheaply, the widow of an Ayr doctor lent Robert *The Spectator* and books, neighbours supplied other books, and William Burnes subscribed to "a book society in Ayr", probably one of the private libraries then being set up in many parts of Scotland. The reading matter thus obtained could not be easily assimilated after a hard day's work in the open air. It must have required tremendous concentration, even from a boy as clever as young Robert Burns, to understand William Derham's *Physio-Theology* and *Astro-Theology*. John Ray's *The Wisdom of God Manifested in the Works of Creation* and Thomas Salmon's *New Geographical and Historical Grammar* were little better, but at least Thomas Stackhouse's retelling of the Bible story, the *New History of the Bible*, came to them in parts during the year 1767. A sound practical leavening was provided by the *Ready Reckoner and Tradesman's Sure Guide*.

One piece of good fortune arose from a mistake by one of Agnes's brothers when he was sent to Ayr to buy a ready reckoner and a guide to letter-writing. He bought the ready reckoner, but instead of the letter-writer he "got by mistake a small collection of letters by the most eminent writers, with a few sensible directions for attaining an easy epistolary style". This was a tremendous stroke of luck because the book, described by Robert as "a collection of letters by the Wits of Queen Anne's reign" and greatly enjoyed by him, had a great influence on his prose style.

Another piece of luck was Murdoch's return to Ayr in the autumn of 1772 as English master at the burgh school. The friendship with the Mount Oliphant folk was quickly resumed and often, on his half-holiday, the teacher would walk out to the farm, accompanied by a few friends, so that Burnes "might enjoy a mental feast" – a feast shared by Robert, who would interrupt with a hundred questions on subjects which were consuming his interest at that moment, and by Agnes, who hung with greedy ear on what her husband had to say.

The following summer Murdoch invited Robert to Ayr to spend some time with him revising his English grammar, in order that he might help to teach his younger brothers and sisters that winter. Teacher and pupil were together in every waking hour – in school, at meals, on walks – and at the end of a week Robert had mastered enough grammar for Murdoch to try to teach him a little French so that he might understand phrases he met with in his reading. Robert attacked the language (in Murdoch's words) "with great courage", practising verbs and memorizing the names of objects by a kind of simple look-say method of pointing, hearing the word and repeating it. Not only did he soak up enough French to drop a phrase into his correspondence and conversation thereafter, he also soon began to read Fénélon's *Aventure de Télémaque* in the original. Harvest time arrived, and Robert had to leave the congenial atmosphere of Ayr and continue his studies on his own. He took with him a Latin grammar but never made much of the language. Gilbert recalled that he would pick up Ruddiman's *Rudiments of the Latin Tongue* "on any little chagrin or disappointment, particularly in love affairs"; it never lasted, and once he sheepishly wrote a few stanzas on love, all ending: "So I'll to my Latin again."

Ayr gave him a glimpse of the world beyond the narrow furrow. Here was a bustling seaport, full of characters, life and joviality. Return to the farm must have caused much regret and longing for what had to be left behind. He must have missed especially the lively minds against which he had pitted his wits and the generous hearts who offered him friendship and lent him books.

Gilbert suggested that his brother was jealous of the rich and successful, but this is not true. Robert himself said that his sociability, when not checked by what he called his "spited pride", enabled him to cultivate those who were better off. "I formed several connections with other Younkers who possessed superior advantages," he wrote, "the youngling Actors who were busy with the rehearsal of PARTS which they were shortly to appear on that STAGE where, alas! I was destined to drudge behind the SCENES ... My young superiors never insulted the clouterly appearance of my plough-boy carcase, the two extremes of which were often exposed to all the inclemencies of all the seasons."

Far from being jealous, Robert formed genuine affections.

"Parting with these, my young friends and benefactors, as they dropped off for the east or west Indies, was often to me a sore affliction." What Gilbert and many others mistook for jealousy was his bitterness of tongue or pen when those who were better off than himself flaunted their advantages or used them unfairly. Many of the epigrams written in such circumstances were no more than the instinctive reaction of a cornered animal, and usually he bitterly regretted them afterwards.

Murdoch's influence came to an abrupt end when the schoolmaster, in his cups one evening, criticized Dr Dalrymple of the Auld Kirk. In Ayr such talk was blasphemy, and Murdoch was dismissed his post and forced to leave the town. He settled in London, where in due course he enjoyed seeing his old pupil's poems "relished by the Caledonians ... full as much as they can be by those of Edinburgh". Murdoch made a living teaching French, but after the French Revolution so many native speakers better able to teach the language fled to England that he fell on hard times and died a poor man in 1824.

While Robert was completing his formal education in the early 1770s the financial burden of Mount Oliphant was increasing alarmingly, and soon Burnes was in difficulties. Provost Fergusson was patient, but after his death on 7th November 1769, only three years after Burnes took the lease, a factor who would not tolerate delays in payments took control. From that moment, Burnes was badgered and hounded for money which he just could not find.

The older children, especially Robert, were well aware of the situation, and it caused them great anguish. Gilbert said: "To think of our father growing old (for he was now above fifty) broken down with the long continued fatigues of his life, with a wife and five other children, and in a declining state of circumstances, these reflections produced in my brother's mind and mine sensations of the deepest distress."

In Robert's it stirred up anger: "A Novel-Writer might perhaps have viewed these scenes with some satisfaction, but so did not I; my indignation yet boils at the recollection of the scoundrel tyrant's insolent threatening epistles, which used to set us all in tears."

It was that dunning factor who "sat for the picture" which Robert drew in his "Tale of Twa Dogs". The brass-collared, well-bred Caesar, in conversation with Luath, the "faithfu' tyke" of a ploughman's collie, describes the agony of rent day:

> I've notic'd, on our Laird's *court-day*,[1] [¹rent-day
> An' mony a time my heart's been wae,
> Poor *tenant-bodies*, scant o' cash,
> How they maun thole[2] a factor's snash; [²suffer
> He'll stamp an' threaten, curse an' swear,
> He'll *apprehend* them, *poind* their gear,
> While they maun stand, wi' aspect humble,
> An' hear it a', an' fear an' tremble!

The cost to Robert of the Mount Oliphant factor's snash was high: Gilbert traced his later fits of depression and the illness which was to claim his life back to this period: "At this time he [Robert] was almost constantly afflicted in the evenings with a dull head-ache, which, at a future period of his life, was exchanged for a palpitation of the heart, and a threatening of fainting and suffocation in his bed at night time."

It was during these cheerless years, too, that Robert first "committed the sin of rhyme".

He was now fifteen, working at the harvest like a grown man, a girl called Nelly Kilpatrick beside him in the usual country habit of pairing a man and a woman in the field. Nelly was a "bonie, sweet, sonsie lass", only a year younger than he, and she willingly loitered behind with him on the way home in the evening and gave him her hand to pick out thistles. "I did not know myself why ... the tones of her voice made my heart strings thrill like an Eolian harp; and particularly why my pulse beat such a furious ratann when I looked and fingered over her hand ...," Robert wrote, but it initiated him into "a certain delicious passion, which, in spite of acid Disappointment, gin-horse Prudence, and bookworm Philosophy, I hold to be the first of human joys, our dearest pleasure here below".

Nelly taunted him with a song composed by a local laird's son for one of his father's maids with whom he was in love. "I saw no reason why I might not rhyme as well as he," said Robert, "for, except smearing sheep, and casting peats, his father living in the moors, he had no more Scholar-craft than I had. Thus with me began Love and Poesy."

She hummed a tune to him and to it he set "O Once I Lov'd a Bonie Lass", a song as innocent as the affair that inspired it. Robert remembered it clearly enough to copy it into the Commonplace Book which he started in April 1783.

O once I lov'd a bonnie lass,
　An' aye I love her still,
An' whilst that virtue warms my breast
　I 'll love my handsome Nell.

In spite of his struggles, William Burnes remained obsessed by the importance of education, especially for his eldest son, no doubt hoping that Robert might escape from the snare in which he himself had become so hopelessly trapped. So, in 1775, Robert was sent to Hugh Rodger's school at Kirkoswald, in his mother's home country, to learn "mensuration, surveying and dialling".

Ayr had been one experience: Kirkoswald was another. Although the village lies a few miles inland it was one of the important centres of operations on the notorious smuggling coast of south Ayrshire, a place familiar with "scenes of rioting swagger and roaring dissipation" such as the douce county town had never known. He enjoyed watching the vibrant life of the village, both its smugglers and the band of itinerant masons and joiners who were then building a new church there for the Earl of Cassillis. They filled Jean Kennedy's "Leddies House". Lowff beside the kirkyard, where even on Sundays, mugs of ale were handed through the window to drouthy worshippers. Robert relished it all and bragged about it. He boasted that he learnt to drink in Kirkoswald, to look on a large tavern bill without fear and to mix in a drunken brawl. Money was so short, and relatives were so thick on the ground that all this is very doubtful. The tavern bills were other people's; the drink could have been no more than a dram offered by a companion; and the brawls were viewed from a distance.

For a time Robert made "pretty good progress" in his studies until, in his own words, "the sun entered Virgo, a month which is always a carnival in my bosom". It almost seemed as if the slow-warming Scottish summer sun ripened his passion and muse as surely as it matured the corn. That August he went into the garden one morning to take the sun's altitude, looked over the hedge and saw "a charming Filette who overset my Trigonometry, and set me off in a tangent from the sphere of my studies". He struggled on with sines and co-sines for a few days more, but it was hopeless. "It was vain to think of doing any more good at school. The remaining week I staid, I did nothing but craze the faculties of my soul about her, or steal out to meet with her; and the last two nights of my stay in the country, had sleep been a mortal sin, I was innocent."

Again he committed the sin of rhyme:

Now westlin winds, and slaught'ring guns
  Bring Autumn's pleasant weather;
The moorcock spring, on whirring wings,
  Amang the blooming heather:
Now waving grain, wide o'er the plain,
  Delights the weary Farmer;
The moon shines bright, as I rove at night,
  To muse upon my Charmer.

The charmer was Peggy Thomson, a Kirkoswald girl, of whom he was very fond and to whom he gave a copy of his poems after her marriage to John Neilson of Kirkoswald. Burns later visited them and took a sad leave of her when he set out for home.

But Peggy dear, the ev'ning's clear,
  Thick flies the skimming Swallow;
The sky is blue, the fields in view,
  All fading-green and yellow:
Come let us stray our gladsome way,
  And view the charms o' Nature;
The rustling corn, the fruited thorn,
  And ilka happy creature.

We'll gently walk, and sweetly talk,
  While the silent moon shines clearly;
I'll clasp thy waist, and fondly prest,
  Swear how I lo'e thee dearly:

Not vernal show'rs to budding flow'rs,
   Not Autumn to the Farmer,
So dear can be, as thou to me,
   My fair, my lovely Charmer!

At Mount Oliphant once again, love was soon forgotten, for things were worse than ever, and, with the break in his lease due, William Burnes was anxiously casting around for a way out of the morass of hard work and little return. He could not have been aware of them, but factors beyond his control – probably mostly beyond his comprehension too – were working towards a solution.

Ayrshire's rapidly increasing agricultural improvements had been supported by the Ayr Bank, set up in 1769 by Douglas Heron and Company, which lent money freely (some were inclined to think recklessly) until it had so much in circulation that, if called on to do so, it would have been unable to meet its commitments. The inevitable crash came in 1772 and was a resounding one. The Bank's debts amounted to more than half a million pounds, and scarcely a landowner in the county was left unaffected: many old families were ruined and had to sell off their estates, and an inrush of new landlords meant a reshuffle of tenants. William Burnes found the larger farm of Lochlie near Tarbolton, only a few miles further inland, but in a more fertile part of the country. It had 130 acres and so should have supported Burnes's growing family far better than Mount Oliphant ever could. Fortunately the Fergusson family had not been forced to realize their assets after the crash, so Burnes was able to carry some of his debt over to Lochlie. On 9th November 1776 an instrument of seisin was drawn up in favour of Fergusson's daughters, Elizabeth, Jean, Eleonora, Margaret and Susanne, and Jean's husband, John Hunter, by which Burnes was lent £145 on the security of the cottage at Alloway, which was still unsold.

This allowed Burnes to accept the tenancy of Lochlie from an Ayr merchant, David McLure, at the high price of twenty shillings an acre. There was no written agreement between landlord and tenant: the bargain was sealed on a handshake as so many were in Ayrshire two centuries ago and still are. Under the agreement, William Burnes was to lime and fence the land, with a financial contribution from McLure. It all seemed straightforward when the family moved on Whit Sunday 1777, but the bargain was soon to turn sour. Mount Oliphant, a nightmare left behind, had cost the Burnes family much in health and contentment, but it had raised William's status from hired gardener to tenant farmer, quite a step up the social ladder. The price had been high: he was now an old man, worn out by work and beaten down by the factor's dunning letters. Only pride in his family, the sole consoling feature of his life, drove him on. He and Agnes now had seven fine children, who helped to carry the burden of the farmwork. Robert was eighteen, a thoughtful youth with ideas which sometimes worried his father. He had built well on the educational foundations laid by his father, and now he was delving into new authors. He read rapidly, and remembered what he read. The path ahead was now clearer than it had ever been.

3

Pride and Poverty

The blessed relief of Lochlie! This was the rolling, rumpled, hillocky heartland of Kyle – wet, but in better condition altogether than Mount Oliphant had ever been. Most important of all, from the point of view of William Burnes, there was more of it. One hundred and thirty acres promised a fair living and postponed any possibility of dispersal of the family. The situation must have reminded Burnes of his own father's position in Kincardineshire a generation before – the desperate search for capital and a larger, more viable unit of land to hold the family together and his ultimate failure, even with a loan and additional farms. If William thought of that, he did not discuss it with his sons: Lochlie would be different.

Robert suggests that the move was more than a mere transfer of debts and worries. The nature of the bargain gave his father a little ready money, although it is hard to see where this came from. Perhaps he was thinking of McLure's contribution to the improvements and the extra time granted by the Fergussons for repayment of their loan. Whatever relief there was was short-lived, although the first years at Lochlie were the only time of utter contentment that the Burneses were ever to know.

The move took them out of slowly-developing southern Ayrshire into the northern half of the county, where industrial and agricultural progress were already moving fast. Deep pits were being sunk to produce coal for burning lime which farmers needed to fertilize their fields, and in time this was to bring iron-smelting and other industries. Although it was a move of no more than ten miles, it took them into a new world.

The Burnes family were not against progress: William

never was among those farmers who refused to use newly-introduced carts even when they were supplied free from improving landlords. He and his sons were interested in innovations, and because Tarbolton, only two miles away, was a centre for handloom weaving Robert and Gilbert rented some land from their father on which they tried to grow flax. In 1780 they had three acres of "pretty good flax", and in January 1783 the *Glasgow Mercury* reported that Robert had been awarded a prize of £3 for his crop.

Robert was by now a grown man, five feet nine inches tall, though he looked rather shorter because he had already developed a farmer's stoop. His looks were attractive enough, although his broad forehead and coarse features inherited from his mother prevented him from being handsome. His complexion was dark, his countenance rather serious, and his melancholy eyes penetrated the heart of everyone who looked into them. He had a taste for high fashion by now and was the only young man in the parish to tie up his brown, curling hair. Young Lochlie was well aware that people turned to stare when he passed by:

My coat and vest, they are Scotch o' the best,
  O' pairs o' guid breeks I hae twa, man:
And stockings and pumps, to put on my stumps,
  An' ne'er a wrang steek[1] in them a' man.   [1stitch

My sarks[2] they are few, but five o' them new,   [2shirts
  Twal'-hundred,[3] as white as the snaw, man,   [3woven in reel
A ten-shillings hat; a Holland cravat;   of 1,200 divisions
  There are no' mony poets sae braw, man.

His appearance was striking, but as soon as he spoke features and dress were forgotten, for his conversation was sheer sorcery. Maria Riddell, who knew him later in life, wrote: "His voice alone could improve upon the magic of his eye; sonorous, replete with the finest modulations, it ... captivated the ear. And what he had to say was worth listening to. By nature kind, brave, sincere and compassionate to a degree, yet he could be proud, irascible and even vindictive."

Burns considered himself a poet first and a farmer second: not that he was a bad farmer, for he could do a day's work as well as any man in the parish. Yet when each day ended he left farming behind and the poet took over: "I spent the evenings in the way after my own heart," he told Dr John Moore of London in a long autobiographical letter, written soon after he became famous.

His heart led him to Tarbolton, where he found the social life of which he had been starved at Mount Oliphant. Proximity to the village was the greatest advantage of the move to Lochlie, although its weaving trade had lost many of its markets as a result of the War of American Independence and it was not as prosperous as it had been.

Economic problems had little visible effect, however. The village was still roused every morning to the tuck of the drum and sent to bed at night the same way. Between the drum calls there was a daily routine of weaving, meetings of the Friendly Society, gossip at the bridge, broken by Kirk attendance on Sunday and a gala day when the Coilsfield hounds were out or the summer cattle fair came round. The townsfolk led an unedifying life, or, as Robert's friend David Sillar put it, they were "uncontaminated by reading, conversation, or reflection".

Any incomer was looked upon with suspicion and accepted either slowly or not at all – and the Burneses arrived with a reputation for pride and poverty. Even in the eighteenth century news travelled, and rumours of the financial standing of the new tenants at Lochlie preceded them. Once they had arrived, the situation was made worse by William Burnes's fine accent and notion for reading books and his son's jaunty appearance, which suggested that he considered himself, a tenant farmer's son, a good cut above the village lads. Robert *did* consider himself superior, for when he came to found the Tarbolton Bachelors' Club (a debating society) in 1780 the preamble to the rules referred to "the self-conceited mechanics of a country town", suggesting that more than a hint of jealousy existed between the town and country factions.

Stories of Burns's relationship with Tarbolton folk lingered long into the nineteenth century, and, even if they cannot be substantiated, they have a ring of truth. Writing towards the end of the century, E.H. Letham quoted an old person as saying of the poet: "He asked my grandmother to go with him to a dance, but she refused." Another said, "My mother and mother-in-law baith shore [reaped] beside him, an' nane o' them liked him." Asked why, she said, "Oh, he was jist that sarcastic a body didna ken what he wad say next".

Burns loved an argument on Sundays, either between sermons or on the way to church. Once he met up with a crofter named Wallace, a seceder, bound for the meeting-house. The opportunity was too good to miss, and the pair argued all the way to the village. On parting, Burns shot at the seceder, "Well, I didna think to meet with the Apostle Paul in Tarbolton parish."

"Naw," replied Wallace, "ony mair than I thought tae forgather wi' the wild beasts o' Ephesus."

Burns's pen was too sharp for his own good; the Ronalds of the Bennals did not care to be told that Robert was as good as they, and it angered the Tarbolton lasses to have fun poked at them: Peggy knew she was a lady, Sophy had little art in courting, Mysie was dour and din, and Jenny was proud of her bonnie looks ...

As ye gae up by yon hillside,
    Spier[1] in for bonnie Bessy: [1]ask
She'll gie ye a beck, and bid ye light,[2]   [2]alight
    And handsomely address ye.

There's few sae bonny, nane sae guid
    In a' King George's dominion;
If ye should doubt the truth o' this –
    It's Bessy's ain opinion.

Worse still were the epigrams at which most people laughed, tempering their amusement, however, when they reflected that they might be the poet's next victim. Would their own epitaph echo that of the laird of Boghead?

Here lies Boghead amang the dead,
    In hopes to get salvation;
But if such as he, in heaven may be,
    Then welcome, hail! damnation –

Or the innkeeper's?

Here lies 'mang ither useless matters,
A. Manson wi' his endless clatters. –

Even the living were unsafe. John Wilson, the schoolmaster,
was honest enough, but he was paid a pittance which fell far
short of his needs. He augmented this by selling groceries and
drugs from his cottage, a very useful service in those days
when medical help was beyond the means of most people.
Burns made the district rock with "Death and Dr
Hornbook", a hilarious satirical poem describing how
Wilson (Dr Hornbook) met Death on the road to Willie's
Mill, a farm just below the village. Death complained bitterly
that there was no trade for his "awfu' scythe" because the
doctor's "cures" were killing off so many people. Death had
fallen on hard times:

See, here's a scythe, and there's a dart,
They hae pierc'd mony a gallant heart;
But Doctor *Hornbook*, wi' his art
          And cursed skill,
Has made them baith no worth a f-t,
          D-n'd haet[1] they'll kill!
                                                              [¹thing

Citing cases and prescribed remedies – sal-alkali of midge tail
droppings and ill-brewed drinks – Death reached his
peroration and vowed to nail the doctor "as dead's a herring"
next time they met. Alas, he had time to say no more:

But just as he began to tell,
The auld kirk-hammer strak the bell,
Some wee, short hour ayont the twal',
          Which rais'd us baith:
I took the way that pleas'd mysel,
          And sae did Death.

Tarbolton laughed, but poor Wilson carried on as if nothing
had happened. He was obviously a man of some character
because he held no grudge against Burns: in fact, he asked the
poet for a reference when he was applying to become a clerk in
a law office in Edinburgh in order to escape the drudgery of
teaching in Tarbolton.

The man who retaliated on behalf of Tarbolton folk was Saunders Tait, and because he did so he is usually dismissed as a jealous toady who was embittered because his own poetry was bad. There was an element of envy in his attacks on Burns, but all the evidence points to the fact that Tait was universally liked in the village and had much good in him. No doubt he was stung by the proud, jaunty, clever poet with unorthodox views and a hint of malice.

However, Robert had his friends as well as his enemies in the village, and these enabled him to escape from his melancholia as well as to find an outlet for his high spirits.

His closest friend, although not the first he made in the district, was David Sillar, a farmer's son from Spitalside, who also was a poet and published his own book of verse in 1789. Robert wrote two "Epistles to Davie", one of which, while exhorting his fellow-poet to continue writing, showed the joy he was deriving from his verse-making:

Leeze me[1] on rhyme! It's ay a treasure,   [1let me enjoy
My chief, amaist my only pleasure,
At hame, a-fiel, at wark or leisure,
    The Muse, poor hizzie!
Tho' rough an' raploch[2] be her measure,   [2coarse
    She's seldom lazy.

Haud tae the Muse, my dainty Davie:
The warl' may play you (monie) a shavie[3];   [3trick
But for the Muse, she'll never leave ye,
    Tho' e'er sae puir,
No, even tho' limpan wi' the spavie
    Frae door tae door.

David Sillar is remembered as a poet only because he was a friend of Burns, but he would not mind that: to make verse was more important than to make great or even good poetry.

Burns had many other acquaintances in the district, young men such as John Rankine of Adamhill, who hardly matched the poet intellectually but, because he was a farmer, was at the right social level. Then there were Hugh Reid, Alexander Brown, Walter Mitchell, Thomas Wright and William McGavin, all of them founder-members of the Bachelors'

Club, which Robert and Gilbert helped to establish. Later they were joined by Sillar, Adam Jamaison, John Orr and Matthew and James Patterson.

According to its rules, the Bachelors' Club was to meet every fourth Monday, debate a topic, choose a chairman and a subject for the next meeting and drink to the members and their mistresses. Fines for non-attendance helped to augment the threepenny subscription which was levied for drinks at each session. The last of the elaborate set of rules bears the marks of Robert's hand:

Every man proper for a member of this Society, must have a frank, honest, open heart, above anything dirty or mean; and must be a professed lover of one or more of the female sex. No haughty, self-conceited person, who looks upon himself as superior to the rest of the club, and especially no mean-spirited, worldly mortal, whose only will is to heap up money, shall upon any pretence whatever be admitted. In short, the proper person for this society is, a cheerful, honest-hearted lad; who, if he has a friend that is true, and a mistress that is kind, and as much wealth as genteelly to make both ends meet – is just as happy as this world can make him.

Subjects debated also suggest Robert's influence: "Whether we derive more happiness from Love or Friendship?", "Whether is the savage man or the peasant of a civilised country in the most happy situation?" and a long motion asking whether a farmer without prospects should marry a rich girl with neither beauty nor conversation or one "every way agreeable in person, conversation and behaviour, but without any fortune".

By June 1782, the number of members had grown to thirteen, and on the night of Tarbolton races the following month they held a dance to which every member invited a partner.

Dancing was something new to Robert, who described himself as "the most ungainly, awkward boy in the parish", so he decided to attend a dancing-class to give himself polish. This resulted in high feeling between the poet and his father, which deeply affected both. It seems a trivial incident, yet years later Robert wrote of it in a kind of disjointed almost distraught manner, mixing repentance with accusation and defiance.

> My father had an unaccountable antipathy against these meetings, and my going was what to this moment I repent, in opposition to his wishes. My father ... was subject to strong passions; from that instance of disobedience in me, he took a sort of dislike to me, which, I believe, was one cause of the dissipation which marked my succeeding years. I saw Dissipation, comparatively with the strictness, and sobriety, and regularity of Presbyterian country life. ...

Since William Burnes permitted the other members of the family to attend similar classes, it would appear that the old man's rage was not so much against dancing as against his son's attendance at the classes, and perhaps it stemmed from general worry over the way in which Robert, a headstrong lad at the best of times, was throwing himself into the social life of Tarbolton regardless of consequences. Perhaps he was hearing tales of his son's unpopularity in some quarters, and if, as Gilbert avers, Robert excelled at dancing "and was for some time distractedly fond of it" then the old man had reason to fear.

On the evidence of this incident it would be wrong to assume that Burnes was an old curmudgeon who disliked or disapproved of his son. William must have been proud of and felt sympathy towards Robert's genius to spend so much money and effort cultivating it – time which he never gave to the other members of the family. He must have admired his son's warm-heartedness, his ability to mix at all social levels and his wizardry with words. But, like so many fathers in the same mould, he would not have admitted it openly.

His father's rage was small enough in itself, but it affected Robert deeply. His way was pointed by "will-o' wisp meteors of thoughtless whim" countered by early ingrained piety and virtue, he told Dr Moore. He himself saw that he lacked an aim in life, although ambition stirred in him. There appeared to be only two ways to success – niggardly economy or "the chicaning art of bargain-making", neither of which was acceptable to him.

Robert alternated between sociability and lonely summer

Sundays by the River Ayr, between winter walks in the lee of a wood, listening to the sough of the wind high in the trees, and standing on a hilltop just letting the storm engulf him.

On 4th July 1781, he became a freemason at Tarbolton, joining the St David Lodge. Freemasonry, like the Kirk, was full of schisms and disputes, and the Tarbolton masons broke up into two factions, with Robert among the seceders who set up the St James Lodge. Becoming a mason was important to Burns because it introduced him to powerful and useful people such as Gavin Hamilton, the Mauchline lawyer, and James Dalrymple of Orangefield.

.He did not satirize all the Tarbolton lasses whom he met. "My heart was completely tinder," he admitted, "and was eternally lighted up by some goddess or other; and, as in every other warfare in this world, my fortune was various; sometimes I was received with favour, and sometimes I was mortified with a repulse." He worked hard, and in the evenings he escaped to some romantic adventure or another, his own or someone else's. "A country lad seldom carries on a love adventure without an assisting confidant. I possessed a curiosity, zeal and intrepid dexterity, that recommended me as a proper second on these occasions; and I dare say, I felt as much pleasure in being in the secret of half the loves of the parish of Tarbolton, as ever did statesman in knowing the intrigues of half the courts of Europe."

His sister Isabella remembered how in church he became infatuated with a girl who was housekeeper at Coilsfield and that she inspired "Montgomerie's Peggy". In November 1780 he told William Niven, a friend of Kirkoswald days, that he now had a sweetheart or two, but with as little a view of matrimony as ever. The following June he again confided in Niven that "by strange conjuncture of circumstances, I am intirely got rid of all connections with the tender sex, I mean in way of courtship ... though how long I shall continue so, Heaven only knows; but be that as it may, I shall never be involved as I was again". This refers to Alison Begbie, a servant-girl from a neighbouring farm who had just rejected him. A few passionate letters, some which we can only guess are addressed to Alison, are all we have to trace the affair.

Alison was clearly a girl of above average education and

must have appealed to his intellect in some degree – he praised
her "charming qualities, heightened by an education much
beyond anything I have ever met in any woman I ever dared to
approach". His letters to her were both passionate and
literate, and they culminated in a proposal of marriage. Alison
prevaricated, until he begged that she should "either put an
end to my hopes by a peremptory refusal, or cure me of my
fears by a generous consent". Alison declined his hand but
wished him all kinds of happiness. Robert read the letter over
and over again, then wrote to her protesting that he never
again expected to meet charming qualities in such a degree in
this world. But he did not seem heartbroken.

   Alison Begbie probably inspired three songs, "Bonie Peggy
Alison" (also claimed to be written to Montgomerie's Peggy),
"The Lass of Cessnock Bank" and – most beautiful of all –
"Mary Morison".

> O Mary, at thy window be,
>   It is the wish'd, the trysted hour;
> Those smiles and glances let me see,
>   That make the miser's treasure poor:
> How blithely wad I bide the stoure,[1]   [1battle
>   A weary slave frae sun to sun;
> Could I the rich reward secure,
>   The lovely Mary Morison!

If the song was written so early in his career (and some claim
that it is too good to have been) it was quite the best he had
composed to date, and if Alison Begbie did indeed inspire it
then the rejection of his proposal must have been felt deeply.

> O Mary, canst thou wreck his peace,
>   Wha for thy sake wad gladly die!
> Or canst thou break that heart of his,
>   Whase only faute is loving thee!

This also would confirm the theory that Alison's rejection was
a reason for Burns's decision, taken at about this time, to move
to Irvine to learn flax-dressing. Gilbert believed that his
brother wanted to gain financial independence so as to marry,
and Robert himself suggests that the decision was partly taken

on a whim and partly in an effort to find a career for himself. Whatever the reason, the plan had a sound practical basis, for he and his brother were already growing flax at Lochlie, and they would obtain a much better return if they were able to dress and spin it themselves. Like many other industries, the textile trade was passing through a bad phase because of the War of Independence with America, but the government was offering subsidies to encourage production of which the Burns brothers were businessmen enough to take advantage.

They chose Irvine because it was then the main centre in the county for flax-dressing, or heckling as it was called, and by good fortune Agnes Burnes's half-brother, Alexander Peacock, was in the trade there. Irvine was a new experience for young Lochlie: this was a place even larger than Ayr, a busy, bustling seaport, full of characters who had seen the world and lived well and sometimes wildly. It was like Kirkoswald on a grander scale, equally dissipated, and arrival there must have seemed to Robert as exciting as reaching Samarkand itself.

Our knowledge of Burns's Irvine period is full of uncertainties – even to the exact location of the heckling-shop, which is thought to have been in a small thatched house at the back of the Glasgow Vennel, in premises where workhorses were also stabled. Of one thing we are sure: Burns found flax-dressing painful, monotonous, uncongenial work, carried out in an atmosphere which was dusty and ill-smelling, and a complete contrast to the fresh air life he had known at home. Soon he became ill and depressed and suffered violent headaches which made life almost intolerable. A visit from his father at Martinmas did little to raise his spirits, and on 27th December 1781 he wrote an anguished letter home, explaining that he could not be with the family for New Year's Day because of pressure of work and for other reasons which he would not give in his letter.

The weakness of my nerves has so debilitated my mind that I dare not either review past events, or look forward into futurity; for the least anxiety, or perturbation in my breast, produces most unhappy effects on my whole frame. – Sometimes, indeed, when for an hour or two, as is sometimes the case, my spirits are a little lightened, I glimmer a little into futurity; but my principal, and

indeed my only pleasurable employment is looking backwards
and forwards in a moral and religious way – I am quite
transported at the thought that ere long, perhaps very soon, I
shall bid an eternal adiew to all the pains, & uneasiness &
disquietudes of this weary life; for I assure you I am heartily tired
of it, and, if I do not very much deceive myself, I could
contentedly & gladly resign it. ...

He already had high hopes which he thought were likely to be
dashed. "As for this world," he told his father, "I despair of
ever making a figure in it – I am not formed for the bustle of
the busy nor the flutter of the Gay. I shall never again be
capable of it. – Indeed, I am altogether unconcerned at the
thoughts of it. I foresee that very probably Poverty &
Obscurity await me & I am, in some measure, prepared &
daily preparing to meet & welcome these."

The letter was a typical product of the bouts of depression
from which he suffered. In this state of hypochondria, to give it
its fashionable eighteenth-century name, he became heedless
of the present and the future.

The letter must have alarmed his father, even though the
high-sounding phrasing suggests that it was written partly for
effect, and made him wonder once again if he would ever
understand his strange, brilliant son. Perhaps he realized that
Robert was drawing the long bow a little, because he made no
move to go to Irvine to sort things out.

Six years later, when Robert came to describe his stay at
Irvine and its undignified end, there was no Augustan
grandeur about his description of his flax-dressing experience,
his partner or the heckling-shop: "This turned out a sadly
unlucky affair, – My Partner was a scoundrel of the first water
who made money by the mystery of thieving; and to finish the
whole, while we were giving a welcome carousal to the New
Year, our shop, by the drunken carelessness of my Partner's
wife, took fire and was burnt to ashes, and left me a true poet,
not worth sixpence."

Again there was trouble with girls. "A belle-fille whom I
adored and who had pledged her soul to meet me in the field
of matrimony, jilted me with peculiar circumstances of
mortification."

If this refers, as is sometimes suggested, to Alison Begbie, then Robert was lying to save face, but Robert Burns never lied to save face or for any other reason, and in any case it was hardly necessary in 1788 (when he wrote about the belle-fille) to hide the truth. One must assume therefore that there was some brief, wounding affair in Irvine and that Robert, in his disturbed state of mind, was mortified at his rejection.

He made one important friend in Irvine: Richard Brown, a young sailor, who was to influence his future greatly. Brown was six years older than Robert and had a wealth of knowledge of the world which any young poet would envy. Good fortune, bad fortune, adventure, shipwreck, piracy, sexual experience – Richard Brown had sampled them all. Burns wrote of him:

> He was the son of a plain mechanic, but a great man in the neighbourhood taking him under his patronage gave him a genteel education with a view to bettering his situation in life. – The Patron dieing, just as he was ready to launch forth into the world, the poor fellow in despair went to sea; where after a variety of good and bad fortune, a little before I was acquainted with him, he had been set ashore by an American Privateer on the wild coast of Connaught, stript of everything. ...

This was the kind of stimulus a melancholic like Burns needed:

> This gentleman's mind was fraught with courage, independence and Magnanimity, and every noble, manly virtue. – I loved him, I admired him, to a degree of enthusiasm; and I strove to imitate him. – In some measure I succeeded; I had the pride before, but he taught it to flow in proper channels. – His knowledge of the world was vastly superior to mine, and I was all attention to learn. – He was the only man I ever saw who was a greater fool than myself, when WOMAN was the presiding star; but he spoke of a certain fashionable failing with levity, which hitherto I had regarded with horror. Here his friendship did me a mischief. ...

A *certain fashionable failing* – later this was to embarrass Brown, by then a successful sea-captain with a wife and children. Brown denied that he had ever encouraged Burns to sexual intercourse, but the events which followed after 1781 suggest that Robert was telling the truth.

More important for posterity, Brown was the first person to suggest that Robert should publish his poems. In December 1787 the poet reminded him of this: "Do you recollect a Sunday we spent in Eglinton woods? You told me, on my repeating some verses to you, that you wondered I could resist the temptation of sending verses of such merit to a magazine: 'twas actually this that gave me an idea of my own pieces which encouraged me to endeavour at the character of a Poet."

Irvine was an unproductive period for the poet, giving only a few melancholy pieces such as the "Prayer on the Prospect of Death" and "Stanzas on the Same Occasion", so it could not have been newly-composed verses which impressed the sailor. In fact, Burns was two men in his Irvine period: the depressed young apprentice heckler and the ambitious youth who poured out his passions and poetry on long walks by the River Irvine. It was probably an effort to preserve the latter personality that kept the poet on in Irvine after the shop was burned down. He could not bear to face up to Lochlie and all its problems, especially the new one which had become apparent – his father's advancing consumption. By March 1782 he had no choice, however: return was vital.

A dispute had arisen between Burnes and his landlord as to how much each should pay towards liming the soil, fencing off the fields and putting up new farm buildings. McLure claimed £775, but Burnes maintained that £543 of this should be written off because of improvements which he had made to the farm. It was all the result of the lack of any written agreement, and by September 1782, when neither side could agree, the dispute was submitted to arbitration. Charles Norval of Coilsfield represented Burnes and James Grieve of Boghead represented McLure. William withheld rent pending a decision.

The period of waiting was a sorry time for all the family. The harvest of 1782 was so slow to ripen and was brought in so late that there was little time for pleasure, hardly time even for a visit to Ayr. There is a kind of defiance in the extempore verses which Robert produced at this time:

O why the deuce should I repine,
   And be an ill foreboder;
I'm twenty-three, and five feet nine,
   I'll go and be a sodger.

I gat some gear wi' meikle[1] care,   [¹much
   I held it weel the gither;
But now its gane, and something mair,
   I'll go and be a sodger.

At length the arbitrators told Burnes and McLure that they could not agree either, so John Hamilton of Sundrum was brought in as referee. While Hamilton sifted through the complicated accounts, claims and counter-claims, Burnes salted away every penny he could find so that if McLure's claim succeeded he would be able to pay his debt. The winter of 1782 and the spring and summer of 1783 produced a harvest no better than the previous one, and ruined crops brought starvation to many people. William Burnes's health continued to decline: he knew that he was dying.

In August 1783, Hamilton at last announced his decision, in Burnes's favour. By this time, however, McLure had become caught up in the chain of collapses that followed the closure of the Ayr Bank and was beset by debtors, so he took out a writ of sequestration on the stock and crops of Lochlie in an attempt to force Burnes to pay the full amount. Burnes was stubborn: he took his case to the Court of Session in Edinburgh and must have been in despair when it was thrown out on a technicality. He still did not give up but submitted a new petition, and while this dragged its way through the court he held on to life tenaciously. His appearance changed dramatically. Suddenly he grew frail and thin, and when Dr John Mackenzie was called in from Mauchline he confirmed that William's consumption was advancing mercilessly and death could be held off for little longer. This prognosis brought to Robert the terrible realization that he would soon have to shoulder the full responsibility of the family.

He was working hard on the farm, but his real work was being done in the field of literature. He told Murdoch of his discoveries: "My favourite authors are of the sentimental kind,

such as Shenstone, particularly his Elegies, Thomson, Man of
Feeling, a book I prize next to the Bible, Man of the World,
Sterne, especially his Sentimental journey, Macpherson's
Ossian, &c. these are the glorious models after which I
endeavour to form my conduct."

From all of these authors he picked up points of style which
helped to shape his own writing. His greatest discovery,
among all the conventional writers of this Augustan age, was
the rebel Robert Fergusson. This greatly gifted poet had died
in Edinburgh in 1774 when he was only twenty-four, and it
was probably soon after leaving Irvine that Burns encountered
his poems, at a time when he was at a low ebb. "Rhyme ... I
had given up; but meeting with Fergusson's Scotch poems, I
strung anew my wildly-sounding rustic lyre with emulating
vigour."

Fergusson was thus to point the way towards many of
Robert's irreverent barbs at society and to show him the merit
of vernacular verse. He had a great influence on Burns's life
and work. He was responsible for great bursts of enthusiasm between the bouts of melancholy, for this still remained
a time of inconsistent effort. Burns would dabble with verse,
then drop it, though his "rustic lyre" was kept busy
enough trying out many tunes. There were songs such as
"Mary Morison" and "John Barleycorn", and pawky poems
such as the "Death and Dying Words of Poor Mailie, the
Author's Only Pet Ewe" and "Poor Mailie's Elegy". The ewe
and two lambs had been bought from a neighbour and
tethered near Lochlie farmhouse while Robert was out
ploughing. A simple herd-boy, Hugh Wilson, came rushing
out to the field crying that the sheep had strangled herself in a
ditch, but when Robert and Gilbert dashed home they found
her caught up but far from dead. Robert was greatly amused
by the whole incident, and on the way home that evening he
produced the poem in almost its final form.

The idea for "Poor Mailie" was not new: poets had been
putting words into the mouths of animals for centuries, but
Burns brought to the device his own brilliant touch. The ewe,
Mailie, makes a dying speech to the herd-lad, instructing him
to tell his master to let his sheep wander at will in future, to
look after her lambs and to ensure that her son behaves

himself and never strays and that her daughter consorts only
with "sheep o' credit like thysel".

Songs were now coming to interest Robert more and more.
He carried a book of English songs in his pocket all the time. "I
pored over them driving my cart or walking to labor, song by
song, verse by verse; carefully noting the true tender or
sublime from affectation and fustian."

More mundane matters had to be attended to, however.
Gavin Hamilton, the Mauchline lawyer and fellow-mason at
Tarbolton, heard of the family's plight – no doubt common
knowledge in the neighbourhood – and offered a solution. He
had recently leased the farm of Mossgiel from the Earl of
Loudon. He did not want to farm it himself and so offered the
tenancy to the Burns brothers at a modest rent of £90 a year.
The farm, 118 acres in extent, was good land, situated on a
ridge only a mile away from Lochlie, and the plan which
Hamilton suggested was one which would save the family if
the decision of the Edinburgh courts should go against them.

It is said that Hamilton disliked McLure personally and,
although there is no proof of this, he certainly went out of his
way to protect Burnes against the landlord. He suggested that
the girls of the family should be made employees of their
father retrospectively, just as the boys already were, so that
they could claim wages for several years and would have first
call on William Burnes's money. Secondly, he proposed that
the moment the new crops were sown at Lochlie they should
be sold in the field. Thus McLure could not seize them in part
payment for monies owed.

This escape plan allowed Robert and Gilbert to move
forward into 1784 with easier minds about the future,
although they were now desperately worried about the state of
their father's health. On 27th January news arrived from
Edinburgh that Burnes had won his case, although it was a
Pyrrhic victory, for it had cost almost every penny of his
savings apart from the money he had set aside to meet his just
debts to McLure.

William Burnes could die contented but for one thing – he
had to leave the family in the charge of Robert, and his eldest
son was in many ways ill-suited to guide the fortunes of a
family through the quicksands of life at Lochlie. Robert's

health was far from robust, and he was subject to moods which ranged from black depression to joyful conviviality. His mind was filled with poetry to the exclusion of farming. It was a worrying situation to the dying man who knew nothing of Mossgiel.

Yet death could not be staved off. By now someone had to sit with the old man through the night as they waited for the end. On the night of 12th February it was the turn of Robert and Isabella, and as they sat there through the early wintry hours of the morning they saw their father stir, draw himself up from his pillow and call to Isabella. He told her always to lead a virtuous life, then paused as if he found the next thought difficult to express. There was one member of the family about whom he worried for the future, he said. Robert came close to his father and asked anxiously, "Father, is it me you mean?"

The old man replied that it was, and Robert turned quickly aware to stare at the window, his whole body shaking as he tried to hold back the tears which ran down his cheeks.

William Burnes said no more: a few hours later he died.

William's coffin was slung between two ponies and carried in a sad little procession back to Alloway where he had begun his married life so hopefully nearly a quarter of a century before. In the Auld Kirkyard, only half a mile from the cottage which he had built to hold his family and his future, he was laid to rest. This man of such high ideals, hope, enterprise and hard work had been dogged to the end of the road by debt and worry. In many respects his life was harder than anything his son ever knew: in many ways he bore himself more nobly through adversity.

But that famous son wrote him an epitaph, the final line borrowed from Goldsmith, the words of which are as timeless as any he was ever to write and speak for the generations of Ayrshire farmers, including my own forebears, who lie in the Auld Kirkyard:

O ye whose cheek the tear of pity stains,
    Draw near with pious rev'rence and attend!
Here lie the loving Husband's dear remains,
    The tender Father, and the gen'rous Friend.

The pitying Heart that felt for human Woe;
  The dauntless heart that feared no human Pride;
The Friend of Man, to vice alone a foe;
  "For ev'n his failings lean'd to Virtue's side."

Only a month later the Burns family moved to Mossgiel,
wiping out the heartache of the last years at Lochlie. Robert
had high hopes which he was not afraid to express, for he was
now a man, matured in the hard world of farming and
industry. He was close to being a poet of note too, for Lochlie,
for all its troughs, had been a time of many peaks, of much
reading and a little writing – a time of preparation.

4

The Kirk's Alarm

At sowing time 1784 they moved to Mossgiel. The new farm was a joint enterprise stocked by the savings of all the family. Gilbert kept the books with such meticulous care that he was able to swear that his brother's allowance never exceeded seven pounds a year and he never spent more. "His temperance and frugality were everything that could be wished," he said.

The pattern was very similar to that at Lochlie: hard work and determination pitted against undeveloped land and lack of capital to improve and stock it. Robert, now head of the family, was more determined than ever to succeed, and this resolve was reflected in the fact that he now began to keep a Commonplace Book or Journal in which he recorded comment and verse.

"Come, go to, I will be wise," he wrote. And he did, reading farming books, calculating crops, attending markets and all the time watching, listening and learning, for he was acutely conscious of his burden of responsibility and lack of skill.

He also was aware of his failings. "In spite of 'the devil, the world and the flesh', I believe I could have been a wise man," he wrote, "but the first year from unfortunately buying in bad seed the second from a late harvest, we lost half of both our crops: this overset all my wisdom." Gilbert added another reason: the farm at that time lay "mostly in a cold wet bottom" and for the first four years spring arrived late and frost lasted well past sowing time. This brought on another attack of the depression Robert had experienced at Irvine. He worried about his responsibilities to the family, for he was still very immature, and through that first spring and summer at Mossgiel he felt low – so low that he wrote in his

Commonplace Book a poem which he had probably composed at Irvine, "a prayer, when fainting fits, and other alarming symptoms of a pleurisy or some dangerous disorder, which indeed still threaten me, first put Nature on the alarm".

It is difficult at this distance of time and from the poor medical knowledge of the period positively to identify Robert's illness. Sir James Crichton-Browne diagnosed it as advancing endocarditis and described it thus: "His sensations, which only those who have suffered can fully realise, were terrible, kept him in fear of sudden death and led to acute compunction for errors real or imaginary."

There was no stethoscope, no clinical thermometer and little scientific diagnostic experience to help Dr Mackenzie when he was called in to examine the poet. The doctor prescribed plunges in cold baths for the physical condition and harder work on the farm to combat the melancholy. This was disastrous treatment for Robert's complaint, and he felt very much better by the end of the summer in spite of, rather than because of, the doctor's ministrations. By August he was almost restored to full vigour.

He spent much time at Largieside, drawn there by Elizabeth Paton, a girl who had helped out at Lochlie while his father was on his deathbed. Lizzie had a plain face, but that did not matter. Gilbert has said that love transported his brother from this world and that he immediately invested any girl for whom he had fallen with imagined charms. Gilbert said, "There was often a great disparity between his fair captivator and her attributes."

So it was with Lizzie Paton. This was harvest time, the sun was in Virgo, carnival burst in Burns's bosom, Lizzie became a goddess, and a farm had many quiet corners where two people could be alone. Robert and Lizzie lay together and forgot Mossgiel and all the world. Autumn was making way for winter when the farmgirl told him she was pregnant.

By the time this news came, Robert was firmly established in the social life of Mauchline. Although he kept in touch with his masonic friends at Tarbolton he found the new town gayer and its taverns more jovial and spent more and more time there. Mauchline life – even its inns – clustered round the old Kirk, though not the building which is its centre today. The parish church of Burns's time was pulled down in 1827 and replaced by the present building two years later. Around it lie many of the people who were to shape the poet's life. Gavin Hamilton, responsible for bringing the poet to Mauchline, is here; so is his clerk, John Richmond, a wild young companion of Burns; and here are James Armour and his wife, Burns's future parents-in-law, with four little daughters of Robert and Jean Armour who died in infancy. Not far away lie the ale-house keepers, Agnes Gibson (Poosie Nansie) from the inn which still stands across the road, her daughter "Racer Jess", and Nanse Tinnock, whose inn stood on the other side of the kirkyard.

On the side of respectability lies Dr William Auld – "Daddy" Auld, the parish minister to whom Robert brought a certificate of good conduct for the family from Tarbolton Kirk. That must have given "Daddy" Auld food for thought in later days, at least in so far as it referred to Robert. And here too lies Kirk Elder "Holy Willie" Fisher, as frail as any of those lads whose houghmagandie (fornication) made him purse his thin lips in disapproval. In 1790 Fisher was officially rebuked by the minister for drunkenness, and a little later he was suspected of taking money from the poor box. "Holy Willie's" hypocritical existence ended tragically on a frozen roadside one stormy night in February 1809. His narrow life and sad end would be forgotten today were it not for the young man who had just arrived at Mossgiel.

Some of those who were proving troublesome to "Daddy" Auld (and we must have some understanding for the minister who was responsible for such a wayward flock in a wayward age) became Robert's closest friends. Richmond was one; James Smith, a linen draper in the town, was another. Both were some six years older than the poet and practised fornicators. In their crude, immature, rebellious way they and Burns flouted their prowess with women, forming the comic Court of Equity to try to punish fornicators who would not acknowledge the girls whom they had seduced. The Court is described vividly and brilliantly in a poem which shows the craftsmanship of Burns, who was now reaching the peak of his powers:

First, POET Burns, he takes the CHAIR,
Allow'd by a', his title's fair;
And pass'd nem. con. without dissension,
He has a DUPLICATE pretension. —

Next Merchant Smith, our worthy FISCAL,
To cow each pertinacious rascal;
In this, as every other state,
His merit is conspicuous great;
Richmond the third, our trusty CLERK,
Our minutes regular to mark,
And sit dispenser of the law,
In absence of the former twa;
The fourth our MESSENGER AT ARMS,
When failing all the milder terms,
Hunter, a hearty willing brother,
Weel skill'd in dead an' living leather.[1] —   [[1] a tanner

Without preamble less or more said,
We BODY POLITIC aforesaid,
With legal, due WHEREAS and WHEREFORE,
We are appointed here to care for
The interests of our constituents,
And punish contravening truants;
Keeping a proper regulation
Within the lists of FORNICATION.

The four — judge, fiscal, clerk and messenger-at-arms — were all
well-equipped to try their peers. Lizzie Paton's condition was
becoming all too obvious, and Robert acknowledged
responsibility. Richmond found himself in trouble over Jenny
Surgeoner (whom he married six years later) and had to get
out of Mauchline and go to Edinburgh, while Smith had to
flee also, first to Linlithgow and later to the West Indies.

Before the Court of Equity stood John Brown and Sandy
Dow, two transgressors:

YOU Coachman DOW, and Clockie BROWN,
Baith residents in this town;
In other words, you, Jock and Sandy
Hae been at wark at HOUGHMAGANDIE:
And now when facts are come to light,
The latter ye deny outright. —

FIRST, YOU JOHN BROWN, there's witness borne,
And affidavit made and sworn,
That ye hae bred a hurly-burly
'Bout Jeany Mitchell's tirlie-whirlie,
And blooster'd at her regulator,
Till a' her wheels gang clitter-clatter ...

NEXT SANDY DOW you're here indicted
To have, as publicly you're wyted,[1]   [¹blamed
Been clandestinely upward whirlin
The petticoats o' MAGGY BORLAN;
And gie'in her canister a rattle,
That months to come it winna settle. –

Robert's mother, mortified at her son's transgression, wanted him to marry Lizzie Paton, but Gilbert and his sisters counselled strongly against this, and Robert heeded them. This was a coarse age, and Mauchline and Tarbolton enjoyed the discomfiture of flamboyant, wild Mossgiel when he was duly summoned before the congregation to be rebuked by "Daddy" Auld. Even in that humiliating moment Burns was defiant:

Before the Congregation wide
    I pass'd the muster fairly,
My handsome Betsey by my side,
    We gat our ditty[1] rarely;   [¹rebuke
But my downcast eye by chance did spy
    What made my lips to water,
Those limbs so clean where I, between,
    Commenc'd a Fornicator.

Among his friends he showed equal bravado. John Rankine, who lived between Mossgiel and Largieside and thus knew more about Burns's frequent visits, poked fun at the poet and was rewarded with an "Epistle" in which Robert likened himself to a poacher who had taken a "paitrick hen" (partridge) with his gun and now had to pay the fine. He told Rankine that when the child was born he intended to have further sport to get his guinea's worth. Even at a distance of two centuries the poem's sentiments are coarse, vulgar and in terrible taste. Had Lizzie seen it, and she might well have

Robert Burns by Alexander Nasmyth, 1828

Robert Burns by
Alexander Nasmyth,
1787

Robert Burns.
Engraving by J. Beugo
from the Nasmyth
portrait

Robert Burns. Chalk
drawing by A. Skirving

Robert Burns. Miniature
by Alexander Reid, 1795

The birthplace of Robert Burns, Alloway, Ayrshire

Mount Oliphant, looking across the Firth of Clyde to Arran.
From *The Life of Burns* by P. Hateley Waddell

Lochlie by W. H. Bartlett. From Allan Cunningham's *Life and Complete Works of Burns* (1842 edition)

Mossgiel in the early nineteenth century by J. K. Hunter

Ellisland from the River Nith. From *The Life of Burns* by
P. Hateley Waddell

The house in which Burns died, Dumfries

Agnes Burnes, the poet's mother

Jean Armour, the poet's wife, and her favourite granddaughter

Burns centenary celebrations, 1859, (*above*) at Dumfries and (*below*) at Crystal Palace, London. From *The Illustrated London News*

Maria Riddell by Sir Thomas Lawrence, in the collection of
R. Bankes, Esq.

William Creech   George Thomson

Sibbald's Circulating Library, Edinburgh, by W. B. Johnstone, 1786, showing some of the people Burns met in Edinburgh : (*left to right*) Dr Hugh Blair, Henry Mackenzie, Robert Burns, Alexander Nasmyth, David Allan, James Bruce, Lord Monboddo, Miss Elizabeth Burnett, James Sibbald, Dr Adam Ferguson and young Walter Scott. (The picture is on view at Huntly House Museum, Edinburgh.)

Mrs Frances Anna Dunlop

Margaret Chalmers

Clarinda—Mrs Agnes Maclehose

Gilbert Burns

done so or at least heard a garbled version of it, it would have hurt her very deeply, although it certainly was never intended to do so. Indeed, it was nothing more than bragging before male friends, for when the child was born on 22nd May 1785 Robert showed great gentleness and responsibility in fatherhood:

> Welcome! My bonie, sweet, wee Dochter,
> Tho' ye come here a wee unsought for,
> And tho' your comin' I hae fought for,
>   Baith Kirk and Queir;
> Yet by my faith, ye're no unwrought for,
>   That I shall swear!
>
> ... if thou be, what I wad hae thee,
> And tak the counsel I shall gie thee,
> I'll never rue my trouble wi' thee,
>   The cost nor shame o't,
> But be a loving Father to thee,
>   And brag the name o't. –

While other fathers might have denied parenthood, Robert was open and honest. He acknowledged the child, and she was brought to Mossgiel to be reared by old Mrs Burnes as her own. "Dear bought Bess", as Robert called her later, lived in the Burnes household until her father died, when she returned to her mother, who had by that time married a ploughman and settled down. Bess eventually married John Bishop, overseer at Polkemmet, West Lothian. She died in 1817 and was buried at Whitburn.

After Bess's birth, Lizzie Paton only once reappeared in Robert Burns's life, to make a claim on behalf of her daughter after Robert became famous. She accepted £20 from the proceeds of the first edition of Burns's poems.

The year 1785, which saw a new child in the house at Mossgiel, also saw one leave it. John, the youngest child of the family, died that October, aged fifteen and was buried in Mauchline churchyard in a second-quality shroud, the best his brother could afford.

By the time of John's death Robert Burns's zeal, so intense on moving to Mossgiel, had been sorely dampened by the poor harvest, and he now spent most of his energy carousing with his bawdy friends in Mauchline, with the Bachelors and masons in Tarbolton and with grander friends such as Gavin Hamilton and Robert Aiken ("Orator Bob"), an Ayr lawyer who, although considerably older, was to be a useful ally and patron.

Robert's rhymes were earning him a reputation: he was firing barbs at the prim Tarbolton folk, and now he turned also on Mauchline. Epigrams continued to give delight or annoyance, depending upon the target, and many of his friends received a treasured poetic letter from Mossgiel. There were epistles to Davie Sillar, John Rankine, Willie Simpson, John Goldie, John Lapraik and James Smith, many of which give clues to Burns's progress as a poet and as a man. Allan Ramsay and Fergusson still thrilled Robert enough to make him cry out to John Lapraik:

> O for a spunk o' ALLAN's glee,
> Or FERGUSSON's, the bauld an' slee ...

And to "Winsome Willie" Simpson he described how he was inspired to work:

> Yet when a tale comes i' my head,
> Or lasses gie my heart a screed,
> As whiles they're like to be my dead,
>   (O sad disease!)
> I kittle up¹ my rustic reed;   [¹rouse up
>   It gies me ease ...

> The Muse, nae Poet ever fand her,
> Till by himsel he learn'd to wander,
> Adown some trottin burn's meander,
>   An' no think lang;
> O sweet, to stray an' pensive ponder
>   A heart-felt sang!

This was the time of long poems such as "The Twa Dogs", "Hallowe'en", "The Cotter's Saturday Night" and "The Vision", as well as "Man Was Made to Mourn", which serves as a reminder that depression and ill health were enemies which seldom left his side for long:

> O Death! the poor man's dearest friend,
>   The kindest and the best!
> Welcome the hour, my aged limbs
>   Are laid with thee at rest!
> The Great, the Wealthy fear thy blow,
>   From pomp and pleasure torn;
> But Oh! a blest relief to those
>   That weary-laden mourn!

Though the influence of the sentimental and Augustan authors shows strongly, Robert was gradually discovering his own real self and was turning towards vernacular poetry, often topical, and not without a breath of irreverence. When a Bill came before Parliament to control Scottish distillers he wrote "The Author's Earnest Cry and Prayer, to the Right Honorable and Honorable, the Scotch Representatives in the House of Commons", at the beginning of which he makes a drouthy, irresistible cry:

> Alas! my roupet[1] Muse is haerse[1]!   [1husky
> Your Honors' hearts wi' grief 'twad pierce,
> To see her sittan on her arse
>   Low i' the dust,
> An' scriechan[2] our prosaic verse   [2screeching
>   An' like to brust[3]!   [3burst

An incident or encounter would suddenly spark off a poem, as on the night at Poosie Nansie's when he and his cronies Richmond and Smith happened to fall in with a crowd of beggars. A few days later he showed Richmond a draft of the cantata "The Jolly Beggars".

Good as all this poetry was, it was Burns's defiance of the Kirk which first made him stand out as someone far beyond the run of minor poets in the district. His first brush with the ecclesiastical authorities had been over Lizzie Paton, and he had made "profane rhymes" on the subject. Soon he broadened his warfront.

"I now began to be known in the neighbourhood as a maker of rhymes," he wrote to Dr Moore. "The first of my poetic offspring that saw the light was a burlesque lamentation on a quarrel between two revd Calvinists, both of them *dramatis person* [sic] in my Holy Fair. – I had an idea myself that the piece had some merit; but to prevent the worst, I gave a copy of it to a friend who was very fond of these things, and told him I could not guess who was the Author of it, but that I thought it pretty clever. – With a certain side of both clergy and laity it met with a roar of applause. – Holy Willie's Prayer next made its appearance, and alarmed the kirk-Session so much that they held three several meetings, to look over their holy artillery, if any of it was pointed against profane Rhymers."

The Kirk was facing a number of problems in the late eighteenth century. The Presbyterian Church of Scotland was founded on John Knox's *Scottish Confession of Faith*, which laid down as one of its tenets Calvin's doctrine of predestination: that is to say, a small part of mankind was chosen by God to enjoy salvation, while the great majority of people were doomed to eternal damnation.

Appropriately, those chosen were called the Elect, and it made no difference what kind of lives they led or what moral or civil crimes they committed – they were God's chosen people and singled out for His grace. Others might live saintly lives to no avail.

By the middle of the century the absurdity of this theory was accepted by enlightened churchmen, mainly those in the larger centres of population, but for country ministers like "Daddy" Auld the doctrine stood intact as it had done since 1560. Even in country districts, however, there was a growing body of people to whom the theory of predestination was unacceptable, and they were bitterly opposed by their stricter brethren.

Predestination was not the only division within the Kirk. There was also a long-running dispute over a system of patronage under which ministers were appointed by a lay patron, usually a local landowner, and not by the call of the congregation as the original established form of the Church of Scotland had decreed. After the Treaty of Union in 1707 a Tory government in London, anxious to foist episcopacy on the Scots, passed an Act withdrawing the congregation's authority to choose its own minister and giving that right to patrons. Scottish novelist John Galt's *Annals of the Parish*, written at a time when the war of patronage was still far from over, shows how bitter the opposition to this Act was.

The question of state-church relations further divided the Kirk into Burghers and anti-Burghers and points of theology into New Lights and Old Lights (commonly called New Lichts and Auld Lichts). As a result a series of schisms and secessions ran through the eighteenth century and into the nineteenth, culminating in the Great Disruption of 1843, when a large number of ministers walked out to form their own Free Church. It is ironic that by then the wheel had turned full circle and that it was the Auld Lichts and not the New who had the courage to break away and thus re-establish themselves as the moral leaders of the country.

Naturally the whole quarrelsome affair had a bad effect on the Scottish people. For two hundred years the Kirk had ruled their lives, sometimes tyrannically, and even at its most liberal it still had the power to destroy a man: it could drive him out into a wilderness from which he could never return; it could compel him to attend worship; and it could rebuke him or fine him for moral transgression.

It is often assumed that Burns attacked religion in general in his poems, but this is not so. Like all Presbyterians, he had a mixture of respect for the Kirk and healthy refusal to be overawed by it; he was opposed to the Auld Licht section, and in a poem to the Reverend John McMath, accompanying a copy of "Holy Willie's Prayer", he showed where his target lay:

But I gae mad at their grimaces,
Their sighan, cantan, grace-prood faces,
Their three-mile prayers, an' hauf-mile graces,
   Their raxan conscience,
Whase greed, revenge, an' pride disgraces
   Waur nor their nonsense ...

They take religion in their mouth;
They talk o' mercy, grace an' truth,
For what? – to gie their malice skouth[1]   [1freedom
   On some puir wight,
An' hunt him down, o'er right and ruth,
   To ruin streight.

All hail, Religion! maid divine!
Pardon a muse sae mean as mine,
Who in her rough imperfect line
    Thus daurs to name thee;
To stigmatize false friends of thine
    Can ne'er defame thee.

There was much to criticize in the abuse of power in the Kirk
of the 1780s: nevertheless it would be wrong to side wholly
with Burns and his associates. Look at the issues in the
context of the period. In a time of enormous social turmoil
resulting from agrarian and industrial revolutions people were
unsettled – often literally uprooted from the life and
environment they had known – and social values had become
seriously undermined. It was a permissive age, with lax
morals, and the Kirk saw it as its duty to fight this decay.
There were many sore sinners in Mauchline, Robert Burns
among them, and "Daddy" Auld would have been neglecting
his duty if he had not tried to bring them to book. And narrow
as he might appear to us, William Auld was more deeply loved
than ever he was feared or despised in Mauchline parish.

So Burns's battle was not as simple an issue as it is usually
made out to be: it was more than a profane rhymer against a
canting Kirk. In the years between 1784 and 1786 Mauchline
parish had within its bounds an articulate rebel smarting
against the creepie stool as well as against an old-fashioned
minister. Conflict was unavoidable, and at first sight the poet
seemed at a disadvantage.

Burns's first skirmish was not against the local church but
against two ministers in the Kilmarnock area who were
embattled over parish boundaries. The community savoured
the verbiage which was hurled between the Reverend John
Russell of Kilmarnock and the Reverend Alexander Moodie of
Riccarton, and in "The Twa Herds" Burns ridiculed the pair
as a couple of herdsmen squabbling over land. Although the
poem is full of references to local, long-forgotten issues, it is
easy to share Burns's enjoyment of the ridiculous situation:

The twa best herds in a' the west
That e'er gae gospel horns a blast
This five and fifty simmers past,

O dool¹ to tell!   [¹sad
Hae had a bitter, black outcast
  Atween themsel …

Sic twa – O, do I live to see 't,
Sic famous twa, sud disagree't
And names like, 'Villain, Hypocrite,'
  Each other giein;
While enemies wi' laughin spite
  Say, 'Neither's liein'.'

Worse was to follow for the Auld Lichts, and right on the doorstep of "Daddy" Auld's Kirk too.

It had all begun that first summer after the Burnes family had moved to Mossgiel, when a quarrel had broken out between their landlord, Gavin Hamilton, and the Mauchline Church leaders, the Kirk Session. Urged on by "Holy Willie" Fisher, the Session decided to act against those who were considered to be doctrinally unsound, and at the top of the list was Hamilton, a well-known liberal thinker, who was doubly suspect because he had an Episcopalian family background. Hamilton responded sharply to the Kirk's carping and provoked the elders into producing a detailed list of charges. These accused the lawyer of being absent from church without adequate reason on five Sundays, of setting out on a journey into Carrick on the third Sabbath in January 1785, of habitually neglecting family worship in his home, and of writing an abusive letter to the Session on 13th November 1784.

Hamilton would not be cowed. He took his case to the Presbytery at Ayr, where it was ably put by "Orator Bob" Aiken, and won. The Kirk Session went higher – to the Synod of Ayr – but again were defeated. The whole community followed the quarrel with fascination and a great deal of sympathy for Hamilton. Burns, indebted to the lawyer for the tenancy of Mossgiel, fired a hail of arrows into the stronghold of Fisher and his allies in a bitingly satirical poem called "Holy Willie's Prayer". The poet eavesdrops on the elder at prayer:

O Thou that in the heavens does dwell!
Wha, as it pleases best thysel',
Sends ane to heaven an' ten to hell,
    A' for thy glory!
And no for onie guid or ill
    They've done before thee. –

Willie knew that God had chosen him for the Elect,
predestined him to salvation:

Yet I am here a chosen sample,
To shew thy grace is great and ample:
I'm here, a pillar o' thy temple
    Strong as a rock,
A guide, a ruler and example
    To a' thy flock. –

Willie had sins to confess and he laid these before his Maker –
he confessed he had lifted a "lawless leg" over Meg and lain
with Leezie's lass (but of course only because he had taken
drink). Pushing his own sins behind him, Willie turned to
Hamilton's:

Lord mind Gaun Hamilton's deserts!
He drinks, and swears, and plays at cartes,
Yet has sae mony arts
    Wi' Great and Sma',
Frae God's ain priest the people's hearts
    He steals awa. –

And when we chasten'd him therefore,
Thou kens how he bred sic a splore,
And set the warld in a roar
    O' laughin at us:
Curse thou his basket and his store,
    Kail and potatoes. –

The Old Testament ring, which pervades the whole poem, is
crystallized in the last smug verse:

But Lord, remember me and mine
Wi' mercies temporal and divine!

That I for grace and gear may shine,
    Excell'd by nane!
And a' the glory shall be thine!
    Amen! Amen!

The poem must have set the country in uproar as the Auld
Lichts raged and New Lichts laughed. Robert was appalled,
and possibly more than a little frightened, at the effect it had
on the community. Why else did he feel it necessary to send a
long poem of justification, together with a copy of the
"Prayer", in answer to the request of the New Licht minister,
the Reverend John McMath?

I own 'twas rash, an' rather hardy,
That I, a simple, countra bardie,
Shou'd meddle wi' a pack sae sturdy,
    Wha, if they ken me,
Can easy, wi' a single wordie,
    Louse[1] hell upon me.   [[1]loose

Fired by the success of "The Twa Herds" and "Holy Willie's
Prayer", Robert continued his onslaught on the Auld Lichts
during the autumn of 1785 with "The Holy Fair", a poem set
at one of the great religious festivals held at Communion time
– fairs which ended in an orgy of preaching, eating, drinking,
laughing, and worse. They were an absurd mixture of the
serious and the comic, of the moral and the immoral, of
genuine religious fervour and hypocritical cant. People came
from all sides, the faithful and the faithless, the Elect and the
damned, to hear a torrent of Auld Licht preaching. Deftly the
poet summed up the scene as he joined the throng in the
churchyard:

Here stands a shed to fend the show'rs,
    And screen our countra Gentry;
There, Racer-Jess, an' twathree whores,
    Are blinkan' at the entry;
Here sits a raw o' tittlin' jads,
    Wi' heaving breasts an' bare neck;
An' there, a batch o' Wabster[1] lads,   [[1]weaver
    Blackguarding frae Kilmarnock
            For fun this day.

Here, some are thinkan on their sins,
 An' some upo' their claes;[2]   [2clothes
Ane curses feet that fyl'd[3] his shins,   [3dirtied
 Anither sighs an' prays:
On this hand sits a Chosen swatch,
 Wi' screw'd-up, grace-proud faces;
On that, a set o' chaps, at watch,
 Thrang[4] winkan on the lasses   [4busy
  To chairs that day.

And what did the "grace-proud" faces gaze upon? The
improvised pulpit from which a succession of preachers hurled
an endless assault upon sin. Listen to one:

Hear how he clears the points o' faith
 Wi' rattlin an' thumpin'.
Now meekly calm, now wild in wrath,
 He's stampan, an' he's jumpan',
His lengthen'd chin, his turn'd up snout,
 His eldrich squeel an' gestures,
O how they fire the heart devout,
 Like Cantharidian plaisters
  On sic a day!

When Smith begins his "cauld harangues" on practice and
morals the congregation has had enough and flocks to the
refreshment tent, where things already are hectic:

The lads an' lasses, blythely bent
 To mind baith saul an' body,
Sit round the table, weel content,
 An' steer[5] about the Toddy.   [5stir
On this ane's dress, an' that ane's leuk,[6]   [6look
 They're makin observations;
While some are cozie i' the neuk,
 An' forming assignations
  To meet some day.

No matter how hard the ministers preach or how contrite the
sinners claim to be, the end is always the same:

How monie hearts this day converts,
  O' Sinners and o' Lasses!
Their hearts o' stane, gin night are gane
  As saft as ony flesh is.
There's some are fou o' love divine;
  There's some are fou o' brandy;
An' monie jobs that day begin,
  May end in Houghmagandie[7]   [7 fornication
    Some ither day.

Other Kirk-inspired pieces followed during the winter of 1785-
6, "The Address to the Deil", "The Ordination" and "The
Kirk's Alarm", all of which were received with acclaim by
outward-thinking members of the community. The Kirk's
Auld Licht army was defeated in 1785, but it had not yet lost
the war. A new campaign was about to open on a
battleground chosen by the Kirk, a subject on which it had
already wounded the rhymer from Mossgiel. Burns's own
"holy fair" was bound to end in houghmagandie – and the Kirk
was lying in wait.

5

Plans Overturned

It was when the Lizzie Paton scandal was at its height in 1785 that Robert Burns went to the Mauchline race-week dance, and we hardly need tradition to tell us that he was not given an enthusiastic welcome by the girls. Suddenly his faithful collie dog appeared in the hall and the poet, sending it away, commented that he wished he could find a lass who would love him as well as his dog did.

A week later, as he was crossing the village green, a girl who had overheard the remark about the dog asked if he had found his faithful lass yet. The girl was Jean Armour, daughter of a Mauchline stone-mason, James Armour. She was a lively, attractive girl, just turned eighteen, and had pride and spirit to match that of the lad from Mossgiel.

Although he was preoccupied with Lizzie Paton and her pregnancy that summer, the poet began to see a lot of Jean, and in January 1786, wrote to his friend, David Sillar:

> This life has joys for you and I;
> And joys that riches ne'er could buy;
>   And joys the very best.
> There's a' the pleasures o' the Heart,
>   The Lover and the Frien';
> Ye hae your Meg, your dearest part,
>   And I my darling Jean!
>   It warms me, it charms me,
>   To mention but her name:
>   It heats me, it beets me,
>   And sets me a' on flame!

Inevitably, ardour led to pregnancy, but this time parenthood was not a subject for coarse jokes with male friends. He was still proud of his physical prowess and defiant of authority, but his relationship with Jean was very different from that with Lizzie Paton. The song he wrote has a frail beauty, an almost wistful gentleness which he had never shown even in the tenderest moment towards Lizzie or "dear-bought Bess".

O Wha my babie-clouts will buy,
O Wha will tent[1] me when I cry;   [1tend
Wha will kiss me where I lie
The rantin dog the daddie o't.

O Wha will own he did the faut,[2]   [2fault
O Wha will buy the groanin maut,[3]   [3ale for visitors at
O Wha will tell me how to ca't,   the lying-in
The rantin dog the daddie o't.

When I mount the Creepie-chair,[4]   [4repentance stool
Wha will sit beside me there,
Gie me Rob, I'll seek nae mair,
The rantin dog the Daddie o't.

Wha will crack to me my lane;
Wha will mak me fidgin fain;[5]   [5excited
Wha will kiss me o'er again
The rantin dog the Daddie o't.

This time Robert was prepared – even anxious – to marry the mother of his child. Jean, too, wanted to marry him, and the two signed a document pledging themselves to each other. It was a common enough form of marriage in Scotland at that time (and for a long while afterwards), one that was legal and binding.

Fearing the consequences, Jean withheld the news from her parents until it could no longer be concealed at the end of February or in the first days of March 1786. They were horrified and heart-broken: it was bad enough that a daughter of James Armour, pillar of the Kirk and image of respectability, should be pregnant, but worse that the child should be fathered by the profane rhymer Rab Mossgiel, who had already done penance with Lizzie Paton. Jean produced the marriage document and told them of her vows. Armour

swooned away and had to be revived with a cordial, which gave
him strength to rush off to Ayr to lay the paper before "Orator
Bob" Aiken. For some unexplained and inexplicable reason,
Aiken mutilated the document by cutting out the two names.
Looking back, it seems inconceivable that a respectable
lawyer should do such a thing – after all, it in no way
invalidated the marriage – and one wonders whether in fact
the defacing was done by Armour himself or whether Aiken
did it in the belief that he was protecting Burns from his own
folly.

Reassured in his own mind that his daughter was neither
married nor betrothed to the poet, Armour sent Jean off to
Paisley to stay with relatives, in the hope that the Kirk Session
might not hear of her pregnancy and that she might marry a
man named Robert Wilson, who had shown interest in her.

Burns was hurt, humiliated and enraged. He cared neither
for Armour nor for the Kirk's wrath: what hurt him was the
betrayal by Jean. He wrote to Hamilton on 15th April, an
almost demented letter, in which anger and deep love were
juxtaposed: "Perdition seize her falsehood and perjurious
perfidy! but God bless her and forgive my poor, once-dear,
misguided girl. – She is ill-advised."

In a long letter to John Arnot of Dalquhatswood, he laid
bare his feelings, though he maintained enough control to turn
literary cartwheels and pirouettes in his description of the
seduction of Jean and her rejection of him. This part of the
letter developed into an involved coarse military metaphor, in
which he was a general who had "made a practicable breach
behind the curtain in the gorge of the very principal bastion".
Just when he had slipped "a choice detachment into the very
citadel ... Fortune took alarm, and pouring in her forces on all
quarters, front, flank, & rear, I was utterly routed, my
baggage lost, my military chest in the hands of the enemy; &
your poor devil of a humble servant, commander in chief
forsooth, was obliged to scamper away, without either arms or
honours of war, except his bare bayonet & cartridge-pouch;
nor in all probability had he escaped even with them."

Pausing for breath after this literary climax he suddenly
remembered the seriousness of his letter's purpose. He
admitted that he was silent, sullen and stunned at first, then

furious. The letter ended with a blast against the Kirk, which had been alerted in spite of Armour's carefully-laid scheme for his daughter's escape. "Already the holy beagles, the houghmagandie pack, begin to snuff the scent, & I expect every moment to see them cast off, and hear them after me in full cry: but as I am an old fox, I shall give them dodging and doubling for it; & by & by, I intend to earth among the mountains of Jamaica. ...."

So now Robert planned to escape from his misery and commitment by emigrating. Some authors have suggested that the idea of 'going to earth' in Jamaica was mere bluster on the poet's part, and that he had no intention of leaving the country, but this seems most unlikely since he laid his plans carefully and even after he had become famous he kept his emigration plans in reserve. The facts are that he had arranged to take a job in Jamaica and made all the preparations for the journey, so clearly he intended to go. His trunk was on the way to the ship when events made him change his mind.

Thus, during the first half of 1786, while he matured a "delicious idea" for publication of his poems and for emigration, Robert lived wildly, attending meetings of the freemasons, holding drinking contests with his friends and gathering names of subscribers for his book.

Of course, women were a part of that life, and a new involvement gave him a further reason for getting out of Scotland. After Jean abandoned him, Burns met a Highland girl, Mary Campbell, who was employed as a nursemaid in the Hamilton household. Mary Campbell, the romantic, mysterious Highland Mary cherished by so many Burns idolators, was born in 1763, the daughter of Archibald and Agnes Campbell, from Argyll. Presumably, Mary came to Ayrshire in search of work, and the Hamilton situation was her first post. Later, she is supposed to have become a dairymaid at Coilsfield, near Mauchline. Robert's sister Isabella claimed that the Highland Mary affair was a case of love on the rebound and that her brother took up with the girl only after Jean Armour had been packed off to Paisley. He wrote, in a note only published for the first time by R.H. Cromek in his *Burns Reliquies* in 1808, but held to be authentic by many Burns scholars of today: "My Highland Lassie was a warm-hearted, charming young creature as ever blessed a man with generous love. After a pretty long trace of the most ardent reciprocal attachment, we met by appointment, on the second Sunday of May, in a sequestered spot by the Banks of Ayr, where we spent the day taking farewell, before she should embark for the West Highlands to arrange matters among her friends for our projected change of life."

This 'change of life' included emigration to Jamaica with Mary, and one piece of evidence suggests that what Robert said was true. Tradition has it that the two exchanged Bibles that day, and, although Burns's Bible has never been found, Mary's has and can be seen at Burns Monument at Alloway. The Bible, two volumes published in Edinburgh in 1782, was in Mary's sister's home in Ardrossan for a time and was taken to Canada by her sister's son when he emigrated there. It was discovered at Caledon, near Toronto, in 1840.

The fly-leaf of the first volume is inscribed with Mary's name, and the second volume contains Robert's, but both names have been deliberately mutilated, leaving only the 'M' and 'a' of her name and the name 'Robert' and the 's' of his surname, together with what appears to be the old spelling of Mossgiel – "Mossgaville". Underneath this are the poet's mason's mark and texts from Leviticus and Matthew. There can be no doubt that this is the Bible which Robert gave to Highland Mary, and the obliterations may well be the work of her father, who is said to have destroyed all the poet's letters to his daughter, presumably because she was carrying Burns's child and intended to go to the West Indies with him. The song "The Highland Lassie O", written at this time, shows that he was seriously involved with Highland Mary:

She has my heart, she has my hand,
By secret Truth and Honor's band:
Till the mortal stroke shall lay me low,
I'm thine, my Highland Lassie, O. –

He also confirmed that he intended to take her with him to Jamaica in a later song, "Will ye go to the Indies, my Mary".

I hae sworn by the Heavens to my Mary,
   I hae sworn by the Heavens to be true;
And sae may the Heavens forget me,
   When I forget my vow! ...

We had plighted our truth, my Mary,
   In mutual affection to join:
And curst be the cause that shall part us,
   The hour, and the moment o' time!!!

If the sentiments of his song are true, then Burns had given his
heart and his hand twice within six months and was on a
straight path to bigamy. But if they were true, would he not
have referred to Mary in his letters that summer, when he
made plenty of references to Jean Armour? And why did it
take several years for him to produce "Will ye go to the Indies,
my Mary" and "Thou Lingering Star", which describes "that
sacred hour" when he parted from her? One must assume that,
as his physical condition deteriorated, he became more and
more conscience-stricken. His involvement with Mary had
begun purely as a reaction to Jean's conduct, but it progressed
further and faster than he can have wanted, and Burns must
have had second thoughts and qualms of conscience all
summer if he ever seriously intended to take Mary with him.

In May 1786, Robert was doing his best to forget Jean, but
the houghmagandie pack was determined that he should not
do so. They were in pursuit and, realizing that the game was
up, the Armours capitulated. Jean's return to Mauchline on
Friday 9th June brought all the love and tenderness flooding
back into Robert's heart. He probably heard of her return at
the Kirk on the Sunday, for on the following day he wrote to
David Brice, a Mauchline friend now in Glasgow:

Poor, ill-advised, ungrateful Armour came home on Friday last. –
... What she thinks of her conduct now, I don't know; one thing I
know, she has made me completely miserable. – Never man lov'd,
or rather ador'd, a woman more than I did her: and, to confess a
truth between you and me, I do still love her to distraction after
all, tho' I won't tell her so, tho' I see her, which I don't want to
do. – ... I have tried often to forget her: I have run into all kinds of
dissipation to drive her out of my head, but all in vain: and now

for a grand cure: the Ship is on her way home that is to take me
out to Jamaica; and then, farewel dear old Scotland, and farewel
dear ungrateful Jean, for never, never will I see you more!

But not a word of Mary!

Events moved fast: the Kirk Session summoned Jean
Armour to appear before it the following Sunday, 18th June
and she responded with a confession to "Daddy" Auld: "I am
heartily sorry that I have given and must give your Session
trouble on my account. I acknowledge that I am with child, and
Robert Burns in Mossgiel is the father."

While he awaited his call from the Kirk, Robert worried
about Jean and actually visited the Armours' house to ask
after her, (as he told John Richmond in a letter) not with "the
least view of reconciliation, but merely to ask for her health,
and ... from a foolish hankering fondness, fondness – very ill-
plac'd indeed".

He was sent packing by Mrs Armour without seeing her.

In the letter he gave Richmond another interesting piece of
news: "The Priest, I am informed, will give me a certificate as
a single man, if I comply with the rules of the Church, which
for that very reason I intend to do."

Clearly Robert was prepared to accept his freedom, even
though he knew this could not alter the legal position any
more than Aiken's defacing of the marriage document had
done. He was in an impossible tangle and probably saw this as
his only way out.

Before he despatched the letter to Richmond he added a
jaunty postscript on the following Sunday morning: "I am just
going to put on sackcloth & ashes this day, – I am indulged so
far as to appear in my own seat. *Peccavi, Pater, miseri mei*. ...
The Lord stand wi' the righteous. – Amen, Amen."

The unrepentant double sinner did not even have to face the
congregation while he received his reprimand – the Armours
were furious and demanded that Jean be permitted to stand
beside him, but the minister would not allow it. "Which bred
a great trouble ... and I am blamed as the cause of it," the
poet complained. Now Robert Burns was a free man, free to
marry whomsoever he pleased, free to rush off to the West
Indies, free to begin a new life. Or so he thought. But fate had

other plans in store. John Wilson of Kilmarnock had agreed to print a small book of Burns's poems, and now – despite his notorious reputation – the poet had enough subscribers to enable printing to go ahead. It would be Rab Mossgiel's last defiant gesture to prim Ayrshire, a memento along with his broken loves and bastard weans. In Jamaica he would savour the thought of it.

On 13th July, the book went to press and copies were promised for before the end of the month. It was the gossip of the town, and when the news reached James Armour it gave him something to savour too – Mossgiel would not escape from the law as lightly as he had from the Kirk. A book was bound to bring in money, at least some of which was due to Jean's expected child. Armour had to act quickly, however, before the poet disappeared beyond the control of the Scottish courts, and so he persuaded his daughter to sign a complaint against Robert as father of her unborn child. Then he obtained a writ against the poet.

The moment Robert got wind of this writ he moved quickly to thwart Armour's claim – on 22nd July he executed a deed of trust in favour of his brother Gilbert, conveying to him all his property and "the profits that may arise from the Publication of the Poems presently in the Press". At the same time Gilbert was appointed trustee of "dear-bought Bess", who was to be clothed and educated with the monies from the poems. The document, written in Burns's own hand, was very probably drafted by the Ayr lawyer, "honest" Willie Chalmers, who announced it publicly at the mercat cross in the town. The lawyer was rewarded with a poem, "To Willie Chalmers' Sweetheart", aimed at convincing Willie's ladylove of his worth as a husband. Burns was better informed about events than Armour. Unaware of the poet's disposal of his assets, Armour took out a warrant for Robert's arrest, but Robert learned of it in time "by a channel they little dreamed of". Did Jean herself send word of the imminent arrest? Did lawyer Aiken let it slip in Ayr? Did Gavin Hamilton learn of it on the legal grapevine and pass the information on? Or did "Daddy" Auld, sickened by Armour's greed, warn Mossgiel? The legal grapevine seems the most likely source, but we can only guess at the identity of his informant. At any rate it enabled the poet to go into hiding in time, to move about Ayrshire as he continued his preparations for emigration. On 30th July he wrote to Richmond from Old Rome near Irvine: "My hour is now come. – You and I will never meet in Britain more, – I have orders within three weeks at farthest to repair aboard the Nancy, Capn Smith, from Clyde to Jamaica."

He could not resist dramatizing the situation.

I am wandering from one friend's house to another, and like a true son of the Gospel, 'I have no where to lay my head.' – I know you will pour execration on her head, but spare the poor, ill-advised girl for my sake; tho', may all the Furies that rend the injured, enraged Lover's bosom, await the old harridan, her Mother, until her latest hour! May Hell string the arm of Death to throw the fatal dart, and all the winds of warring elements rouse infernal flames to welcome her approach!

On the following day *Poems, Chiefly in the Scottish Dialect* appeared, overturning Robert Burns's plans once again.

There were thirty-six poems in the book, which became known as the Kilmarnock Edition because it was printed there. They ranged from the long, much-admired "Cotter's Saturday Night" to a group of brief epitaphs, and they were just as varied in subject matter. Burns borrowed ideas and verse forms freely from traditional Scottish folksongs and literature – from men he admired, among them Ramsay and Fergusson – and, although this was still early in his career, built on these foundations poems touched with genius.

The Kilmarnock Edition opened with his recently completed "The Twa Dogs", which not only picked up the old Scottish literary device of giving human feeling to animals, but also affirmed his strong sympathy for the poor and the downtrodden. He put into it all the bitter experience of his father's treatment at the hands of his landlord and produced from an apparently meandering duologue sharply-barbed satire.

"Scotch Drink", which follows, again concerns the poor and their escape and is not just a bacchanalian eulogy. It contains acute observation and assessment of the Scottish way of life. Thus the harvest night,

That merry night we get the corn in
O sweetly, then, thou reams the horn in!
Or reekan on a New-Year-mornin
   In cog[1] or bicker[1],   [[1]drinking vessel
An' just a wee drap sp'ritual burn in,
   An' gusty sucker.

or the smoothing over of a quarrel:

When neebors anger at a plea,
An' just as wud[2] as wud can be,   [[2]angry
How easy can the barley-bree
   Cement the quarrel!
It's ay the cheapest Lawyer's fee
   To taste the barrel.

And at the end there is a moral – a confession of the poet's
contentment with few material possessions and a simple life:

Fortune, if thou'll but gie me still
Hale breeks, a scone, an' Whisky gill,
An' rowth[3] o' rhyme to rave at will,   [[3]abundance
   Take a' the rest,
An' deal't about as thy blind skill
   Directs thee best.

"Scotch Drink" introduces readers of Burns to that favourite
verse form, the "Standard Habbie". This was used by the
seventeenth-century poet Robert Semple of Beltrees in a semi-
comic, semi-serious epitaph on Habbie Simson the Piper of
Kilbarchan:

Kilbarchan now may say alas!
For she has lost her game and grace,
Both Trixie and the Maiden-Trace;
   But what remead?
For no man can supply his place –
   Hab Simson's dead ...

Ramsay, Fergusson and then Burns took it up in turn, though
no one used it to better effect than the Ayrshire bard.
   After "The Author's Earnest Cry and Prayer", a plea for

repeal of the heavy taxation on whisky, the reader is brought up with a start as Burns breaks into brilliant satire with the first of the religious pieces in the book, "The Holy Fair". Many of his readers had probably seen the poem in manuscript already as it circulated his home area, but to his new audience it must have come as an astonishing experience. Here is genius from beginning to end – brilliance of concept, brilliance of execution and the richest language and observation of a scene all fused into a scathing attack on the abuses of the Church of his day. The "greedy glower" of the elder presiding over the collection plate, the "screw'd-up, grace-proud faces" of the congregation and the "eldrich squeel" of the minister had all been observed Sunday by Sunday, but never had they been described so well.

Although many of the poems in the Kilmarnock Edition do not match up to "The Holy Fair", the poet's skill is to be found from cover to cover as he takes Scottish folk themes and language and orderly Augustan English and adds to them his own dimension of genius. Perhaps of all the other poems, the one most admired by his readers then was "The Cotter's Saturday Night", which critics have for generations dismissed as artificial, aping English poets and lacking in the basic truth of most of Burns's work. None the less the poem struck a chord throughout Ayrshire and brought him his introduction to the great Mrs Dunlop, who became a valued correspondent.

"The Death and Dying Words of Poor Mailie" gave a hint of the poet's ability to laugh at a comic situation, "A Dream" a hint of his future unpopular political views; "Hallowe'en" showed how he loved tradition; and "The Vision" illustrated his skill at painting a detailed canvas within the scope of a few lines of verse. In this last poem the end of a winter day is caught in the first stanzas:

> The sun had clos'd the winter-day,
> The Curlers quat their roaring play,
> And hunger'd Maukin[1] taen her way   [¹hare
>   To kail-yards green,
> While faithless snaws ilk step betray
>   Whare she has been.

The Thresher's weary flingin-tree,
The lee-lang day had tired me;
And when the Day had closed his e'e,
    Far i' the West,
Ben i' the Spence, right pensivlie,
    I gaed to rest.

The relationship which grows between a man and his faithful
work-animal – or equally between a man and another man or
woman – is shown in "The Auld Farmer's New-year-morning
Salutation to his Auld Mare, Maggie". It is astonishing that a
Scotsman (for the Scots are a sentimental race) should escape
the trap of ending such a poem on a maudlin, self-pitying
note. Throughout its eighteen "Standard Habbies", the poet
never once becomes emotional or drifts off into a romantic
search for the animal's soul. He simply describes a scene, the
traditional custom of giving the animals a handful of corn each
New Year's morning. In doing so the farmer pauses to recall
what the mare once was:

Thou ance was i' the foremost rank,
A filly buirdly,[1] steeve[2] an' swank,   [[1]stalwart [2]strong
An' set weel down a shapely shank,
    As e'er tread yird;
An' could hae flown out-owre a stank,[3]   [[3]stagnant pool
    Like onie bird.

and what they once were together:

Monie a sair daurk[4] we twa hae wrought,   [[4]day's work
An' wi' the weary warl' fought!
An' monie an anxious day, I thought
    We wad be beat!
Yet here to crazy Age we're brought,
    Wi' something yet.

The final verse glows with a deep affection which has been
likened to "John Anderson My Jo":

We've worn to crazy years thegither;
We'll toyte about wi' ane anither;

Wi' tentie care I'll flit thy tether,
  To some hain'd rig,
Whare ye may nobly rax your leather,
  Wi' sma' fatigue.

The sheep Mailie, the mare Maggie, and a mouse, a louse and a mountain-daisy all appear in the Kilmarnock Edition. The least successful of these is "To A Mountain-Daisy, On turning one down, with the Plough in April, 1786", which rings untrue throughout, largely because of the high-flown language, so unexpected after what has gone before:

The flaunting flow'rs our Gardens yield,
High-shelt'ring woods and wa's maun shield. ...

"To A Mouse, On turning her up in her Nest, with the Plough, November, 1785" is much more effective, from the descriptive opening – "Wee, sleekit, cowran, tim'rous beastie" – to the moral at the end which touches every man. The language is rich, the philosophy perhaps homespun, but it penetrates to the core of us all:

I doubt na, whyles, but thou may thieve;
  What then? poor beastie, thou maun live!
A daimen-icker in a threave[1]   [¹ear of corn in a sheaf
  'S a sma' request:
I'll get a blessin wi' the lave,[2]   [²rest
  An' never miss 't!

The poet feels for the mouse, whose home has been destroyed just when there is no material left to build a new one and December winds threaten. He sympathizes over the hard work it has taken to make the home, so quickly destroyed by the cruel coulter of the plough. But suddenly the poet brings the reader up quite sharply: he has something in common with the mouse:

But Mousie, thou art no thy-lane,
In proving foresight may be vain:
The best laid schemes o' Mice and Men,
  Gang aft agley,[3]   [³ astray

An' lea'e us nought but grief an' pain,
  For promised joy!

Then the poet presses his point home; the animal has the advantage over the human being who is able to understand the bleakness of the future that lies ahead for him:

Still, thou art blest, compar'd wi' me!
The present only toucheth thee:
But Och! I backward cast my e'e,
  On prospects drear!
An' forward, tho' I canna see,
  I guess an' fear!

The louse, least of all the creatures in the Kilmarnock Edition, shows Burns at his best, extracting from every syllable glee at the incongruity of the louse on a lady's bonnet in church. It was just the kind of happening to appeal to Burns – he could hardly wait to be at the insolent creature as he opened the poem with the cry:

Ha! whare ye gaun, ye crowlan ferlie![1]   [1creeping brute
Your inpudence protects you sairly:
I canna say but ye strunt rarely,
  Owre gawze and lace;
Tho' faith, I fear ye dine but sparely,
  On sic a place.

The words build up with a kind of Old Testament zeal:

Ye ugly, creepan, blastet wonner,
Detested, shunn'd, by saunt an' sinner,
How daur ye set your fit upon her,
  Sae fine a Lady!
Gae somewhere else and seek your dinner,
  On some poor body.

A beggar's hair would be a more suitable perch for such a creature, says the poet, and for four more stanzas he watches the louse's progress on the lady's hat, and the reader follows the chase with mounting excitement:

Now haud you there, ye're out o' sight,
Below the fatt'rels, snug and tight,
Na faith ye yet! ye'll no be right,
    Till ye've got on it,
The vera tapmost, towrin height
    O' Miss's bonnet.

But suddenly the lady turns round and we expect to see the
laird's daughter at the very least. But no, it is only Jenny, a
plain country girl:

O Jenny dinna toss your head,
An' set your beauties a' abread!
Ye little ken what cursed speed
    The blastie's[2] makin!   [2ill-disposed creature
Thae winks and finger-ends, I dread,
    Are notice takin!

Having brought us to a point at which we are laughing
nervously at the plight of this poor girl, sitting there at her
devotions, unaware that all the airs she might have been
putting on are rendered comic by this insect, Burns suddenly
strikes home with one of those staggeringly obvious truths
which he was expert at expressing:

O wad some Pow'r the giftie gie us
To see oursels as others see us!
It wad frae monie a blunder free us
    An' foolish notion:
What airs in dress an' gait wad lea'e us,
    And ev'n Devotion!

In the Kilmarnock Edition the public was given glimpses of
three other aspects of Burns – as writer of epigrams, as verse
letter-writer and as song-writer. The epistles to various friends
– a couple to John Lapraik, and one each to David Sillar,
William Simpson and John Rankine – provide a lively insight
into Burns the man and Burns the poet. Here he is among his
male friends, talking freely and with verve on many subjects,
especially on poetry. Here is the man among his own folk
rather than a writer posturing to impress strangers. To
Lapraik he says:

Gie me ae spark o' Nature's fire,
That's a' the learning I desire;
Then tho' I drudge thro' dub an' mire
    At pleugh or cart,
My Muse, tho' hamely in attire,
    May touch the heart.

But it was to Simpson that he presented himself as the bard of his native Ayrshire:

Ramsay an' famous Ferguson
Gied Forth an' Tay a lift aboon;
Yarrow an' Tweed, to monie a tune,
    Owre Scotland rings,
While Irwin, Lugar, Aire an' Doon,
    Naebody sings.

It was early in the poet's career but he was already well on the way to taking his place among Scotland's poets and to singing of the rivers of his beloved western Scottish countryside.

Burns was to sing of much more than a few rivers, although there were few songs in his first volume of poetry – only three in fact, and of these only one of great merit. But what a song! "Corn Rigs" is a masterpiece, one of the best pieces he was ever to write. He took an old tune and an old chorus and fused them simply and skilfully into a song which captures sexual surrender better than any other song in the language – Scottish or English. It is a song to be sung, not read, for the air and the lyric are essential to give the rhythm of the sexual act, building slowly from a simple country scene in which the poet and Annie setting out to walk among the corn rigs:

The time flew by, wi' tentless heed,
    Till 'tween the late and early;
Wi' sma' persuasion she agreed,
    To see me thro' the barley.

Gradually the pace quickens to total sexual satisfaction:

I lock'd her in my fond embrace;
Her heart was beating rarely:

My blessings on that happy place,
    Amang the rigs o' barley!
But by the moon and stars so bright,
    That shone that hour so clearly!
She aye shall bless that happy night,
    Amang the rigs o' barley.

And for the poet too, this was something beyond other earthly
pleasures:

I hae been blythe wi' Comrades dear;
    I hae been merry drinking;
I hae been joyfu' gath'rin gear;
    I hae been happy thinking:
But a' the pleasures e'er I saw,
    Tho' three times doubl'd fairly,
That happy night was worth them a',
    Amang the rigs o' barley.

Corn rigs, an' barley rigs,
    An' corn rigs are bonie:
I'll ne'er forget that happy night,
    Amang the rigs wi' Annie.

Six hundred and twelve copies of *Poems in the Scottish Dialect*
were printed and sold at three shillings each. At once the
poet's fame spread beyond Ayrshire into Galloway, where
servant men and women gave money they could ill-afford to
buy a copy. By the end of August there were only a few copies
left and soon these disappeared. By the time the volume sold
out news of the new poet was just beginning to reach
Edinburgh and a clamour was being set up there for copies.

Influential friends were soon begging Robert Burns to think
hard about going to the capital to show himself off to the
literary lions and to arrange a new printing of his poems.

6

New Friends ... New Love

One early result of Robert's success in print was that Armour, reassured that there was plenty of money available to recompense his daughter and partly out of awe for the printed word, withdrew his warrant and the poet was able to come out of hiding. Armour's intelligence was not as good as Robert's, so he was unaware that all rights to the money had already been passed on to Gilbert. The Kirk Session carried through the process of declaring Burns a single man, which he allowed because he remained doggedly determined to have nothing to do with Jean Armour, although it was not so easy to cast her out of his thoughts. He told his friend Smith:

O Jeany, thou has stolen away my soul!
In vain I strive against the lov'd idea:
Thy tender image sallies on my thoughts,
My firm resolves become an easy prey.

"Against two things however, I am fix'd as Fate: staying at home, and owning her conjugally. – The first, by Heaven I will not do! the last, by Hell, I will never do!"

And yet there remained a sneaking regard for the girl, for he added, "If you see Jean, tell her, I will meet her. So help me in my hour of need!"

He continued to make preparations to join the *Nancy* at Greenock, spending much time riding round the countryside to take farewell of friends and collect subscriptions for his poems. At Kirkoswald he called on Peggy Thomson, the girl who had overset his trigonometry and who was now married and settled in the village. He gave her a present of his poems, and when he left her husband escorted the poet three miles along the road, presumably to Maybole, and they parted in tears. He took leave of his masonic colleagues in Tarbolton and visited Dr Patrick Douglas in Ayr, brother of the man on whose estate he was to work in Jamaica. Here he met a Mr and Mrs White who had just returned from the West Indies. They were horrified to hear of his plans to sail to Savannah-la-Mar and make a dangerous two hundred mile cross-country journey to his destination, Port Antonio. They suggested that he should sail instead in the *Bell* which was due to leave Greenock for Kingston a little later in September under the command of Captain Cathcart, a friend of Gavin Hamilton. This idea appealed to Robert and he set out for Greenock, presumably to make arrangements. On the journey he called on the Reverend George Lawrie at Loudon, who advised Burns strongly that this was no time to rush off abroad just when success had arrived. He told the poet that he would contact some of his influential friends in Edinburgh to see what could be done to make staying at home a more attractive proposition. Burns heeded the minister and returned to Mauchline, explaining to his friend Richmond in Edinburgh that the captain of the *Nancy* had not given him enough notice of the sailing date to allow him to wind up his affairs in Scotland.

As soon as he reached Mauchline he called to see Jean and found her "threatened with pangs of approaching travail". He still had a compartment in his heart for her and told Richmond, "I cannot help being anxious for her situation. But," he added, "she would gladly now embrace that offer she once rejected, but it shall never more be in her power. –"

Two days later, on 3rd September, he again wrote to Richmond, "Wish me luck dear Richmond! Armour has just brought me a fine boy and girl at one throw, God bless the little dears!"

Two days later "Daddy" Auld baptized the twins with the names Jean and Robert, so clearly Jean cannot have thought too unkindly of Mossgiel. As the baptism was taking place the *Nancy* was casting off from Greenock and heading into the Firth of Clyde, and Robert Burns was not aboard.

This was a crowded month. Harvesting had to be done at home, and he visited Kilmarnock in the hope of arranging a second edition of his poems, because all but thirteen copies of the first printing had been sold and demand was far from satisfied. Wilson, the printer in Kilmarnock, refused to risk a new edition unless Robert would pay £27 for the paper required to produce a thousand copies.

Wilson's caution was doubly annoying because the Loudon minister, as promised, had sent a copy of the Kilmarnock Edition to Dr Thomas Blacklock, the blind poetaster, who was an influential figure in the Edinburgh literary world, and a reply at last reached Robert during the third week of September. The letter was grandiloquent, lofty and restrained, but through every line of the doctor's careful prose could be read enthusiasm. Blacklock had already heard of Burns's poems through Dugald Stewart, an Ayrshire man who was Professor of Moral Philosophy at Edinburgh University and who had tried without success to subscribe to the Kilmarnock Edition. The blind poet wrote:

> There is a pathos and delicacy in his serious poems; a vein of wit and humour in those of a more festive turn, which cannot be too much admired, nor too warmly approved; and I think I shall never open the book without feeling my astonishment renewed and increased. ... It has been told me by a gentleman ... that the whole impression is already exhausted. It were therefore much to be wished ... that a second edition could immediately be printed.

Unfortunately, even the enthusiasm of Dr Blacklock could not persuade the canny Wilson to reprint, so Robert had to set his mind to finding another publisher to back a new edition. In the meantime, he enjoyed the adulation of the highest and humblest in Ayrshire, dining at Dugald Stewart's home, Catrine Bank, in the company of Lord Daer, the brilliant young brother of the Earl of Selkirk. Stewart was immensely shrewd in his summing up of Burns, whom he found simple, manly and independent, without arrogance or vanity. The poet took his share in the conversation, but no more, and when talk turned to subjects beyond his ken, he listened. The professor summed up:

> If there had been a little more of gentleness and accommodation in his temper, he would, I think, have been still more interesting;

but he had been accustomed to give law in the circle of his ordinary acquaintance, and his dread of any thing approaching to meanness or servility, rendered his manner somewhat decided and hard.

During that autumn he made one other vitally important friendship. On 14th November he received an order for half a dozen copies of his poems, accompanied by a letter from Mrs Dunlop of Dunlop at Stewarton. Mrs Dunlop had been extremely depressed following a long illness, but she had read "The Cotter's Saturday Night" with such pleasure that she at once sent a message to Mossgiel begging Robert to visit her. Mrs Dunlop was a daughter of Sir Thomas Wallace of Craigie at Ayr, and she was proud of her family's descent from Sir William Wallace, who was, of course, one of Burns's heroes. Robert replied enthusiastically, telling her how his heart had glowed when he visited the haunts of Wallace and promising to call at Dunlop House.

Mrs Dunlop took the closest interest in the poet's life; she scolded, she badgered, but by and large the bard ignored her advice – much to her annoyance. She even accused him of not reading her letters, which is perfectly possible and quite understandable since they were long, ill-written and unpunctuated. The friendship, with Mrs Dunlop in the role of mother-confessor, lasted for many years and was only broken by Robert's foolishness in his last years. With Dr Blacklock, Lord Daer, Professor Stewart, Mrs Dunlop and all his influential friends to occupy him it is not surprising that the *Bell* sailed for Jamaica without Burns, and he began to think about some more congenial and more remunerative means of making a living at home than farming.

Probably at the instigation of his friend Alexander Findlater, an exciseman who lived in Tarbolton, he began to consider the Excise Service as a career, although he feared that his past "follies" might debar him. He wrote to Aiken about the matter:

I have for some time been pining under secret wretchedness, from causes which you pretty well know – the pang of disappointment, the sting of pride with some wandering stabs of remorse, which never fail to settle on my vitals like vultures, when attention is not called away by the calls of society, or vagaries of the Muse. Even in the hour of social mirth, my gaiety is the madness of an intoxicated criminal under the hands of the executioner. All these reasons urge me to go abroad, and to all these reasons I have only one answer – the feelings of a father. This, in the present mood I am in, overbalances everything that can be laid on the scale against it. ...

The pang of disappointment, the sting of pride, stabs of remorse ... what could they be? Did the pangs come from frustration at Wilson's refusal to reprint? Was the sting of pride the indignity of having to pay penance in church? And what were the wandering stabs of remorse, if not for the Highland girl who waited for his call to go with him to Jamaica? Perhaps it was nothing more than general repentance for a year spent in wild dissipation and sexual adventure, and perhaps the remorse and hurt pride were brought on by a fear that this might jeopardize the prospect of a career in the Excise Service.

At Mossgiel one afternoon towards the end of October a letter arrived for Robert. His sister Isabella watched him open it and cross the room to the window to read it more easily. As he read, he turned pale and, without a word, strode out of the house and away from the farm.

The news the letter contained was that Mary Campbell was dead and had been buried in the old West Highland churchyard of Greenock: it was too late to hurry to her side or even to follow her coffin to the grave. We shall probably never know exactly how Mary died. The popular theory is that she had come to Greenock from Campbeltown to stay with relatives and have her baby away from censuring tongues. But this seems impossible for she could have been no more than seven months pregnant, although she may have died as a result of a miscarriage which cost the baby's life as well.

It seems very likely that Mary was expecting Robert's baby and, tired of waiting for the call to accompany him to Jamaica, came to her Macpherson relatives in Greenock, which was the port from which he would be likely to sail. And while she waited for her lover and her child she caught typhus, which was then raging in the town, and died.

This would be a good reason for Robert's enormous burden

of guilt; that she should die whilst carrying his child was bad
enough, but that her visit to Greenock should be to intercept
him was too much. By the time he received the letter he knew
that he would never go to the West Indies; he probably knew
too that he would never have married Mary. He had let her
down in the most cruel and horrible way, and if he carried a
burden of guilt he deserved to. The Highland Mary episode
could not be wiped out from his memory by a night's drinking
or whoring.

The legend of Highland Mary was one of the first to grow
up round the poet's life, and she has not been permitted to lie
in peace in that grave in a Greenock cemetery. As early as 1808
the Greenock Burns Club, the first to be formed in the
country, asked Macpherson for permission to add a tablet to
the memory of Mary Campbell to the grave, and presumably
he agreed. This request alone – made while many people were
still alive who knew Mary and must have known something of
the background to her relationship with Burns – suggests that
there is some substance in the belief that Highland Mary was
important in Robert's life. It was forty years later that a
monument was erected over the grave, a monument at
which Victorian adulators of Burns worshipped as they built
Mary Campbell's story into a legend.

In 1920 the churchyard was needed to give a nearby ship-
building yard space to expand, and after much argument and
discussion it was decided to move all the bodies to the newer
Greenock West Cemetery. On 5th November, in the presence
of a number of municipal officials and representatives of the
Burns Federation, Mary Campbell's grave was opened and
among the remains found was the bottom board of a child's
coffin. At once it was assumed that this was certain proof that
Mary had indeed died in childbirth, bearing Robert's child,
until it was pointed out that a lair is not a single grave but
holds several coffins, and in the Macpherson lair, where Mary
was buried, there were found three skulls and a number of
other bones. Unfortunately, it does not seem to have occurred
to anyone to allow a forensic expert to examine the remains
before they were reinterred and the monument replaced.

Perhaps one can glean as much about Mary Campbell from

Robert's reactions as from the facts, surmises and legends which have grown up round her.

After he received that letter at Mossgiel, Robert kept silence even to his closest friends for three years, until 7th July 1789, when he wrote to Mrs Dunlop. She had sent a letter reprimanding him, and he replied that her letter had given him "more pain than any letter, one excepted, that I ever received".

Five months later, in a moment of illness and depression, he wrote again to Mrs Dunlop on 13th December, telling her that he wished he could believe in a "World to come", for there he would meet "an aged Parent, now at rest from the many buffetings of an evil world against which he so long and bravely struggled. ... There should I, with speechless agony of rapture, again recognize my lost, my ever dear MARY! whose bosom was fraught with Truth, Honor, Constancy & Love. ..." He then quoted the first stanza from "To Mary in Heaven" and added: "Your goodness will excuse this distracted scrawl which the writer dare scarcely read, and which he would throw into the fire, were he able to write any thing better, or indeed any thing at all."

Thus he purged his conscience of Highland Mary, who clearly meant much to Burns, despite the modern Burnsians' attitude, which probably stems from the fact that she detracts from the romantic image which they have tried to attach to Jean Armour. Undoubtedly he felt in some degree responsible for her death. Perhaps this is why he wrote no poetry of great worth about his liaison with her – the hurt of her death was too keen. Highland Mary inspired only "The Highland Lassie O", "Will Ye Go to the Indies, my Mary", "To Mary in Heaven", and possibly (as Gilbert claims but few students of Burns agree) "Flow Gently Sweet Afton". Perhaps the reason was simply that the wound was too deep, his conscience too stricken, his feelings too numb for him to produce more than a "distracted scrawl" when he thought about her even years later.

7

Into the Gay World

Even in moments of despair or depression, Robert did not repine for long when a pretty girl came on the scene. As he was walking by the River Ayr one evening just about sunset at the beginning of November 1786 – "a golden moment for a Poetic heart", he called it – his attention was caught by a young woman who seemed far beyond him socially (although the position might have been very different only a few weeks later). He did not speak to her but went home and wrote:

> O if she were a country Maid,
>   And I the happy country Swain!
> Though shelt'red in the lowest shed
>   That ever rose on Scotia's plain:
> Through weary Winter's wind and rain,
>   With joy, with rapture I would toil,
> And nightly to my bosom strain
>   The bony Lass o' Ballochmyle.
>
> Then Pride might climb the slipp'ry steep
>   Where fame and honours lofty shine:
> And Thirst of gold might tempt the deep
>   Or downward seek the Indian mine:
> Give me the Cot below the pine,
>   To tend the flocks or till the soil,
> And ev'ry day has joys divine
>   With th' bony Lass o' Ballochmyle.

The woman who inspired the verses was Wilhelmina Alexander of Ballochmyle, and on 18th November Burns sent the poem to her accompanied by a letter apologizing "for the liberties that a nameless stranger has taken with you in the

inclosed poem, which he begs leave to present you with". She
did not even reply, and no doubt the result was another small
irritation in Burns's mind against the rich and socially
established. But there was little time to pine over the rebuff.

Robert still had plenty of friends anxious to help him, and
they buoyed his hopes for an Edinburgh printing of the
poems. With that in view he set off for the capital on Monday
27th November on a borrowed pony, though still with
emigration at the back of his mind as a last resort; for he had
noted that the *Roselle* was due to sail from Leith on 17th
December for Savannah-la-Mar. The ride to Edinburgh
occupied two pleasant days, for his fame had spread
sufficiently for him to be entertained on the way. He arrived
on the evening of 29th November and went straight to the
lodgings of his friend John Richmond, whose landlady, Mrs
Carfrae, allowed the poet to share Richmond's bed for a
payment of an extra three shillings a week.

During the first week Burns suffered from a miserable
headache and a stomach complaint, so he did little but
observe the city and its alien way of life. What a contrast it
was to Mauchline: tall tenements, called lands, pierced the
sky, with people packed together on every floor like herrings in
a barrel. Across the valley of the Nor' Loch could be seen the
first elegant New Town terraces, but the old High Street
remained the heart of the capital, with its crowds and its
smells.

Baxter's Close, where Richmond lodged, was typical of
other lands; the lower floors closest to the odours of the street
housed the poorest; the rich and successful lived in the middle
storeys; shopkeepers and merchants occupied the upper
floors; and the garrets housed the working men.

Although every class maintained its place in the social scale,
all lived together in ill-assorted juxtaposition. Mrs Carfrae's
overhead neighbours were a group of prostitutes whose trade
outraged the "staid, sober, piously-disposed, sculdudery-
abhoring Widow" and gave amusement to Robert –
amusement which bubbled over into a glorious letter to John
Ballantine in Ayr:

My Landlady who ... is a flesh-disciplining, godly Matron, firmly believes that her husband is in Heaven; and having been very happy with him on earth, she vigorously and perseveringly practises some of the most distinguishing Christian virtues, such as, attending Church, railing against vice, &c. that she may be qualified to meet her dear quondam Bedfellow in that happy place where the Unclean & the ungodly shall never enter. – This, no doubt, requires some strong exertions of Self-denial, in a hale, well-kept Widow of forty-five; and as our floors are low and ill-plaistered, we can easily distinguish our laughter-loving, night-rejoicing neighbours – when they are eating, when they are drinking, when they are singing, when they are &c., my worthy Landlady tosses sleepless & unquiet, "looking for rest but finding none", the whole night. – Just now she told me, though by and by she is sometimes dubious that I am, in her own phrase, "but a rough an' roun' Christian" that "We should not be uneasy and envious because the Wicked enjoy the good things of this life; for these base jades who, in her own words, lie up gandygoin with their filthy fellows, drinking the best of wines, and singing abominable songs, they shall one day lie in hell, weeping and wailing and gnashing their teeth over a cup of God's wrath!"

Burns always reacted to people, and the warmth of the community life in Edinburgh stimulated him. The rich had not yet deserted the ancient city for the New Town, leaving the old capital to the poor and any cold charity they might find. In such a beehive the news of Robert's arrival spread quickly, and the poet soon found himself in the midst of a literary whirl such as he could never have imagined. To Hamilton back in Mauchline he wrote:

I am in a fair way of becoming as eminent as Thomas a Kempis, or John Bunyan; and you may expect henceforth to see my birthday inserted among the wonderful events, in the Poor Robin's and Aberdeen Almanacks, along with the black Monday, and the Battle of Bothwel Bridge. – My Lord Glencairn & the Dean of the Faculty, Mr H. Erskine, have taken me under their wing; and by all probability I shall soon be the tenth Worthy, and the Eighth Wise Man, of the world.

The Earl of Glencairn and Henry Erskine were influential men and Robert was doing well to be taken up by them so soon. Glencairn, who had already heard of the poet through his poem "The Ordination", was to be his most important patron, and this was Burns's only friendship with a member of the aristocracy that survived for any length of time. Erskine, one of the most brilliant Scottish lawyers of the day, also took to Robert warmly and opened many doors for him.

What doors! What society! Nobility, the law, literature, scholarship ... all welcomed him.

The Duke of Gordon and his gay, unconventional duchess were among the first, and they were quickly followed by the great eccentric, Lord Monboddo, the old judge who believed that men were born with tails which midwives docked secretly, and his daughter, the beautiful Elizabeth Burnett, whom Burns praised in his "Address to Edinburgh":

> Fair Burnet strikes th' adoring eye,
>   Heav'n's beauties on my fancy shine,
> I see the Sire of Love on high,
>   And own his works indeed divine!

At last Robert met Henry Mackenzie, whose *The Man of Feeling* he had admired so much and who had reviewed the Kilmarnock Edition for the *Lounger* just before the poet arrived in the city. Dugald Stewart he already had met, but 'the professor now became a valued friend and the two Ayrshire men used to take early morning walks together to the Braid Hills. Stewart recalled that on these walks Burns charmed him "still more by his private conversation than he had ever done in company". The poet would talk politics or religion or recite great screeds of verse, mostly Scottish ballads, which he said he had learnt from his mother as a child.

The blind poet Dr Blacklock, who had praised the Kilmarnock Edition so warmly, was delighted to meet Burns; Dr Hugh Blair, the precise kirkman and man of letters was greatly taken by the poet; he was elected a member of the Canongate Kilwinning Masonic Lodge, and Francis Charteris, its Grand Master, praised him as "Caledonia's Bard, Brother Burns".

Within weeks there was no one worth knowing in the capital who had not met Robert or who was not anxiously engineering an introduction to him. On 30th December old

Mrs Alison Chambers, author of *The Flowers of the Forest* and a great character in the town, was able to write to a friend:

> The town is at present agog with the ploughman poet who receives adulation with native dignity, and is the very figure of his profession – strong and coarse – but has a most enthusiastick heart of LOVE. He has seen dutches Gordon and all the gay world. His favourite for looks and manners is Bess. Burnet – no bad judge indeed.

Less than a fortnight later she wrote again: "The man will be spoiled if he can spoil, but he keeps his simple manners and quite sober. No doubt he will be at the Hunter's Ball tomorrow, which has made all women and milliners mad."

So the poet was accepting society's adulation with dignity. This suggests that he was ill at ease in this hothouse society, and prim Dr Blair's approval of the poet points to the care with which he was behaving. Professor Stewart reported that Burns had made a good impression, his manner was unaffected and his dress that of a plain countryman with one single concession to fashion – buckskin breeches for special occasions. Blair was pleased to note that Burns spoke English well "and avoided more successfully than most Scotchmen the peculiarities of Scottish phraseology". Praise, indeed, from the minister.

Young Walter Scott remembered Burns as he appeared in the drawing-room of Professor Adam Ferguson at Sciennes:

> His person was strong and robust, his manners rustic, not clownish; a sort of dignified plainness and simplicity, which received part of its effect perhaps from one's knowledge of his extraordinary talents. His features are represented in Mr Nasmyth's picture, but to me it conveys the idea that they are diminished in perspective. I think his countenance was more massive than it looks in any of the portraits. I would have taken the poet, had I not known what he was, for a very sagacious country farmer of the old Scotch school – i.e. none of your modern agriculturists, who keep labourers for their drudgery, but the *douce gentleman* who held his own plough. There was a strong expression of sense and shrewdness in all his lineaments; the eye alone, I think, indicated the poetical character and temperament. It was large, of a dark cast, and glowed (I say literally *glowed*)

when he spoke with feeling or interest. I never saw such another
eye in a human head. ...

Most members of Edinburgh society thought, as they shook
the hand of the ploughman-poet, that they were meeting an
ill-educated natural genius, and Robert cunningly let them
think so. In fact his education was as good as that of most of
those whom he met, so when the fashionable and learned
came to enjoy him as a novelty they quickly fell under his spell
and accepted him for his real worth. Yet Robert was not taken
in and refused to give himself over wholeheartedly to this
society, which he regarded as a quicksand which might suck
him down at the first false step. He expressed this fear to the
Reverend William Greenfield, minister of St Andrews Church,
in a letter whose tone was cooler and more objective than any
other the poet ever wrote:

"Never did Saul's armour sit so heavy on David when going to
encounter Goliath", [he told Greenfield] as does the
encumbering robe of public notice with which the friendship and
patronage of some "names dear to fame" have invested me. – I do
not say this in the ridiculous idea of seeming self-abasement, and
affected modesty. – I have long studied myself, and I think I know
pretty exactly what ground I occupy, both as a Man & a Poet;
and however the world, or a friend, may sometimes differ from me
in that particular, I stand for it, in silent resolve, with all the
tenaciousness of Property. – I am willing to believe that my
abilities deserved a better fate than the veriest shades of life; but
to be dragged forth, with all my imperfections on my head, to the
full glare of learned and polite observation, is what, I am afraid, I
shall have bitter reason to repent. – I mention this to you, once for
all, merely, in the Confessor style, to disburthen my conscience,
and that – "When proud fortune's ebbing tide recedes" – you
may bear me witness, when my bubble of fame was at the
highest, I stood unintoxicated, with the inebriating cup in my
hand, looking forward, with rueful resolve, to the hastening time
when the stroke of envious Calumny, with all the eagerness of
vengeful triumph, should dash it to the ground.

And as if to underline this, he had a stone erected over the
unmarked grave of his idol Robert Fergusson in the
Canongate churchyard. Edinburgh did not take Robert Burns

in, just as he could not continue to deceive it indefinitely.

In fact in the midst of the adulation of that first winter in the capital it should have been possible for others to see, as Burns did, the first shadows of his rejection because of his outspokenness – even rudeness – and the way in which he seemed to go out of his way to cultivate both those whom society considered beneath it and the drunken, wild element within its bounds. A man might be a man for a' that in the eyes of God and Robert Burns, but not in the eyes of Edinburgh society.

The fact is he felt at home in a drinking-club much more than in a drawing-room. For him there was far greater safety in a roistering crowd than in conversation with a single delicate flower of the nobility. It was this that drew him to "Dawney" Douglas's tavern in Anchor Close where the Crochallan Fencibles met.

The improbably named Crochallan Fencibles was one of those drinking-clubs which formed an important part of the Old Town social life during the late eighteenth century. It derived its name from "Dawney" Douglas's liking for a Gaelic song called "Crodh Chaillan" ("Colin's Cattle"), which was easily corrupted by Lowlanders to Crochallan. The Fencible part of the title was a piece of fun-poking at the volunteer corps then being raised for defence against growing threats from Europe which was on the verge of the French Revolution and all the turmoil of Napoleon's wars.

The Crochallan Fencibles, with Robert in their midst, must have been Edinburgh's most lively club. The company was all male, its humour bawdy, and Burns brought to it a literary flourish which it would not otherwise have enjoyed. The Fencibles had a strong legal core, with Erskine and Lords Hailes, Monboddo, Newton and Gillies among the members, who included also Alexander Cunningham, "rattlin', roarin' Willie" Dunbar, Hugh Blair, Adam Ferguson the moral philosopher, Henry Mackenzie, the historian Gilbert Stuart, Robert Cleghorn, a jovial farmer from Saughton Mills, and William Smellie, scholar, translator, first editor of the *Encyclopaedia Britannica* and Robert's next printer. Individually, the Fencibles were valuable friends, but collectively they formed an association with which the poet, as far as society was concerned, should have had rather less contact.

Undoubtedly Burns's broad humour added mightily to his popularity as a Fencible. He already collected and wrote bawdy verses just as he collected folk songs, and he must often have regaled his fellow-members with these. He continued to send bawdy verse to Cleghorn and others, but most of this has been destroyed and for a century and more was judged by the comments of others. Smellie's biographer took it upon himself to destroy Burns's bawdy poems sent to the printer and commented that they were totally unfit for publication. Most of Cleghorn's letters and poems from Burns also disappeared and have been judged for generations by the fact that Lord Byron described them as "full of oaths and obscene songs".

Unfortunately, garbled versions of some of Burns's bawdy poetry and much that was not his at all were published surreptitiously after the poet's death under the title *The Merry Muses of Caledonia*, and while one half of the poet's following sniggered over these, the other half, intent on preserving his good name, pretended that the merry muses either did not exist or had nothing to do with Burns. However, an edition of the *Merry Muses*, with poems carefully authenticated or at least attributed to Burns on solid literary grounds, was published in 1965 under the joint editorship of James Barke and Sydney Goodsir Smith. Even if no more of Burns's Merry Muses come to light we now have enough to show that the poems are masculine, coarse, seldom particularly witty, and certainly not of very high literary quality. Above all, they are not likely to give great offence to anyone today.

However, Robert Burns did not spend the entire winter in Edinburgh regaling the Crochallan Fencibles with erotic verse or waiting nervously for "the stroke of Calumny". Soon after his arrival he appointed William Creech, one of the best-known publishers in the capital, to be his literary agent and publisher. Creech was some fourteen years older than the poet and firmly established as a man of great importance, with a flourishing business linked with the London publisher, Cadell.

Creech, a neat little man in black silk breeches and with generously powdered hair, had a shop at the foot of the luckenbooths, those little lock-up shops which surrounded St

Giles and spilled down the middle of the High Street. A little further up the street towards the Castle, Allan Ramsay had his famous shop. Creech attracted many notables of society, literature and printing to his home in Craig's Close, where he held court every day up to noon, when he hurried off to attend to his business. By two o'clock he was back with his literary salon to talk until four. Everybody of importance came to Craig's Close to enjoy his company and that of other lights in the capital, yet they complained ungenerously about the meanness of Creech's hospitality – which hardly seems fair in view of the large numbers he had to entertain.

It did not take long to get a new edition of the poems under way, although Creech was really little more than an agent, since all the printing costs were borne by Burns himself. Early in December the poet and Creech came to an agreement, details of which we do not know, and before Christmas 1786 subscription notices were printed – notices which claimed that the edition was already in the press.

Robert's noble friends rallied to him: the Duke and Duchess of Gordon subscribed for two dozen copies; through Lord Glencairn influential people such as the Marquis of Graham, the Duke of Montague and the Duke of Portland added their names; and the Caledonian Hunt took up a hundred copies, which earned them the dedication of the work.

By 14th January 1787, Burns had corrected the first hundred and fifty two pages, but he seems to have run into difficulties then, for he did not report completion of the task until 22nd March, when he wrote to Mrs Dunlop:

> I have today corrected the last proof sheet of my poems, and have now only the Glossary and the subscribers names to print. – Printing this last is much against my will, but some of my friends whom I do not chuse to thwart will have it so. – I have both a second and a third Edition going on as the second was begun with too small a number of copies. – The whole I have printed is three thousand. ...

Unfortunately the type for the second edition had been distributed before a decision was taken to print a third, so it had to be reset as quickly as possible, with the result that it contained a number of errors.

As subscribers came forward so fast Creech began to realize that his homespun farmer was the most valuable literary commodity in Scotland at the time, and he took up his option to resell five hundred of the subscription copies at a profit of a shilling each. He also made what he believed was an agreement with Burns to purchase the copyright of the poems, which would give him the right to issue further editions as he chose. But the rights to many of the poems were not Robert's to sell – he had made them over to his brother the previous year to be used for the upbringing of "dear bought Bess". However, before leaving for Edinburgh on 27th November, the poet had instructed Gavin Hamilton to arrange a settlement with Elizabeth Paton, and this was done on 1st December. So Gilbert no longer had need of the monies from the poems.

Burns met Creech on the evening of 17th April 1787 at the home of Henry Mackenzie and asked him to suggest a suitable price for the rights of the poems. Mackenzie proposed a fee of one hundred guineas, which in retrospect seems bad advice on two accounts – the poems should not have been sold outright and the sum was far too low. However, one must realize that poetry then (as now) did not make money, nor was Burns a long-established figure in the literary world. He had blossomed suddenly the previous summer and might wither as quickly. After all, as his letter to Greenfield suggests, Robert himself half expected this to happen, and he was satisfied with the hundred guineas. What displeased him was the time Creech took to pay up.

The memorandum, drawn up by Mackenzie, stated that since Scotland "was now amply supplied with the very numerous edition now printed, he [Creech] would write to Mr Cadell of London to know if he would take a share of the book". Although he had received no reply from Cadell, on 23rd April Creech accepted total responsibility and assignation was made on that day.

Two days earlier, the second edition, usually called the Edinburgh Edition, had appeared.

This new edition was the Kilmarnock one with about a hundred pages more, twenty-two additional poems, few of

which were actually new. "Death and Dr Hornbook", "The
Ordination" and "The Address to the Unco Guid" were all
well known in Burns's circle, although unfamiliar to his
Edinburgh audience. Perhaps the "Unco Guid" struck home
in the smug, successful world of Edinburgh, for it was aimed
at the self-righteous, of whom there were plenty in the capital.

> O ye wha are sae guid yoursel,
>   Sae pious and sae holy,
> Ye've nought to do but mark and tell
>   Your neebours' fauts and folly!
> Whase life is like a weel-gaun mill,
>   Supply'd wi' store o' water,
> The heaped happer's ebbing still,
>   And still the clap plays clatter.

The poem ranges from the caddish, mean jibe of which Burns
was capable at times,

> Ye high, exalted, virtuous Dames,
>   Ty'd up in godly laces,
> Before ye gie poor Frailty names,
>   Suppose a change o' cases;
> A dear-lov'd lad, convenience snug,
>   A treacherous inclination –
> But, let me whisper i' your lug,
>   Ye're aiblins[1] nae temptation.   [[1]perhaps

to the gentler, much-quoted closing stanzas which reveal the
true humanity of the man:

> Then gently scan your brother Man,
>   Still gentler sister Woman;
> Tho' they may gang a kennin wrang,
>   To step aside is human:
> One point must still be greatly dark,
>   The moving Why they do it;
> And just as lamely can ye mark,
>   How far perhaps they rue it.
>
> Who made the heart, 'tis He alone
>   Decidedly can try us,

He knows each chord its curious tone,
   Each spring its various bias:
Then at the balance let's be mute,
   We never can adjust it;
What's done we partly may compute,
   But know not what's resisted.

There were also half a dozen religious poems, "The Calf", and
a number of gloomy pieces including "Stanzas on the Prospect
of Death". Seven new songs included "Green Grow the
Rashes O", "John Barleycorn" and "My Nannie O". A
compliment to his host city, "Address to Edinburgh", had to
be included, but "Tam Samson's Elegy" brought the new
poetry back to life – although it "killed off" one of the poet's
Kilmarnock friends who was very much alive. Tam, a keen
sportsman, had expressed a wish to be buried on the moors
over which he had shot game so often and Burns, on hearing
this, at once wrote an elegy to him.

Rejoice, ye birring Paitricks[1] a';   [1partridges
Ye cootie Moorcocks, crousely craw;
Ye Maukins,[2] cock your fud fu' braw,   [2hares
   Withoutten dread;
Your mortal Fae is now awa',
   Tam Samson's dead!

Tam was a curler of note and he would be missed on the ice in
winter:

When Winter muffles up his cloak,
And binds the mire like a rock;
When to the loughs the Curlers flock,
   Wi' gleesome speed,
Wha will they station at the cock,
   Tam Samson's dead?

He was the king of a' the Core,
To guard, or draw, or wick a bore,
Or up the rink like Jehu roar
   In time o' need;
But now he lags on Death's hog-score,
   Tam Samson's dead!

Tam was indignant at this untimely epitaph and is supposed
to have cried out when he heard it, "I'm no' deid yet." So the
poet added the "Per Contra":

> Go, Fame, an' canter like a filly
> Thro' a' the streets an' neuks o' Killie,
> Tell ev'ry social, honest billie
>   To cease his grievin,
> For yet, unskaith'd by Death's gleg gullie,[1]   [1deft knife
>   Tam Samson's livin!

"The Brigs o' Ayr", another of those jaunty pieces written to
entertain a friend, was a long duologue similar to "The Twa
Dogs". The poet wrote the poem in 1786 for his Ayr friend
John Ballantine, who was one of the civic leaders involved in
building a new bridge across the River Ayr to replace the
ancient arched one which had stood since 1232. The Auld
Brig boasts that it will still be standing when its successor is in
ruins:

> Conceited gowk! puff'd up wi' windy pride!
> This mony a year I've stood the flood an' tide;
> And tho' wi' crazy eild[1] I'm sair forfairn,[2]   [1old age 2worn-out
> I'll be a Brig when ye're a shapeless cairn!

And it was. It happened in 1877 when

> Arous'd by blustering winds an' spotting thowes,
> In mony a torrent down the snaw-broo rowes;
> While crashing ice, borne on the roaring speat,
> Sweeps dams, an' mills, an' brigs, a' to the gate;
> And from Glenbuck, down to the Ratton-key,
> Auld Ayr is just one lengthen'd, tumbling sea;
> Then down ye'll hurl, deil nor ye never rise!

The bridge did rise, but the Auld Brig still spans the Ayr, too,
and carries its share of traffic.

   To persuade Creech actually to publish his poems had been
hard work, and by now Burns felt thoroughly disenchanted
with printers, Edinburgh society and his own future
prospects. He needed time to think, a chance to escape to the

pure air of the country, an opportunity to make up his mind about the future.

If Edinburgh felt that it had summed up Burns, the poet also had fathomed Edinburgh. When Ramsay of Ochtertyre asked whether the *literati* of the capital had improved his poems by their criticisms, Robert replied: "Sir, these gentlemen remind me of some spinsters in my country, who spin their thread so fine, that it is neither fit for weft nor woof."

He was prepared to tell them this to their faces, too, and made no secret of the fact that he preferred rough, rebellious Fergusson's poems to the mim English-aping verse so popular in New Town drawing-rooms. But Burns was worried enough to repeat to the Reverend George Lawrie of Loudon what he had said to Greenfield about his insecurity in Edinburgh.

The future worried him greatly, and he told Robert Muir in Kilmarnock that he had neither house nor home that he could call his own. "I ... live on the world at large."

Yet he knew he could no longer ignore the future: the time had come to set down some roots into the healthy Scottish earth, well away from Edinburgh.

8

The Passionate Pilgrim

Robert's immediate problem was to settle himself in a career which would allow him to continue to write poetry yet provide a living with none of the hardship which his father had known. He had already thought seriously enough about the Excise Service to talk it over with 'Orator Bob' Aiken in Ayr before he left home. He must also have considered the possibility of obtaining some sinecure in Edinburgh, but his brief experience of society there, and what he had heard of its treatment of the unfortunate Fergusson, who had eked out a living as a poet with office work, destroyed any desires in that direction.

Mrs Dunlop had suggested an army career and, although the poet had rejected the idea politely, he must have known in his heart that he could never suffer the social life of an army officer. In the same letter to Mrs Dunlop he made it clear that he would probably stick to what he knew and "commence Farmer" with the capital of two to three hundred pounds which he expected to clear from his poems.

The opportunity came sooner than he expected. Patrick Miller, a director of the Bank of Scotland and chairman of the Carron Iron Company, had bought the estate of Dalswinton on the River Nith just a few miles north of Dumfries, and he offered Robert a lease of one of the farms on the estate. Burns had reservations on two counts: he was diffident about his ability as a farmer and he was unsure of the quality of the farm. He wrote to Ballantine in Ayr expressing this second doubt, for he knew Miller was no judge of land. "And though I dare say he means to favour me, yet he may give me, in his opinion, an advantageous bargain that may ruin me."

But at least he could go and look at the farm, and that gave him an excuse for leaving Edinburgh.

The trip to Dumfriesshire was linked with another reason for leaving the capital. On 7th February he had written to the Earl of Buchan: "I wish for nothing more than to make a leisurely Pilgrimage through my native country; to sit and muse on those once hard-contended fields, where Caledonia, rejoicing, saw her bloody lion borne through broken ranks to victory and fame."

Notice the reason was not to admire the scenery – Robert Burns, like so many who have to earn a hard-won living from the soil, did not have time to look at the countryside for mere pleasure. He was too much concerned with guiding the heavy plough as it cut its shallow furrow or with gathering the meagre harvest before the clouds, which looked so powerful against the mauve hills in the distance, brought rainstorms to destroy the season's work. To the farmer the country either yielded or withheld a living: it was left to Sir Walter Scott to discover its beauty.

Thus, in 1787, when Robert Burns went on his "pilgrimages through Caledonia" he made little comment on the grandeur of the scenery or even on its historic associations. Of Bannockburn he said no more in his journal than this: "Came to Bannockburn – shown the old house where James 3d was murdered – the field of Bannockburn – the hole where glorious Bruce set his standard – Came to Stirling." Even when he wrote to his friend Robert Muir in Kilmarnock he said of this part of the journey: "Knelt at the tomb of Sir John the Graham, the gallant friend of the immortal Wallace; and two hours ago I said a fervent prayer for Old Caledonia over the hole in a blue whinstane, where Robert de Bruce fixed his royal standard on the banks of Bannockburn."

Robert kept records of his tours and these first appeared, edited by Allan Cunningham, in 1834, with a number of additions and deletions to the original text made by Cunningham – alterations which the editor no doubt thought flattering to Burns or to Scotland. He was giving the public of 1834 what it wanted to read rather than what Burns wrote. Instead of the brief note about the visit to Bannockburn, Cunningham took the comment "fervent prayer for Old Caledonia" and built it up into a heroic jingoistic exultation for Bruce, almost as if Robert had sat down on the "blue whinstane" and tossed off "Scots Wha Hae".

But Burns's first tour was not to Bannockburn: it was to the Borders, with the object of looking at the Dalswinton farm, and it was taken during the early summer after the publication of the Edinburgh Edition when Creech was trying to make up his mind about buying the copyright of the poems. Early on the morning of Saturday 5th May, mounted on his mare Jenny Geddes, Burns set out on the Borders tour, accompanied by Robert Ainslie, a law student who was rather in the mould of the poet's Mauchline friends, Richmond and Smith – an easy-going, hard-living, hard-drinking, womanizing young man, who later (like Richmond) became mighty respectable and spoke very vaguely of his adventures with Burns.

Ainslie's home at Berrywell, near Duns, made a useful headquarters for the tour, and they arrived there on the Saturday evening. On Sunday they attended Duns Church and the following day crossed the Tweed at Coldstream, when Burns set foot in England for the first time. Robert was already enjoying his release from bondage in Edinburgh, and he celebrated his arrival in England, Ainslie said, by praying, blessing Scotland and "pronouncing aloud, in tones of deepest devotion, the two concluding stanzas of 'The Cotter's Saturday Night'".

Returning to Scotland, the pair breakfasted at Kelso on Tuesday 8th May and went on to visit Roxburgh Castle and the ruins of the old castle where James II was killed by a bursting cannon. By the time they reached Jedburgh, Burns was beginning to fall under the spell of the Border towns, which he found "had the appearance of old rude grandeur".

At Jedburgh he also fell under the spell of Miss Isabella Lindsay, "a good-humor'd amiable girl; rather short *et embonpoint*, but handsome and extremely graceful". Perhaps his infatuation was the more enjoyable because it annoyed an oldish spinster, also present, whom Burns wished "curst with eternal desire and damn'd with endless disappointment".

On Thursday 10th May he reached Wauchope House, where he looked forward to meeting Mrs Elizabeth Scot, who had sent him in Edinburgh a verse-letter in Scottish dialect, doubting his rustic origin because of the quality of his verse.

She regretted that she could not hear him recite his poetry and promised to send him a plaid to keep him warm. The letter had been a refreshing breath of the country in the stuffy society of Edinburgh, and he responded with the poem "The Gude-Wife of Wauchope". On meeting the "gude-wife" he described her as having "exactly the figure and face commonly given to Sancho Panza", but with "all the sense, taste, intrepidity of force, and bold critical decision which usually distinguishes female Authors".

Ainslie took the poet back to Kelso, then to Dryburgh, "a fine old ruined Abbey"; Melrose, "far-fam'd glorious ruins"; Selkirk, Traquair, Elibanks and Elibraes, and then to Berwick, where Robert was flattered to be recognized by Lord Erroll. After brief visits to St Abbs and Dunbar they returned to Berrywell, and Ainslie, who had to return to Edinburgh, left the poet there in the care of his sister Rachel. Burns spent a few days at the Ainslie home, flirting with Rachel, before he continued his journey to Newcastle in the company of a Mr Robert Kerr and an elderly gentleman named Hood.

His new travelling companions were less congenial company and at Newcastle he wrote to Ainslie: "I dare not talk nonsense lest I lose all the little dignity I have among the sober sons of wisdom & discretion, and I have not had one hearty mouthful of laughter since that merry-melancholy moment we parted."

The trio crossed the Pennines to Carlisle, where Robert was left – thankfully – to continue his journey back to Scotland alone. He reached Dumfries on 4th June, but the warm welcome and honorary freedom of the town which he was given did little to compensate for a worrying letter from Edinburgh which awaited him.

Meg Cameron, a servant-girl he had known in the capital, was pregnant. Going by what he called "the Devil's Day-book" Robert reckoned that he could not yet have "increased her growth much". In fact he had doubted whether he was responsible for her condition at all, adding mysteriously in a letter to Ainslie: "I begin, from that, and some other circumstances to suspect foul play."

However, having thought matters over, he wrote to Ainslie on 25th June, asking him to get in touch with the girl.

Please call at the Jas. Hog mentioned, and send for the wench
and give her ten or twelve shillings, but don't for Heaven's sake
meddle with her as a *Piece*. – I insist on this, on your honour; and
advise her out to some country [friends]. You may perhaps not
like the business, but I must tax your friendship thus far. – Call
immediately, or at least as soon as it is dark, for God's sake, lest
the poor soul be starving.

In response to this, Ainslie broke the news that he, too, had
just become father of an illegitimate son and received from
Burns in return a roaring welcome "to the venerable Society of
Fathers". It seems unfair that Robert's friends were able to
father illegitimate children without reprimand, lawsuit or
any other inconvenience, but that Robert's misdeeds were
always trumpeted aloud.

Robert visited Dalswinton, and although he had had
reservations from the start about the farm's suitability he was
disappointed to discover when he actually saw it that it
seemed unsatisfactory. He therefore made no decision but
agreed to meet Miller again in August and left. He was less
than fifty miles from home, so instead of turning towards
Edinburgh he headed west and rode into Mossgiel
unannounced on 9th June.

He was disgruntled with life, upset to return in such an
uncertain state, and desperately worried to find the situation
at Mossgiel nearly as bad as Lochlie had ever been. Gilbert
was in appalling financial straits, and Gavin Hamilton
approached Robert to stand security for his brother. With
great reluctance the poet refused. "I never wrote a letter which
gave me so much pain in my life," he told Hamilton. He knew
that the refusal to stand guarantor for Gilbert would give
offence to Hamilton, and it did. From then on the relationship
was never the same again.

Gilbert did not hold this decision against his brother,
although others have since suggested that Robert might have
helped the family out. He had already given to them
generously and it is grossly unfair to suggest that this was
conscience money to make up for his abandoning them to go
to Edinburgh. Robert always was a loyal member of the
family: he gave so generously to his mother and to his family
that he jeopardized his own success as a farmer.

Mauchline hardly knew what to make of Robert: the rebel had returned the hero of Edinburgh, for they knew nothing of how the visit to the capital had begun to turn sour. Even the Armours fawned on him so much that Burns was disgusted by "their mean, servile compliance", but they were soon to regret this change of heart for reunion with Jean led to a second pregnancy.

Burns was ill at ease in Mauchline now, not through any fault of Mauchline but because of his own unsettled state. He told his friend Smith on 11th June that he still could not make up his mind about the future. "Farming, the only thing of which I know anything, and heaven above knows but little do I understand of that, I cannot, dare not risk on farms as they are. If I do not fix, I will go for Jamaica." There was a shrewd, canny side to his nature though, for he added, "Should I stay in an unsettled state at home, I would only dissipate my little fortune, and ruin what I intend shall compensate my little ones for the stigma I have brought on their names."

He now set off on another journey – this time to the West Highlands. Many reasons have been given for this tour. Franklin Bliss Snyder suggests in his biography of the poet that it was conscience over the death of Highland Mary that took him to her home country, and Catherine Carswell states that he actually made a pilgrimage to Mary's grave. But Burns himself says, in his autobiographical letter to Dr Moore, that he went to collect subscriptions for his poems.

He kept no journal of this journey, so we know little of the route, apart from a clue in a letter to Ainslie, written from Arrochar on 25th June, which says, "I write this on my tour through a country where savage streams tumble over savage mountains, thinly overspread with savage flocks, which starvingly support as savage inhabitants. My last stage was Inverary – tomorrow night's stage, Dumbarton."

At Inveraray the Duke of Argyll was holding a large houseparty, and the innkeeper neglected the poet in favour of the Duke's guests. This was just the catalyst needed to rouse the poet's anger and he struck out with an epigram.

Who'er he be that sojourns here,
　I pity much his case,

Unless he comes to wait upon
  The Lord their God, his Grace.

There's naething here but Highland pride,
  And Highland scab and hunger,
If Providence has sent me here,
  'Twas surely in an anger.

The bard did enjoy Highland hospitality elsewhere, however.
At one house they danced until three in the morning. "Our
dancing was none of the French or English insipid formal
movements," Robert wrote, "the ladies sung Scotch songs like
angels at intervals; then we flew at Bab at the Bowster,
Tullochgorum, Loch Erroch Side &c. like midges sporting in
the mottie sun, or craws prognosticating a storm in a hairst
day."

After the ladies left at three in the morning the men sat
around the punch bowl until six o'clock, leaving off only to
watch "the glorious lamp of day" over Ben Lomond. Burns had
a short rest and set off with two companions for Dumbarton. It
was a hectic journey, Robert recalled.

My two friends and I rode soberly down the Loch side, till by
came a Highlandman at the gallop, on a tolerably good horse, but
which had never known the ornaments of iron or leather. We
scorned to be out-galloped by a Highlandman, so off we started,
whip and spur ... my old mare, Jenny Geddes, one of the
Rosinante family, strained past the Highlandman in spite of all
his efforts with the hair halter; just as I was passing him Donald
wheeled his horse, as if to cross before me to mar my progress,
when down came his horse, and threw his rider's breekless a—e in
a clipt hedge; and down came Jenny Geddes over all, and my
Bardship between her and the Highlandman's horse. Jenny
Geddes trode over me with such cautious reverance, that matters
were not so bad as might well have been expected; so I came off
with a few cuts and bruises, and a thorough resolution to be a
pattern of sobriety for the future.

A somewhat chastened bard was made a freeman of
Dumbarton on 29th June, although his name does not appear
on the burgess roll. One reason for this omission may be that
the Reverend James Oliphant, whom Burns had lampooned

in "The Ordination", was now minister there and opposed the honouring of the poet. Dr George Grierson, the poet's travelling companion, says the Dumbarton bailies were denounced publicly by Oliphant "for conferring honours on the author of the vile, detestable and immoral publications".

Burns was back at Mossgiel by the end of the month and spent the whole of July there, moody and unproductive – the only poem he composed was an elegy on the death of Sir James Hunter-Blair, an Ayrshire man who had been Lord Provost of Edinburgh.

He was still thinking about the Dalswinton farm, a settled future, and now about marriage. "I shall somewhere have a farm soon," he told his friend Smith on 30th June; "I was going to say, a wife too; but that must never be my blessed lot. I am but a younger son of the house of Parnassus, and like other younger sons of great families, I may intrigue, if I choose to run all risks, but must not marry."

As he brooded at Mossgiel and nursed his wounds from the Loch Lomond adventure, Robert began to write a long autobiographical letter to Dr John Moore, a Scot living in London, telling his life story up to the time of his departure for Edinburgh. The crafty Mrs Dunlop had engineered this, and we are grateful that she did so, because it fills in many gaps in our knowledge of Burns's early life.

Burns had planned a longer Highland tour in the autumn of 1787, and he went back to Edinburgh at the beginning of August to try to prise money out of the reluctant Creech and to prepare for it. No doubt it was also a relief to escape from the atmosphere of penury at Mossgiel, for he had already lent Gilbert £180 interest free and without a set repayment date, but it was perfectly apparent that more would soon be called for.

On arriving in Edinburgh he found that his friend Richmond had no room for him, so he moved to the house of his prospective travelling companion, William Nicol, in Buccleuch Square. Nicol, a classics master at the High School and a fellow-mason, was one of those friends who did Robert more harm than good. But the poet, although he described his journey with the Latin master as like "travelling with a loaded blunderbuss at full cock", was doggedly loyal and complained remarkably little.

Nicol was a coarse, egotistical, pompous, tetchy character, universally disliked throughout the capital. As a schoolmaster he was a bully and as a friend he was a boor. His ill-temper and hustle spoiled the high moments of the tour, especially the precious time which Burns spent with his family in the north-east, and damaged the poet's relationship with some influential people. Nicol's haste spoiled the poet's composition too: Burns wrote that he tried to polish up the " 'Petition of Bruar Water' as well as Mr Nicol's chat and jogging of the chaise would allow".

The poet and Nicol arranged to leave on 25th August and at the schoolmaster's suggestion travelled by chaise: "Nicol thinks it more comfortable than horseback," commented Burns to Ainslie, "to which I say Amen."

Burns was glad to be on his way because Meg Cameron, learning that he was in the capital, took out a writ against him. The poet admitted liability, which left him free to set out on the tour but committed him to further expense later.

On the journey Robert's mind was on farming, sizing up the land between Edinburgh and Linlithgow as "fine, improven, fertile country", although he would not exchange the people for those of his native Ayrshire. "The more elegant and luxury among the farmers," he commented. "I always observe, in equal proportion the rudeness and stupidity of the peasantry. ... I think that a man of romantic taste, a 'Man of Feeling', will be better pleased with the poverty, but intelligent minds, of the peasantry of Ayrshire."

At Carron he showed one of those flashes of anger to which he was given when thwarted. It was Sunday and he and Nicol were refused admission to the great iron-works. The poet wrote on the inn window with a diamond ring:

We cam' na here to view your warks
    In hopes to be mair wise,
But only, lest we gang to hell,
    It may be nae surprise:
But when we tirl'd at your door
    Your porter dought na bear us,
Sae may, shou'd we to hell's gate come,
    Your billy Satan sair us!

The manager of the blast-furnace reacted equally sharply:

> If you came here to see our Works
>   You should have been more civil
> Than give a fictitious name,
>   In hopes to cheat the Devil.
> Six days a week to you and all,
>   We think it very well;
> The other, if you go to church,
>   May keep you out of Hell.

When he saw the state of ruin into which Stirling Castle had been allowed to decay, nationalism welled up strongly in him and he took his diamond ring and scratched on a window pane the lines:

> The injured Stewart line is gone,
> A race outlandish fill their throne;
> An idiot race, to honor lost,
> Who know them best despise them most.

It cannot be that Burns was a Jacobite: like so many Lowland Scots he suffered from double judgment on the Stuarts – his heart yearned for the ancient house which went back to the establishment of Scotland's independence, while his head told him that the latter Stuarts were unworthy of the throne they claimed. Since Charles Edward, the king over the water, was a dying man and his heir a cardinal of the Roman Catholic Church, it seems unlikely that the Presbyterian Robert Burns supported a Jacobite restoration. Burns quickly realized the enormity of his indiscretion and when he returned to Stirling a few months later he smashed the window pane.

From Stirling the travellers turned east, along the foothills of the Ochils to Harvieston, to spend a night with Gavin Hamilton's step-mother and her family before going on to Crieff, Taymouth and Aberfeldy, where Burns composed the jaunty "Birks of Aberfeldy" on the spot.

> Let Fortune's gifts at random flee,
> They ne'er shall draw a wish frae me,
> Supremely blest wi' love and thee
>   In the birks of Aberfeldy. –

Bony lassie will ye go, will ye go, will ye go,
Bony lassie will ye go to the birks of Aberfeldy.

Pausing only to honour Neil Gow, the great Scottish fiddle-
tune composer, and to hear the master play, Burns and Nicol
arrived at Blair Atholl on the last day of August and were
welcomed at Blair Castle by the Duchess of Atholl in the
absence of the Duke. At table the poet was shrewdly observed
by Josiah Walker, tutor to the Duke's son, who had already
met him at Dr Blacklock's in Edinburgh:

His person though strong and well knit, and much superior to
what might be expected in a ploughman, was still rather coarse in
its outline. His stature, from want of setting up, appeared to be
only of the middle size, but was rather above it. His motions were
firm and decided, and though without any pretensions to grace,
were at the same time so free from clownish constraint, as to show
that he had not always been confined to the society of his
profession. His countenance was not of that elegant cast which is
most frequently among the upper ranks, but it was manly and
intelligent, and marked by a thoughtful gravity which shaded at
times into sternness. In his large dark eye the most striking index
of his genius resided. It was full of mind, and would have been
singularly expressive, under the management of one who could
employ it with more art, for the purpose of expression. He was
plainly but proudly dressed, in a style midway between the
holiday costume of a farmer and that of the company with which
he associated. In no part of his manner was there the slightest
degree of affectation. In conversation he was powerful. His
conceptions and expression were of corresponding vigour, and on
all subjects were as remote as possible from commonplace.

On his return the Duke of Atholl pressed the poet to stay
longer, and he met Robert Graham of Fintry, who had just
been appointed one of the Scottish Commissioners of the
Excise. It was a fortunate meeting, for it revived thoughts of
the Excise Service in Burns's mind; Graham was later to be of
great help to the poet when he came to consider the career
seriously. Unfortunately Nicol nagged Burns to leave and he
missed meeting the great Henry Dundas, "King" Dundas, the
all-powerful Scottish politician who might have helped him
tremendously.

On 2nd September Burns and Nicol left Blair Atholl and headed north, between mountain peaks which bore the first snows of winter, by Dalwhinnie, Aviemore, to Castle Cawdor, where they "saw the identical bed in which Tradition says king Duncan was murdered by Macbeth". Soon they reached Inverness, the Highland capital, so "jaded to death with fatigue" that Robert had to ask the Provost to postpone a meeting.

At Culloden the shallowness of Burns's Jacobite feelings was revealed by the terse comment: "Come over Culloden Muir – reflections on the field of battle." Leaving the scene of Charles Edward Stuart's defeat behind, Burns and Nicol continued through Nairn, Forres and Elgin to Castle Gordon at Fochabers, where Burns was warmly welcomed by his friends the Duke and Duchess of Gordon, who invited him to stay the night. The family were about to sit down to dinner and invited Burns to join them. It was only after he had drunk a few glasses of wine that Robert told them that his friend was at Fochabers, and the Duke offered to send a servant to fetch Nicol. Burns insisted on going himself, but Nicol was furious and slighted and was adamant that he would not accept the invitation. Robert had no choice but to leave.

In a letter accompanying the song "Streams that Glide in Orient Plains" Burns referred to "that unlucky predicament which hurried me, tore me away from Castle Gordon" and blamed "that obstinate son of Latin-Prose", Nicol. The discourteous departure from Fochabers was unfortunate, for it ruined another relationship with influential people who might have been able to help Burns.

Burns now came to the home country of his Burnes forbears. He passed through Aberdeen to Stonehaven where he met some of his relatives. "I spent two days among our relations, and found our aunts, Jean and Isbal still alive and hale old women," he told Gilbert. Robert Burnes, a lawyer in Stonehaven, he found "one of these who love fun, a gill, a punning joke, and have not a bad heart; his wife a sweet hospitable body, without any affection of what is called town-breeding". Robert also arranged to meet his cousin James from Montrose, but his stay was cut short by the hustling Nicol who forced him to leave after breakfast on 13th

September and sail down the coast to Arbroath. They picked up their chaise there and continued by Dundee, Perth and Kinross, and on Sunday 16th September they "came through a cold barren country to Queensferry-dine-cross the Ferry, and come to Edinburgh".

In the capital Robert found much to be done. The Meg Cameron business still hung over him, Creech was prevaricating and Miller was pressing him to reach a decision on the Dalswinton farm. Robert told his prospective landlord that he had to stay in Edinburgh to ensure Creech's settlement and pointed out that if Miller had left Dalswinton by then, his factor would be able to arrange the lease. Miller may not have realized it, but there was another piece of business which Robert had not mentioned but was to delay him.

Robert was now anxious to settle down with a wife, and he realized that this would not only be desirable but essential if he were to become a Dumfriesshire farmer. And were he to choose the Excise Service, the Commissioners were likely to insist on his being settled with a wife before they would accept him.

But whom should he marry? Lizzie Paton and Jean Armour were obvious candidates since they had borne him children; Meg Cameron soon would do so; Mary Campbell was dead, and all his other romances were brief, if passionate, affairs, now forgotten. Although the three women with whom he had had sexual relations all had satisfied him on that level, none had been able to satisfy him intellectually, and he hankered after a woman who could support him in his literary work. Jean had by far the best mind of the three, but she was not an intellectual and was the last to claim to be so.

However, there was one other girl who both appealed to him and was above the others socially and intellectually. Margaret (Peggy) Chalmers was the daughter of an Ayrshire farmer, a girl some years younger than the poet and a connection by marriage of Gavin Hamilton. Robert may well have known her at Mauchline, and he almost certainly met her in Edinburgh the previous winter when she spent much time playing the pianoforte to Dr Blacklock.

Peggy Chalmers was a small, neat girl with hazel eyes, not

particularly beautiful but with a lively personality. She was sensible and much more down-to-earth than Robert could ever have been. She was intelligent and well read, although she rarely talked of books or intellectual matters.

Robert fell head over heels in love with her and sent her letters abounding with quotations and French tags. "My dear Countrywoman," he called her.

I know you will laugh when I tell you that your Pianoforte and you together have played the deuce somehow about my heart, but you know that black story at home. My breast has been endowed these many months, and I thought myself proof against the fascinating witchcraft but I am afraid you will, I feelingly convince me what I am. I say, I am afraid, because I am not sure what is the matter with me, I have one miserable bad symptom which I doubt threatens ill. When you whisper or look kindly to another, it gives me a draught of damnation.

So at the beginning of October the poet left Edinburgh on his last tour in pursuit of Peggy. This time he took as his companion Dr James Adair, the son of an Ayr doctor and a kinsman of Mrs Dunlop. The companions rode to Stirling where they encountered Nicol by chance and spent some time with him drinking toasts, singing songs and reciting poems. Burns wisely took the chance to smash the window on which he had scratched the Jacobite verse during his previous visit.

They continued their journey to Harvieston, where Peggy was staying, and Burns began his wooing. Alas, after directing things from "the distant formal bow" to "the familiar grasp of the waist", Peggy thought he was becoming too ardent.

Miss, construing my words farther I suppose than even I intended, flew off in a tangent of female dignity and reserve, like a mountain lark in an April morning; and wrote me an answer which measured me out very completely what an immense way I had to travel before I could reach the climate of her favour. But I am an old hawk at the sport; and wrote her such a cool, deliberate, prudent reply, as brought my bird from her aerial towerings, pop, down at my foot like Corporal Trim's hat.

He spent eight ecstatic days at Harvieston with Peggy and very likely proposed to her, but was refused. Peggy chose instead the duller, but much more reliable, Lewis Hay, a partner in an Edinburgh banking house. Adair was more fortunate; he fell in love with Charlotte Hamilton, whom he met at Harvieston, proposed, was accepted, and married her on 16th November 1789.

Robert felt the blow of Peggy's rejection deeply, and the feeling of emptiness endured; nearly a year later he wrote to her, "When I think I have met with you, and have lived more of real life with you in eight days than I can do with almost anybody I meet with in eight years – when I think on the improbability of meeting you in this world again – I could sit down and cry like a child."

Poor Robert! At last he had found a girl who was on his intellectual plane, who appealed to him greatly, but who rejected him for the security which he knew in his heart he could never give her.

Rejected Robert and the successful Adair filled the rest of their time visiting important people and places in the district. They saw Castle Campbell, the Cauldron Linn and Rumbling Bridge, and they met Sir William Murray of Ochtertyre in Strathearn, John Ramsay of Ochtertyre in Kincardine, and old Mrs Bruce of Clackmannan Tower, the last of a line descended from a branch of the great Bruce family, who knighted the poet with Robert the Bruce's sword. She had, she told him, a better right to do so than some people.

On the way home the pair stopped at Dunfermline Abbey and, while Adair mounted the cutty stool, Robert – spirits restored – delivered from the pulpit a comic parody of the lecture which "Daddy" Auld had read him in Mauchline Kirk fifteen months before. On Saturday 20th October they crossed the Queensferry and rode into Edinburgh, Robert nursing a heavy cold.

During the ensuing month Burns wrote two songs to Peggy Chalmers, "Where Braving Angry Storms" and "My Peggy's Face", but these did not help him to forget her. He knew that Peggy could give him much more even than Jean Armour. But her intelligence might well have clashed with his, and she certainly would not have tolerated his waywardness. Though he may well have realized this, the wound was none the less deep.

They remained good friends, and near the end of the poet's life, on 12th July 1796, he sent her a song, which he had probably composed many years before, proving that on his visit to Harvieston he had not had eyes for the Rumbling Bridge, the Cauldron Linn or Castle Campbell, or ears even for old Mrs Bruce; he saw and heard only the "Fairest Maid on Devon's Banks", Peggy Chalmers.

How pleasant the banks of the clear-winding Devon,
    With green-spreading bushes, and flowers blooming fair!
But the bonniest flower on the banks of the Devon
    Was once a sweet bud on the braes of the Ayr.

9

Talk Not of Love

Robert returned to Edinburgh from Harvieston to bad news which upset him more than his letter telling his friend Richmond about it would suggest. It is strange how, when he had disagreeable information to pass on to male friends, he would wrap it up in bravado which often amounted to bad taste. At the beginning of October 1787, Jean, the twin daughter of Jean Armour, died, and on the 25th of the month Burns wrote to Richmond:

> By the way, I hear I am a girl out of pocket and by careless, murdering mischance too, which has provoked me and vexed me a good deal. – I beg you will write me by post immediately on receipt of this, and let me know the news of Armour's family, if the world begin to talk of Jean's appearance any way.

He had intended to stay in Edinburgh for no more than a fortnight, but he could not get Creech to settle and so he lingered on, wondering and worrying about his future and things at Mauchline. His only consolation was that his writing had found a new outlet – one very dear to his heart.

In Edinburgh drawing-rooms at this time there was a great fashion for singing old songs – had Peggy Chalmers not spent much of last winter playing and singing to Dr Blacklock, and had Robert not enjoyed the vogue as much as anyone? Music-teaching had been largely taken over by foreigners such as Pietro Urbani and Domenico Corri, who harmonized and otherwise "improved" traditional Scottish airs until they lost their original vigour. Words, too, were not safe in the hands of the improvers, many of whom had neither knowledge of nor feel for poetry. Folksongs were usually about political subjects, jollity, love or plain sex, and when these were considered coarse or improper the "improvers" rewrote them. Worse still, this was the time when mim-mouthed men who should have known better were trying to pass Scotland off as North Britain and were anglicizing the language. Every Scot should be grateful to Burns for making them aware of the Scottish heritage and for preserving so much of it.

In Edinburgh James Johnson had begun work collecting and refurbishing Scottish songs in a work entitled, *The Scots Musical Museum*. Burns had always been interested in Scottish songs, and as soon as he heard of Johnson's enterprise he began to help him. Unfortunately Robert was too late to contribute more than a couple of songs to the first volume, which appeared in 1787. Johnson had taken a great deal of material from Allan Ramsay's *Tea-Table Miscellany*, including English verses of poor quality, and had also included English airs. Burns was determined that only genuine Scottish tunes should be used and that the words should be of high quality. Thus in the autumn, when he wrote to Richmond from Edinburgh, he said: "I am busy at present assisting with a Collection of Scotch Songs set to Music by an Engraver in this town. – It is to contain all the Scotch Songs, those that have been already set to music and those that have not, that can be found."

Soon Burns had virtually taken over the *Museum*, working with its musical editor, Stephen Clarke, organist at the Episcopal Church in the Cowgate. Fortunately Johnson appreciated the ability of his new collaborator and allowed him so much freedom that he became its literary editor in all but title. Burns wrote to all his friends who might be able to help, among them Peggy Chalmers, Dr Blacklock, the Duke of Gordon and Dr John Skinner, author of "Tullochgorum's My Delight". In his letter to Skinner his enthusiasm boiled over:

The world may think slightingly of the craft of song-making, if they please, but, as Job says – 'O that mine adversary had written a book!' – let them try. There is a certain something in the old Scotch songs, a wild happiness of thought and expression, which peculiarly marks them, not only from English songs, but also from the modern efforts of song-wrights, in our native manner and language. ...

Burns did not depend solely on other people's contributions. He set to work himself, recalling the songs his mother and others had sung, songs such as "Ca' the Yowes", which he first heard from Tibbie Pagan, an old drunken wife in Irvine when he lived there to learn flax-dressing. Then he took some of the fiddle-tunes, which were enjoying a great revival now that dancing was considered a respectable pastime in Scotland, and set words to them.

Burns never lost interest in the *Museum*. He constantly badgered both Johnson and Clarke to keep at the work year in, year out. On 15th November 1788, for example, he wrote to Johnson:

> I can easily see, my dear Friend, that you will very probably have four Volumes. – Perhaps you may not find your account, *lucratively* in this business; but you are a Patriot for the Music of your Country; and I am certainly. Posterity will look on themselves as highly indebted to your Publick spirit. – Be not in a hurry; let us go on correctly; and your name shall be immortal.

In 1787 the second volume of the *Museum* appeared, forty of its hundred songs coming from Burns's pen. Volumes three and four, which followed in 1790 and 1792, contained fifty of Robert's songs. By that time, however, Burns had also become involved with George Thomson's *Select Scottish Airs* and so was unable to devote much time to Johnson's work. As a result, the fifth volume of the *Museum* only appeared in 1796, when both Burns and Clarke were dead. Although the poet left much material behind him the sixth and last volume did not appear until 1807. But this is to move ahead too fast: in 1787 Robert was to recruit another helper in his search for songs for the *Museum* and at the same time became involved in a strange love-tangle with a married woman.

It happened at the beginning of December 1787, while Robert was again worrying about his future. He had come to Edinburgh for a couple of weeks in the autumn and had stayed on, trying to get his money out of Creech. Now he simply had to make up his mind about the Dumfriesshire farm because, as he had expected, interest in him was waning in Edinburgh. The reason was partly because the novelty of the "plowman-poet" was decreasing, partly because he was not mixing in Edinburgh society. He also tended to speak over-frankly when it would have been better to keep silent, and he would even turn up in Tory drawing-rooms wearing a waistcoat in the buff and blue Whig party colours. It was all too much for a great many grand hostesses of the capital!

On 6th December, Robert was invited to a tea party at the home of John Nimmo, an Excise revenue officer, where one of the guests was a Mrs Agnes Maclehose, a dabbler in poetry who had carefully engineered the meeting through Nimmo's sister. Agnes – or Nancy – Maclehose was an attractive woman of twenty-nine who was living in Edinburgh after the breakdown of her marriage to a ne'er-do-well law agent, James Maclehose. The daughter of a Glasgow surgeon and the niece of Lord Craig, one of the law lords at the Court of Session in Edinburgh, she had married Maclehose, a heavy-drinking, wild young man, in the face of strong opposition from her family, and now she regretted it. Maclehose had been forbidden the Craig family house in Glasgow but had persisted in seeing Nancy in secret. He once booked every other seat on the Glasgow to Edinburgh coach on which he knew she was to travel so that he could have her to himself for the entire journey. And, of course, the ardent lover won in the end. But after four years of marriage and three children, Nancy left her husband and returned to her father's house with her two surviving children. After her father died in 1782, Nancy moved to Edinburgh, where she lived in a small flat off the Potterrow on an annuity from her father's estate, supplemented by gifts from her uncle. Maclehose continued to live off his family until at length they refused to pay his debts any more and he borrowed money for his fare to Jamaica.

Nancy had come to Edinburgh in search of culture, and as a poetaster she was anxious to meet the man about whom the whole town was talking. No doubt Burns's other reputation had not escaped her either, and she – living alone, with a husband far away in Jamaica – was at least a little intrigued by him. The meeting clearly did not disappoint her, for she went straight home from the Nimmo tea party and invited the poet to tea on the following Thursday. Robert was unable to come on that day but suggested Saturday instead, and so a second meeting was arranged.

Before this second meeting Robert met with an accident, a drunken coachman causing him to fall and suffer "a good, serious, agonising damn'd hard knock on the knee". He must have been annoyed, for here, hard on the heels of the Peggy Chalmers, was a suitable candidate for an intellectual wife, and he was desperately anxious to continue the acquaintanceship. No doubt at this stage he knew little of the husband in the West Indies and, passion aroused, cared even less. At any rate he now wrote Nancy a letter which took a great stride forward in their relationship – a letter which dealt with things more basic than poetry:

I can say with truth, Madam, that I never met with a person in my life whom I more anxiously wished to meet again than yourself. ... I know not how to account for it – I am strangely taken with some people; nor am I often mistaken. You are a stranger to me; but I am an odd being: some yet unnamed feelings; things, not principles, but better than whims, carry me farther than boasted reason ever did a Philosopher.

Her reply was a strange mixture of encouragement and caution, a reciprocation of these "unnamed feelings" tempered with reason and deep Calvinistic fervour – two influences which never held the poet back. She understood his feelings perfectly:

Perhaps instinct comes nearer their description than either "Principles" or "Whims". Think ye they have any connection with that "heavenly light which leads astray?" One thing I know, that they have a powerful affect on me, and are delightful when under the check of reason and religion. ... Pardon any little freedom I take with you.

Nancy tried out her poetry on him and on 12th December he wrote back encouragingly: "Your lines, I maintain it, are poetry, and good poetry." But he was more interested in Nancy herself, for he told her: "Had I been blest as to have met with you *in time*, might have led me – God of love only knows where."

It was the first mention of the word love, and Nancy retorted sharply: "Do you remember that she whom you address is a married woman?"

Despite this reprimand, she did not abandon the friendship: indeed, it blossomed as they adopted classical names in the fashion of the time, and continued their correspondence as passionately as ever. He was to be Sylvander and she Clarinda: it seems out of character for Robert Burns to agree to such an artificial basis for their correspondence, but he did so, no doubt thinking that this was how an intellectual young woman ought to be wooed.

Although Nancy had repulsed the poet's first mention of love, by Christmas she was sending him verses which showed her feelings and how badly her unfortunate marriage still hurt:

> Talk not of Love, it gives me pain,
>   For Love has been my foe;
> He bound me with an iron chain,
>   And plunged me deep in woe.

But she would not budge from her moral standpoint, for she continued in the same poem:

> Your Friendship much can make me blest,
>   O, why that bliss destroy!
> Why urge the odious, one request
>   You know I must deny!

Obviously Robert had lost no time in carrying a casual friendship on to love and intimacy. He was impatient with Nancy, for this was not the kind of love-making to which he was accustomed, but he fell in with her wishes and continued to flatter her poetry to gain his end. But he did baulk at the word "odious" – for the request was far from odious to him! – and when he set the poem to the tune "The Borders of Spey" for the *Musical Museum* he altered "odious" to "only".

But he did not altogether abandon the direct approach. On 28th December he wrote to her: "I do love you if possible still better for having so fine a taste and turn for Poesy. – I have again gone wrong in my usual unguarded way, but you may erase the word, and put esteem, respect, or any other tame Dutch expression you please in its place."

The direct assault, cunningly disguised by a compliment to her poetry, ought to have been irresistible, but she took shelter behind religion. "Religion, the only refuge of the unfortunate, has been my balm in every woe," she told him. "O! could I make her appear to you as she has done for me! ... I entreat you not to mention our corresponding to anyone on earth. Though I've conscious innocence, my situation is a delicate one."

Her situation was indeed delicate. She was a married woman, with two children to whom she was devoted, dependent for financial help on an uncle who certainly would not approve of any liaison, especially one involving a poet whose reputation was known throughout Edinburgh. A crisis was near, yet she could not give him up. Clarinda was desperate to find some ways of continuing the relationship with Sylvander, yet without surrendering to him. It was desperately difficult in those early days of 1788, for Robert was as ardent a lover as ever. He told his old friend Brown, now a sea-captain: "Almighty Love still 'reigns and revels' in my bosom; and I am at this moment ready to hang myself for a young Edinr widow."

At last, with the greatest difficulty and pain, Robert was able to make the journey to Potterrow in a sedan chair, and now the affair reached white heat. While shocking her deliciously as he pursued his love, he horrified her by revealing to her that he admired Milton's Satan and had to explain that he only admired Satan's "manly fortitude in supporting what cannot be remedied – in short, the wild broken fragments of a noble, exalted mind in ruins". He told her about his autobiographical letter to Dr Moore and confessed his sexual relationships with Jean Armour and others and their results. Nancy in turn told him all about Maclehose and her unhappy situation.

She still could not turn him away and on 12th January Burns reached the last stage to which Nancy Maclehose was prepared to go before she pulled down the shutters of religion and ordered him to stop. Her confusion – compounded of continued attraction heaped on shame – sent her to her writing-desk as soon as he left:

I will not deny it, Sylvander, last night was one of the most exquisite I ever experienced. Few such fall to the lot of mortals! Few, extremely few, are formed to relish such refined enjoyment. That it should be so, vindicates the wisdom of Heaven. But though our enjoyment did not lead beyond the limits of virtue, yet to-day's reflections have not been altogether unmixed with regret.

What she did not know – could not know – until much later was that her ardour and caution in close harness had driven Burns to take Jenny Clow, a tavern girl, with the usual results.

In the meantime, perhaps thus relieved, he was able to reassure Nancy: "I would not purchase the *dearest gratification* on earth, if it must be at your expense of worldly censure; far less, inward peace."

So January passed, as letters increased the temperature of the love affair. At last, on the 23rd, Robert again came to Clarinda and pushed his love-making to the limit – short of intercourse. Clarinda knew how slender was the barrier that stopped her and how easily it might be crossed if she did not take care. Neither religion nor reason, which both held her back, troubled Robert, and she was desperately afraid.

"I am neither well nor happy," she wrote to him. "My heart reproaches me for last night. If you wish Clarinda to regain her peace, determine against anything but what the strictest delicacy warrants."

Robert capitulated. "Sylvander's honour ... that you shall never more complain of his conduct."

The poet tried hard to abide by his decision when they met again on the 26th, but had some difficulty. After he left she protested mildly: "Perhaps the line you had marked was a little infringed – it was really; but though I disapprove I have not been unhappy about it. ... I wish our kind feelings were more moderate ... try me merely as your friend."

"Try me merely as your friend."

What a request to make to a man capable of such passion as Robert Burns. It was impossible: friendship was useless to him. He loved with all the desire of a man, and he had to find someone who could give herself to him. It was probably then that the poet realized how hopeless the Clarinda affair was, how utterly hopeless.

But Nancy Maclehose did not want to lose the poet. On 6th February she hinted that she might be free to come to him one day. "Your friend may yet live to surmount the wintry blasts of life and revive to taste a spring time of happiness."

"Name the terms on which you wish to see me, to correspond with me, and you shall have them," he told her. "I must love, pine, mourn, and adore in secret." And at midnight on the same day he wrote a second letter to her: "After a wretched day, I am preparing for a sleepless night." This was prompted by news from Nancy informing him of a "haughty, dictatorial letter" she had received catechizing her. We do not know for sure from whom this letter had come, but it was almost certainly from her uncle, Lord Craig, or from her minister, the Reverend John Kemp, of the Tolbooth Church, who was her confidant at that time. It is unlikely that she had spoken to either of these men: in the tight community of Edinburgh it was unnecessary, for everyone must have been aware of the romance and its increasing tempo. She sent the letter to her lover, and Robert's reaction was anger – anger against the wagging tongues in the first place and secondly against Maclehose, "the man who has repeatedly, habitually, and barbarously broken every tie of duty, nature, or gratitude to you". During the next few days he saw her several times and in between sent letter after letter apologizing for the injury he had caused to her reputation. He protested eternal and disinterested friendship but offered her no hope.

"I esteem you, I love you, as a friend," he told her. "I admire you, I love you, as a woman beyond any one in all the circle of creation."

The poet was almost out of his mind with worry and frustration. Clarinda was tearing his peace to shreds, but he was also worried about the decision on the Dalswinton farm, which he had still not made. His overtures to the Excise Commissioners about an appointment were jeopardized by hints from meddling tongues that he would have to mend his ways if he were to be considered for the service. On top of this there were rumours that Creech was bankrupt and would be unable to pay him. From Mauchline came news which suggested that unless he could do something Gilbert would soon be bankrupt too, and of course Jean was nearing her time again.

At long last, quite unexpectedly, Creech settled with him, probably spurred on by a "frosty keen letter" sent by the poet in January, and Robert for once was well-off. He told Mrs Dunlop that he had cleared £540, and Dr Snyder has calculated that the poet's total receipts would be about £750, of which a little less than half would remain as net profit. With Creech's £100, this would give him in the region of £450. Certainly by the time he had paid £200 and other sums to his brother to keep Mossgiel afloat and lived in Edinburgh for two winters and toured Scotland, he would have little more than £200 left to finance his farm in Dumfriesshire.

Creech had much to answer for: he had caused Robert much worry, and it was his fault that the poet had had to hang around Edinburgh, becoming entangled with Nancy Maclehose, and worse still, losing many friends in the capital.

Now Robert decided to move out of Edinburgh, out of Nancy Maclehose's life, and out of the terrible tangle in which he was enmeshed. To Clarinda he wrote:

Look forward, in a few weeks I shall be some where or other out of the possibility of seeing you: till then, I shall write you often, but visit you seldom. ... Be comforted, my Love! the present moment is the worst; the lenient hand of Time is daily and hourly either lightening the burden, or making us insensible to the weight.

Three days after he wrote that letter, on 18th February, he mounted his mare and turned towards the west. In his saddle-bags he carried two shirts for little Robert, Jean's surviving twin, as a present from Clarinda.

He gave Clarinda a copy of Young's *Night Thoughts* and a pair of drinking glasses accompanied by a poem, which bears all the marks of his anguished mental state:

Fair Empress of the Poet's soul,
    And Queen of Poetesses;
Clarinda, take this little boon,
    This humble pair of Glasses.

And fill them high with generous juice,
    As generous as your mind;
And pledge me in the generous toast –
    'The whole of Humankind!'

'To those who love us!' – second fill;
   But not to those whom we love,
Lest we love those who love not us: –
   A third – 'to thee and me, Love!'

Long may we live! Long may we love!
   And long may we be happy!!!
And may we never want a Glass,
   Well charg'd with generous Nappy!!!!

Neither could have known that this was the end of the affair;
the ache of a broken heart was all that was left for Clarinda.

10

Farewell Rakery!

Once again Robert Burns was glad to leave Edinburgh, but he was in no hurry to reach Mauchline, where Gilbert's financial straits and Jean Armour's impending confinement both had to be faced. So he went first to Glasgow to spend a merry evening with his young brother William and his old friend Richard Brown, whose ship, *Mary and Jean*, was at Greenock. He spent a night at Paisley with Alexander Pattison and rode on the following day to Kilmarnock to see Robert Muir, who was seriously ill with consumption. After that he called at Dunlop House, near Stewarton, to meet Mrs Dunlop, and he was so carried away with enthusiasm that he committed a solecism by sending one of her daughters a copy of Gray's poems after he left. Staid old Mrs Dunlop at once wrote saying that she did not allow her daughters to receive presents from men who were not members of the immediate family and that she proposed to return the book or to allow her daughter to tear out and keep only the pages with the poems which she liked best. Burns must have held Mrs Dunlop in high esteem, for he acquiesced instead of reacting angrily, as he would have done with many another person.

At last, on Saturday 23rd February 1788, he rode into the close of Willie's Mill at Tarbolton, where Jean Armour was staying with his friend William Muir. Jean had either been banished from or left the family home in Mauchline because of her parents' reaction to her pregnancy. With only a few friends to support and comfort her, she was now awaiting her confinement.

Poor Jean was delighted to see him again, but compared to the fine-mannered Clarinda and the Dunlop girls she seemed coarse and uncouth. And her fawning attitude irritated him. He wrote to Clarinda:

Now for a little news that will please you. – I, this morning as I came home called for a certain woman. – I am disgusted with her; I cannot endure her! I, while my heart smote me for the prophanity, tried to compare her with my Clarinda; 'twas setting the expiring glimmer of a farthing taper beside the cloudless glory of the meridian sun. – Here was tasteless insipidity, vulgarity of soul, and mercenary fawning; there, polished good sense, heaven-born genius, and the most generous, the most delicate, the most tender Passion. – I have done with her, and she with me. ...

But he could not abandon Jean in her plight. He found her an upper room in a house in the Back Causeway, overlooking Mauchline Kirk, which, although not very comfortable, was at least her own. It was there, only eight days later (on 3rd March), that she gave birth to twin girls.

Before he heard that he had become a father again Burns wrote to Ainslie, telling him of the situation in Ayrshire as he had found it on his return:

Jean I found banished like a martyr – forlorn, destitute and friendless; all for the good old cause: I have reconciled her to her fate: I have reconciled her to her mother: I have taken her a room: I have taken her to my arms: I have given her a mahogany bed: I have given her a guinea: and I have f–d her till she rejoiced with joy unspeakable and full of glory. But – as I always am on every occasion – I have been prudent and cautious to an outstanding degree: I swore her, privately and solemnly, never to attempt any claim on me as a husband, even though anybody should persuade her she had such a claim, which she has not, neither during my life, nor after my death. She did all this like a good girl, and I took the opportunity of some dry horselitter, and gave her such a thundering scalade that electrified the very marrow of her bones.

Today, one's blood runs cold at the thought of so treating a pregnant woman. The letter was either the most disgusting piece of sexual bravado in the English language, to impress a bawdy friend, or Burns's conduct was beyond human feeling and strangely out of character. And if his account is true, then Burns must bear some responsibility for the deaths of his twin daughters within a few weeks of their birth.

But is it true? All the other facts in the letter are accurate enough – the girl was forlorn, destitute, friendless and in some trouble with her mother; he did rent a room for her and buy her a bed, and very probably he did give her a guinea. So it is reasonable to think that he did attempt sexual intercourse, gave her "a thundering scalade" and made her promise never to make any claim on him as a husband. However, it is possible that he exaggerated his vigour, for his pen always tended to run away with him in letters to lusty young friends.

Nevertheless, in this letter Robert Burns reached the lowest depth of behaviour in his whole life.

There were other things on his mind still, and the letters which he wrote to more important people were much more temperate, the kind he thought the recipient would like to receive.

To Lord Glencairn he said that he intended to give his brother some of the proceeds of the Edinburgh edition of the poems in order to hold the family together and that he intended to bank the £200 or so remaining. He was worried about the future and wrote: "Extraordinary distress, or helpless old age have often harrowed my soul with fears; and I have one or two claims on me in the name of father: I will stoop to anything that honesty warrants to have it in my power to leave them some better remembrance of me than the odium of illegitimacy."

For the moment he was set against farming: the memory of his father's agonies, as he tried to keep above the waves of penury, was too vivid to allow him to take the farm on Dalswinton estate. He told Graham of Fintry:

> I had intended to have closed my late meteorous appearance on the stage of life, in the country Farmer; but after discharging some filial and fraternal claims, I find I could only fight for existence in that miserable manner, which I have lived to see throw a venerable Parent in the jaws of a Jail; there, but for the Poor Man's best and often last friend, Death, he might have ended his days..

He was keen to make a career in the Excise Service, and before leaving Edinburgh had written to Glencairn and Graham of Fintry seeking their assistance in obtaining an appointment. His manner was no longer that of a young rebel but of a man seeking preferment, and he wrote to Glencairn:

> I know your Lordship will disapprove of my ideas in a request I am going to make to you, but I have weighed seriously my situation, my hopes and turn of mind, and am fully fixed to my scheme if I can possibly effectuate it. – I wish to get into the Excise; I am told that your Lordship's interest will easily procure me the grant from the Commissioners; and your Lordship's Patronage and Goodness which have already rescued me from obscurity, wretchedness and exile, embolden me to ask that interest.

To Graham of Fintry he was even more explicit:

> You know, I dare say, of an application I lately made to your Board, to be admitted as Officer of Excise. – I have, according to form, been examined by a Supervisor, and today I give his certificate with a request for an Order for instructions. – In this affair, if I succeed, I am afraid I shall but too much need a patronising Friend. – Propriety of conduct as a Man, and fidety and attention as an Officer, I dare engage for; but with any thing like business I am totally unacquainted. – ... I know, Sir, that to need your goodness is to have a claim on it; may I therefore beg your Patronage to forward me in this affair till I be appointed to a Division; where, by the help of rigid Economy, I shall try to support that Independence so dear to my soul, but which has too often been so distant from my situation.

It is clear that, when it suited him, Burns was glad to accept the patronage of the great whom at other times he denigrated, collectively and individually. And thanks to Graham's influence, he was in due course accepted for the service.

In a month which was an ordeal from start to finish, the Excise Commissioners' examination was particularly unpleasant. "Pride and passion" welled up within him, the poet said, as he was questioned "like a child about my matters and blamed and schooled for my inscriptions on a Stirling window". But at length, on the last day of the month, he was accepted for the Excise Service and instructed to take his three-week course under James Findlay, the excise officer at Tarbolton.

This was a time of tremendous mental anguish, for he

watched his twin daughters hold on to life by a slender thread which finally snapped and left both him and Jean grief-stricken. And as if he had not enough to trouble him, Robert finally reached his decision about the farm. Several letters written at the time make it clear that he had no intention of taking Patrick Miller's farm, and on 23rd February he told Clarinda that he had agreed to visit it "merely out of compliment to Mr Miller". Then on 2nd March he wrote again to her, saying, "I am thinking my farming scheme will yet hold."

Robert did not trust his own judgment on farming matters, perhaps because he realized that his interest was not deep enough, so he asked John Tennant of Glenconner, an older and more experienced man, to accompany him to Dumfries to look over the farm. Together they examined Ellisland, on the Dalswinton estate, and Tennant declared himself "highly pleased with the farm", and advised the poet to accept. On 13th March, Robert signed the lease.

But something else – something mysterious – was happening to Robert Burns at this same time. On the 7th he had written to his sea-captain friend, Brown, to say that he had "towed" Jean "into a convenient harbour where she may lie snug till she unload; and have taken the command myself – not ostensibly, but for a time in secret".

The convenient harbour is obvious enough – it was the room in Mauchline's Back Causeway; but what did he mean by telling his friend that he had taken command in secret? He must have meant more than that he had simply rescued her from her dreadful plight, and another letter, to Peggy Chalmers this time, makes things a little clearer. On 7th April he wrote to her from Mauchline: "I am going on a good deal progressive in mon grand bût, the sober science of life. I have lately made some sacrifices for which were I viva voce with you to paint the situation and recount the circumstances, you would applaud me."

We know he had made progress towards his *grand bût* by taking the farm and being accepted by the Excise Service, but neither had cost him any sacrifice. At last, on 28th April, all was made clear in a letter to his friend Smith, now in Linlithgow: "There is, you must know, a certain clean-limbed, handsome, bewitching young hussy of your acquaintance, to whom I have lately given a matrimonial title to my corpus."

The news was out: Robert Burns had married Jean Armour.

Over the next few weeks he passed the information on to his uncle, Samuel Brown in Kirkoswald (at the same time ordering three or four stones of feathers from Ailsa Craig for his nuptial bed), to James Johnson in Edinburgh – "so farewell Rakery!" – and to Robert Ainslie, who must have been astounded at Robert's volte-face.

We have no idea when or how the marriage took place, but it appears to have been an affirmation or reaffirmation of the vows taken some fourteen months earlier. And if the marriage was confirmed before Robert went off to look at Ellisland and to settle his future in Edinburgh, poor Jean must have wondered if once again she would be made to deny her vows, perhaps by her own husband this time. But Robert did not change his mind: having made his decision he proudly spoke of Jean as his wife, telling Ainslie: "I am truly pleased with this last affair: it had indeed added to my anxieties for Futurity, but it had given a stability to my mind & resolutions unknown before; and the poor girl had the most sacred enthusiasm of attachment to me, and has not a wish but to gratify my every idea of her deportment."

At the end of June the poet wrote to Smith that he had seen "Daddy" Auld about the marriage and that if two witnesses would testify that he had acknowledged the marriage in their presence all would be well. On 5th August 1788 Robert and Jean finally made their peace with the Kirk – Robert gave "a guinea note on behoof of the poor" and Mauchline Kirk Session recorded a minute recognizing them as man and wife.

More intriguing than *when* the marriage took place is the question *why* it took place. And to decide this would help us to establish when. If, when Robert referred to taking command, he meant to marry, then there can be no single reason – he would marry to put his private life in order before he embarked on a career in the Excise or in farming, and perhaps out of pity for Jean as well. If the marriage was the sacrifice referred to in the letter to Peggy Chalmers, then it was probably made merely to appease the Commissioners who were insisting that he should regularize his life. He would thus have sacrificed the possibility of eventual marriage to Clarinda or possibly even to Peggy Chalmers for dull, faithful Jean. This seems the most likely reason which fits the known facts and, while it may not be a pretty reason for marrying a girl, marriages have been contracted for less.

This tallies with Burns's letter to Mrs Dunlop (who appears to have thought he should remain a bachelor) on 10th August 1788 when he wrote:

Circumstanced as I am, I could never have got a female Partner for life who could have entered into my favorite studies, relished my favorite authors, &c. without entailing on me, at the same time, expensive living, fantastic caprice, apish affectation, with all the other blessed boarding-school acquirements which (pardon me, Madame!) are some times to be found among females of the upper ranks, but almost universally pervade the Misses of the Would-be-gentry.

In the final analysis, he told Johnson in Edinburgh, his choice was "as random as Blind Man's buff!"

Then he explained it all to Peggy Chalmers on 16th September:

Shortly after my last return to Ayrshire, I married "my Jean". This was not a consequence of the attachment of romance perhaps; but I had a long and much-loved fellow creature's happiness or misery in my determination, and I durst not trifle with so important a deposit. Nor have I any cause to repent it. If I have not got polite tattle, modish manners, and fashionable dress, I am not sickened and disgusted with the multiform curse of boarding-school affectation; and I have got the handsomest figure, the sweetest temper, the soundest constitution, and the kindest heart in the country.

Apart from reading the Bible and metrical psalms, he told Peggy, he doubted whether Jean had spent five minutes on prose or poetry in her life – except his own book, which she was reading most devotedly.

So there it is: Burns reached the right decision for probably the wrong reason, and he never regretted it. For her part, Jean was well suited to him: she made him a comfortable home, she gave him children, she never was jealous of his writing or of his association with the rich and influential, and above all she was understanding when he erred from the path of virtue.

There was one person who did not hear of the marriage from Robert. Nancy Maclehose learned of it from his friend Ainslie, who, in the absence of the poet, had become friendly with Clarinda. For almost a year she said nothing: she just sat in Edinburgh, feeling angry, jilted and bitter. But finally she sent him a letter which has been lost, but which we can guess at from the poet's reply. It was on 9th March 1789 that he wrote:

As I am convinced of my own innocence, and though conscious of high imprudence & egregious folly, can lay my hand on my breast and attest the rectitude of my heart; you will pardon me, Madam, if I do not carry my complaisance to YOUR opinion; much as I esteem your judgement, and warmly as I regard your worth. – I have already told you, and again I aver it, that at the Period of time alluded to, I was not under the smallest moral tie to Mrs B–; nor did I, nor could I then know, all the powerful circumstances that omnipotent Necessity was busy laying in wait for me. – When you call over the scenes that have passed between us, you will survey the conduct of an honest man, struggling successfully with temptations the most powerful that ever beset humanity, and preserving untainted honor in situations where the austerest Virtue would have forgiven a fall – Situations that I will dare to say, not a single individual of all his kind, even with half his sensibility, and passion, could have encountered without ruin; and I leave you to guess, Madam, how such a man is likely to digest an accusation of perfidious treachery.

This long, defensive letter did not end the Clarinda-Sylvander relationship. Nancy continued to accuse her former lover of perfidy, and when she found out about Jenny Clow and her baby, conceived at the height of her own affair with the poet, she was bitter. She discovered that Jenny was in distress and reprimanded him sharply:

I take the liberty of addressing a few lines on behalf of your old acquaintance, Jenny Clow, who, to all appearances is at this moment dying. Obliged, from all the symptoms of a rapid decay, to quit her service, she is gone to a room almost without common necessaries, untended and unmourned. ... You have now an opportunity to evince you indeed possess these fine feelings you have delineated, so as to claim the just admiration of your country.

The letter stung.

He answered that he would have taken his child from Jenny Clow, but she would never agree to that, and he begged Clarinda to give Jenny five shillings and promised to do what he could during a forthcoming visit to Edinburgh.

Time healed Clarinda's wound at least enough for the correspondence to be resumed, with Burns referring to her as "My Dearest Nancy" but never again writing as a lover. Eventually Clarinda decided to go to Jamaica to join her husband, who had now achieved financial success, and on 6th December 1791 Nancy and Robert met in Edinburgh for the last time. The following month Mrs Maclehose sailed in the *Roselle*, by a strange irony the ship in which Robert was once to have gone to the West Indies. She arrived in Jamaica to find that her husband had installed a negro mistress who had borne him several children, so, complaining of the climate, she returned to Scotland in the same ship.

She kept in touch with Robert and, although they never met again, she remembered those white-hot months in Edinburgh. Forty years later, on 6th December 1831, she wrote in her journal: "This day I can never forget. Parted with Burns, in the year 1791, never more to meet in this world. Oh, may we meet in Heaven."

Nor can the world at large forget Clarinda's love for Sylvander. On 27th December 1791, just before Nancy sailed, the poet sent her three songs, including one of the loveliest love songs Scotland has ever known. "Ae Fond Kiss" reveals the depth of feeling between the two and the agony of parting:

Ae fond kiss, and then we sever;
Ae fareweel, and then for ever!
Deep in heart-wrung tears I'll pledge thee,
Warring sighs and groans I'll wage thee. –

It speaks far more than all the high-flown letters which passed between Clarinda and Sylvander during those brief, passionate days as 1787 turned to 1788.

11

A Farmer Again

In retrospect Burns must have wondered why Tennant of Glenconner had advised him to accept Ellisland and why he himself did not see that it offered poor prospects. Ellisland today is very different from the farm to which Robert moved in 1788: it is good, well-improved land with neat steading standing on a ridge above the rapid-running River Nith, one of the loveliest farms connected with the poet. In Burns's day its land was in poor condition; it was unfenced and it did not have a proper farmhouse. Even its owner, Patrick Miller, had scarcely a good word to say about it, for writing in 1802 he recalled the Dalswinton farms as he first knew them: "When I purchased this estate about five and twenty years ago, I had not seen it. It was in the most miserable state of exhaustion, and all the tenants in poverty. ... When I went to view my purchase, I was so much disgusted for eight or ten days that I meant never to return to the county."

But he did return. And he offered Ellisland to Robert Burns on what he considered generous terms – a rent of £50 a year for the first three years, rising to £70 a year, and with a grant of £300 towards building a farmhouse and enclosing the fields. Robert accepted this, and as soon as he had completed his Excise instruction he rode into Dumfriesshire on his mare Jenny Geddes to take possession.

It was nearly midsummer, but Robert felt far from cheerful when he surveyed the task ahead of him. He was exhausted and depressed after the strain of sorting out his marriage, worrying about Clarinda and studying hard to learn the Excise work. He did not even have the pleasure of the industrious and practical Jean with him, for there was no house to which he could bring her. Instead, Jean moved to

Mossgiel to learn as much as she could about dairying from Robert's mother and sisters and to fit herself to be a farmer's wife when she was called to Ellisland.

That summer he spent fortnight about at Ellisland and Mossgiel, living on his farm in a hovel which had served as a farmhouse for the previous tenant. It was cold, the roof leaked, the fire smoked, and it was lonely, but he made the best of it and spent his evenings writing amazingly cheerful letters to his friends – to Ainslie, Mrs Dunlop, Peggy Chalmers and so on. And no matter how "sore tired" he might be he could still ˙ cull from his enormous knowledge of literature the right phrase. Weary after a day's sowing he quoted Thomson to Mrs Dunlop: "Throwing the grain into the faithful bosom of the ground."

To Hugh Parker he sent a poem with a lonely core:

In this strange land, this uncouth clime,
A land unknown to prose or rhyme;
Where words ne'er crost the muse's heckles,[1]   [1flax-comb
Nor limpet in poetic shackles;
A land that prose did never view it,
Except when drunk he stacher't thro' it;
Here, ambush'd by the chimla cheek,[2]   [2fireplace
Hid in an atmosphere of reek,
I hear a wheel thrum[3] i' the neuk,   [3hum
I hear it – for in vain I leuk. –
The red peat gleams, a fiery kernel,
Enhusked by a fog infernal:
Here, for my wonted rhyming raptures,
I sit and count my sins by chapters;
For lief and spunk like ither Christians,
I'm dwindled down to mere existence,
Wi' nae converse but Gallowa' bodies,
Wi' nae kend face but Jenny Geddes.

He expressed his loneliness in prose too, to Mrs Dunlop on 13th June: "This is the second day, my honored Friend, that I have been on my farm. – a solitary inmate of an old, smoky 'SPENCE'; far from every Object I love or by whom I am belov'd, nor any acquaintance older than yesterday except Jenny Geddes the old mare I ride on."

As with most enterprises Burns embarked on, he began
work with tremendous enthusiasm, fighting off ill-health,
subdued even in his letters to his companion of many
escapades, Ainslie, and experiencing a degree of happiness in
spite of everything. How he slaved; every hour required the
labour of ten; every pound had to do the work of five. Even so,
from the first season it was unrewarding. The accursed
climate took its toll of his enthusiasm and his health and that
autumn he told Mrs Dunlop: "Here I am in the middle of my
harvest, without good weather when I may have Reapers, and
without Reapers when I have good weather. – The
tremendous thunder-storm of yesternight and the lurid fogs of
this morning have driven me for refuge from the
Hypochondria which I fear worse than the devil, to my
Muse."

He contracted influenza, then raging throughout the
district, and was scarcely able to hold up his head for a time,
but he did not give in. Apologizing to Graham of Fintry for the
delay in replying to a letter, Burns told him he had been
working so hard that he had not had time to visit the post-
office to collect letters.

Constant absences to visit Mossgiel and long daily trudges
between his hovel and the fields did not help either. He could
never manage to do as much as he wanted to, and as a result
he always felt frustrated. But it was not merely absence that
handicapped him: Burns was not a good manager of men. He
had too much common humanity in him to drive the kind of
bargain that might have made Ellisland a success. Once,
when a casual labourer was employed to dig drains at
seventeen pence a rood but found that he had badly
underestimated the task, Robert paid him an extra threepence
a rood for his share of the work and twice wrote to ask a
neighbour to do the same. One doubts whether the neighbour
complied.

There was humanity, too, in his relations with the animals
on the farm and the wild life. Jenny Geddes became a firm
friend, and one morning he was deeply moved by seeing a
wounded hare in a field. He was sowing at the time and heard
a shot: soon afterwards he saw the wounded hare limp by.

"This set my humanity in tears and my indignation in

arms," he told Mrs Dunlop. And as a result he wrote the
poem "On Seeing a Fellow Wound a Hare With A Shot".

Go live, poor wanderer of the wood and field,
    The bitter little that of life remains:
    No more the thickening brakes and verdant plains
To thee shall home, or food, or pastime yield.

Seek, mangled wretch, some place of wonted rest,
    No more of rest, but now thy dying bed!
    The sheltering rushes whistling o'er thy head,
The cold earth with thy bloody bosom prest.

Oft as by winding Nith I, musing, wait
    The sober eve, or hail the chearful dawn,
    I'll miss thee sporting o'er the dewy lawn,
And curse the ruffian's aim, and mourn thy hapless fate.

He was lonely at Ellisland and missed Jean with a longing
that produced another beautiful love-song, "Of A' The Airts".
The days at Mossgiel with her were blissful interludes in an
otherwise difficult time.

Of a' the airts¹ the wind can blaw,   [¹directions
    I dearly like the West;
For there the bony Lassie lives,
    The Lassie I lo'e best:
There's wild-woods grow, and rivers row,
    And mony a hill between;
But day and night my fancy's flight
    Is ever wi' my Jean. –

Although the ride to Mauchline produced such lovely
thoughts, it was often undertaken on a winter's night after a
hard day's toil and sometimes made him melancholy or
truculent. One particularly foul night in January 1789, when
he had just settled himself at Bailie Whigham's inn at
Sanquhar, out of the snow-laden wind that was blowing down
the Nith valley, the funeral cortège of Mrs Oswald of
Auchincruive arrived and the poet had to move out. Twelve
miles' hard riding across the desolate moor to the next inn at
New Cumnock did little for his temper, and he sat down and

wrote a bitter ode to the dead woman who, although detested by her servants in life, could hardly be blamed for inconveniencing the bard in death.

As early as 10th September 1788 Burns realized that Ellisland would not be able to support him for some considerable time, and so he wrote to Graham of Fintry, telling him of the financial problems both there and at Mossgiel. Then he suggested a piece of wire-pulling for which he has been much criticized because it seems so out of keeping with his principles. He actually asked for the job of another Exciseman, Leonard Smith. "There is one way by which I might be enabled to extricate myself from this embarrassment," he told Graham, "a scheme which I hope and am certain is in your power to effectuate. – I live here, Sir, in the very centre of a country Excise Division; the present Officer lately lived on a farm which he rented in my nearest neighbourhood; and as the gentleman, owing to some legacies, is quite opulent, a removal could do him no manner of injury; and on a month's warning, to give me a little time to look again over my Instructions, I would not be afraid to enter on business. ... It would suit me to enter on it, beginning of next summer."

With the request he sent a poem, "The First Epistle to Robert Graham, Esq., of Fintry, Requesting a Favor", not even a new set of verses but some taken out of his desk and dressed up for the occasion. Nevertheless Graham received the request favourably, and when Robert wrote to thank him on 23rd September it was clear from the miserable state of the harvest that Burns needed Smith's Excise job more urgently than ever.

He seemed to have no compunction over his request to replace Smith and told Graham: "I could not bear to injure a pòor fellow by ousting him to make way for myself; to a wealthy son of good-fortune like Smith, the injury is imaginary where the propriety of your rules admits."

No doubt Smith, however rich he might have been, did not agree!

While the poet gathered in his harvest and nursed his accursed ill-health, he longed for the companionship of Jean. But eighteenth-century builders were no faster or more reliable than twentieth-century ones, and progress on the house was painfully slow. By January he had to leave the hut in which he had spent the autumn and early winter and was hoping for early completion of his new house. He wrote to Peter Morrison, a Mauchline carpenter, who was making furniture for him and said: "Necessity oblidges me to go into my new house, even before it is plaistered. – I will inhabit the one end until the other is finished. – About three weeks more, I think, will at farthest be my time beyond which I cannot stay in this present house."

In December he was able to rent another house and Jean joined him, leaving young Robert behind at Mossgiel until they were permanently settled. From now on he badgered and cajoled the builders to hurry up the work on the farmhouse. Before leaving for a brief visit to Edinburgh to settle with Creech, he sent an anxious letter to the mason, Thomas Boyd. "I am distressed with the want of my house in a most provoking manner," he said. "It loses me two hours' work of my servants every day, besides other inconveniences. For G-d's sake let me but within the shell of it!"

He succeeded with Creech in Edinburgh, although not as well as he thought he ought to have done, but his other mission failed. He was pursuing the Excise job and proposed to set Gilbert up in Ellisland, but Graham was either unable or unwilling to arrange this, despite pressure from Mrs Dunlop as well as from Robert.

On his return to Ellisland he found that no progress had been made on the house, and he sent another anguished note to Boyd. By this time Jean had taken in Robert's younger brother William, a twenty-two-year-old who could not settle to any job and was a source of worry to the whole family. Burns tried, through Ainslie, to have William apprenticed to a saddler in Edinburgh but without success and so he brought the young man to Ellisland. After some months William found work at Longtown, near Carlisle, and later in Newcastle. Robert lectured his brother to fight like a man, but offered him a home if ever things went wrong. His advice was not all that their mother, back at Mossgiel, would have given the lad though. Once, when William announced that he was in love, the poet wrote to him: "I am, you know, a veteran in these campaigns, so let me advise you always to pay your particular assiduities and try for intimacy as soon as you feel the first symptoms of the passion; this is not only best, as making the most of the little entertainment which the sportabilities of distant addresses always gives, but is the best preservative for one's peace."

From Newcastle William moved to London, where he found another job as a saddler, and Robert asked his old teacher, John Murdoch, to visit him. Unfortunately, before Murdoch could contact him, the young man caught some illness and died suddenly in July 1790. It was left to Robert to pay the expenses of his illness and funeral.

William had left before the farmhouse at Ellisland was ready, and Robert and Jean moved in the following May. It was their first home and the poet's pride bubbled over:

I hae a wife o' my ain,
   I'll partake wi' naebody;
I'll tak Cuckold frae nane,
   I'll gie Cuckold to naebody ...

I'll be merry and free,
   I'll be sad for naebody;
Naebody cares for me,
   I care for naebody.

Robert worshipped Jean with all the passion he had in his heart, even if the terms in which he expressed it were sometimes above her head.

O were I on Parnassus hill;
Or had o' Helicon my fill;
That I might catch poetic skill,
   To sing how dear I love thee.
But Nith maun be my Muses well,
My Muse maun be thy bonie sell,
On Corsincon I'll glower and spell;
   And write how dear I love thee ...

By night, by day, a-field, at hame,
The thoughts o' thee my breast inflame;
And ay I muse and sing thy name,

I only live to love thee.
Tho' I were doom'd to wander on,
Beyond the sea, beyond the sun,
Till my last, weary sand was run;
  Till then – and then I love thee.

Jean soon sank to the level of a dull, hard-working
housekeeper, though with the added bonus that she gave him
a large family. She had neither culture enough nor any desire
to visit the rich and intellectual with her husband, but she did
not hold him back from doing so. Perhaps that was her
greatest virtue: she accepted Robert Burns as he was – for his
many virtues and for his sins as well. She was never jealous,
and she was forgiving far beyond the normal bounds. Once
when she went home to Mauchline, Robert seduced Anna
Park, barmaid at the Globe Inn, with the usual results. Anna
died in childbirth, and Jean took the baby into her home and
reared her as her own child.

The humdrum monotony of Ellisland was broken by
occasional visits from old friends, who often called in
unexpectedly on their way through Dumfriesshire. One day,
during 1790, when Ramsay of Ochtertyre and Stewart of Luss
noticed the poet hurrying past as they were travelling through
Closeburn, they enquired at the inn and were told he would be
back within a few hours. So the pair left a note to say that they
would stop at Ellisland and hoped to see him there. In the
evening he rushed in in high spirits, crying "I come, to use the
words of Shakespeare, stewed in haste." There then followed a
roistering evening, with Robert full of ideas for a play he
wanted to write. Two English travellers on another occasion
found him standing on a rock beside the Nith, angling. He was
dressed in a foxskin cap and a greatcoat pulled together with
a belt from which hung a great Highland broadsword. He
invited them to share his dinner of barley broth and boiled
beef and afterwards produced the toddy bowl, over which he
talked happily of many topics, including his youth and his
poetry.

Not all old friends proved so faithful. Ainslie came to
Ellisland on Friday 15th October 1790 and repaid his friend
by rushing to Nancy Maclehose (with whom he was flirting at

that moment) to report that, while the welcome had been
warm enough, "the house was ill-contrived – and pretty dirty,
and Hugry Mugry". Jean he found vulgar and commonplace,
"pretty round and fat", but "a kind Body in her own way, and
the husband tolerable Attentive to her". Burns's sister and
sister-in-law were present and were "common looking girls".
It was kirn-night (harvest home) and an evening for
jollification, but the other guests did not come up to Ainslie's
high standard. They were "a Vulgar looking tavern keeper
from Dumfries and his wife more vulgar – Mr Miller of
Dalswinton's gardener and his wife – the said Wife's sister –
and a little fellow from Dumfries who had been a clerk".
Ainslie did not approve of the dancing, nor of the kissing at the
end of every dance.

Burns enjoyed the evening hugely, though Ainslie could not
understand why.

"Our Friend himself is an ingenious as ever," he wrote, "and
seems very happy with the Situation I have described – His Mind
however now appears to me to be a great Mixture of the poet and
the Excise Man – One day he sits down a Beautiful poem – and
the Next he Seizes a cargo of Tobacco from some unfortunate
Smuggler – or Roups out some poor Wretch for selling Liquors
without a License. From his conversation he Seems to be
frequently among the Great – but No Attention is paid by people
of any rank to his wife. ..."

The visit all but finished the friendship, which continued in
desultory fashion until early in 1794 when Ainslie sent a letter
"so dry, so distant, so like a card to one of his clients" that
Robert "could scarce bear to read it". And so far as we know
he never answered it.

The summer of 1789 was Robert's deadline for taking up an
Excise appointment, and he did not let Graham forget him.
On 13th May he went to see Mitchell, Excise Collector for the
district, with a letter from Graham in his hand. Mitchell was
busy as it was collection day and asked the poet to call at
another time, but pride held Burns back – "As I don't wish to
degrade myself to a hungry rook gaping for a morsel, I shall
just give him a hint of my wishes," he told Graham. He did
not have to pocket his pride and beg for a job: Mitchell,

probably prompted from above, wrote that Smith could be removed "without any detriment", and so Robert obtained his Excise Service post. An alphabetical list of Excise officers, dated 10th October 1789, contains Burns's name and the remark, "Never tryed – a Poet". Later another hand has added, "Turns out well". And so he did.

Excise work was far from easy in the eighteenth century; a wide range of articles was taxed, and all the monies were collected at source by the revenue officers. R.W. Macfadzean, writing in the *Burns Chronicle* of 1898, has described the complexity of these taxes, which were not levied at a single rate on each type of manufacture. There were, for example, seventy-eight different rates of paper duty, according to size, kind and quality. Needless to say no single officer had to deal with the complete range in his station, but he usually had a number of variations to cope with. An officer had to ride some two hundred miles a week on his own horse and every two months had to assure his employers that it was fit. Each day his books had to be brought up to date, a job which was no formality, since they were examined regularly in minute detail by his superior.

For all this an officer was paid a salary of £50 a year, with the addition of 50 per cent of his "prizes" and another £50 for every arrested smuggler. He had to pay all his expenses out of his own pocket. However in comparison with the average minister, whose stipend was about £35, or schoolmaster, whose salary was unlikely to exceed £25, the Excise Officer was well off. Compared with the farmer, who was lucky if there was any money left at all after he had fed his family, he was rich indeed.

Robert enjoyed the work, which covered a dozen or so parishes, for he met interesting characters and had time to think of his poetry as he jogged through Nithsdale. He was a capable and diligent officer in a neglected division, making excellent reports and acting against offenders without fear. Once, after a busy day rounding up witnesses, he told Mitchell, that he expected to be clapped in jail for annoying the friends of half the gentlemen in the county. There was humanity, too, in his approach to the work. He told Graham: "I recorded every Defaulter, but at the Court, I myself begged off every poor body that was unable to pay, which seeming candour gave me so much implicit credit with the Hon. Bench, that with high Complmts they gave me such ample vengeance on the rest, that my Decreet is double the amount of any Division in the District."

Much has been said of the shame that Scotland's greatest poet (as Coleridge put it) should have been snatched from the sickle and the plough to gauge ale-firkins, and of course there has always been a stigma attached to tax-gathering. Robert was well aware of this but did not really mind:

Searching auld wives' barrels,
   Ochon, the day!
That clarty barm should stain my laurels!
   But what'll ye say?
These movin' things ca'd wives an' weans
Wad move the very hearts o' stanes.

Robert Burns was not ashamed to be an Exciseman. He was not snatched from the plough: he was glad to leave it to ride two hundred miles a week "to inspect dirty ponds and yeasty barrels". Shortly after starting work he told Ainslie:

You need not doubt that I find several very unpleasant and disagreeable circumstances in my business; but I am tired with and disgusted at the language of complaint against the evils of life. – Human existence in the most favourable situations does not abound with pleasures, and has its inconveniences and ills; capricious, foolish Man mistakes these inconveniences & ills as if they were the peculiar property of his own particular situation; and hence that eternal fickleness, that love of change which has ruined & daily does ruin, many a fine fellow as well as many a Blockhead; and is almost without exception a constant source of disappointment & misery. – So far from being dissatisfied with my present lot, I earnestly pray the Great Disposer of events that it may never be worse, & I think I may lay my hand on my heart and say, "I shall be content."

He even derived some fun from the situation, poking fun at himself and all his colleagues in the delightful "The De'il's awa wi' th' Exciseman":

The deil cam fiddlin thro' the town;
  And danc'd awa wi' th' Exciseman;
And ilka wife cries, auld Mahoun,
  I wish you luck o' the prize, man.

The deil's awa the deil's awa
  The deil's awa wi' th' Exciseman,
He's danc'd awa he's danc'd awa
  He's danc'd awa wi' th' Exciseman.

The only drawback, so far as Burns was concerned, was the enormous strain his Excise duties and farmwork together put on his weak constitution. To ease the burden, he bought more dairy cattle, whose care and milking Jean could supervise, but it was still too much. His heart trouble was still with him: his knee, which was injured in the Edinburgh accident, continued to give pain, and in September 1789 he had an attack of "malignant, squinancy and low fever". By the end of the year he was "groaning under the miseries of a diseased nervous system".

Throughout the autumn his spirits flagged until at the turn of the year depression had turned to a kind of dogged anger.

The only activity which cheered him was the theatre at Dumfries. He wrote a Prologue which was given there on New Year's Day 1790 to great applause. This, and the longer days of February, began to raise his spirits. Soon he was again writing cheerful letters to his many friends, to the Edinburgh bookseller Peter Hill, to Clarinda mixing defence of his actions with poetry (he sent her "My Lovely Nancy"), and to William Nicol, whose ailing mare had been sent to Ellisland to be sold but had died on Robert's hands. He wrote an elegy on the mare, Peg Nicholson:

Peg Nicholson was a good bay mare,
  As ever trod on airn.[1]   [[1]iron
But now she's floating down the Nith,
  And past the mouth o' Cairn.

He was almost back to normal.

By the spring he had his eye on a port division where he

would earn more money without as much travelling as in his present post. At once he set about enlisting his influential friends, for he had now written off Ellisland and knew he could make a career as an exciseman.

12

Out of Bondage

Robert Burns was quickly accepted by the Nithsdale community, and soon he became embroiled in local politics and other issues, not always on the side on which one might expect to find him. His Excise work brought him into direct contact with the local people and thus tended to increase his political activities at a time when, as a public servant, he ought to have been silent, or at least discreet.

People of importance in Dumfries and the county befriended him from the start, and from his hovel he frequently visited Friars Carse, the home of Robert Riddell of Glenriddell, a short walk away. Riddell, who was six years the poet's senior, was the eldest son of Walter Riddell of Glenriddell, and after studying at the universities of St Andrews and Edinburgh, he entered the army. He served with the Royal Scots and the Prince of Wales' Light Dragoons, from which he retired as a captain on half-pay in 1782. After his marriage to Elizabeth Kennedy of Manchester he settled at Friars Carse, which he preferred to Glenriddell.

It seems strange that Burns enthusiasts feel it necessary to attack anyone with whom the poet crossed swords in his lifetime, all the more strange since Burns himself was so forgiving to his enemies after an initial outburst. "Daddy" Auld and Saunders Tait are victims of these uncritical worshippers, and so too is Walter Riddell, whom they dismiss as a pretentious dabbler in the arts. Robert Burns certainly never found Riddell so, and the captain enjoyed a deservedly high reputation amongst his contemporaries. George Paton called on Riddell as an authority on antiquities to help him with local material for a new edition of Camden's *Britannia*, which was then in preparation, and Riddell duly supplied information on Nithsdale and Galloway antiquities which was published in the book.

Riddell had some musical ability also, for he produced *A Collection of Scotch, Galwegian and Border Tunes for the Violin and Pianoforte*. Burns supplied the words for a number of the songs. Indeed, it was probably the poet's interest in Scottish songs that first brought the two men together and enabled them, despite their different backgrounds, to find enough in common to become friends. In that first difficult summer at Ellisland Riddell lent Burns help to gather in his harvest and gave him a key to his newly-built gazebo in the grounds of Friars Carse so that he could escape to write his poetry.

Riddell introduced Burns to the Monkland Friendly Society, a private circulating library for local tenant farmers of the kind then so popular in Scotland. Burns ran the society – as librarian, treasurer and censor – and ordered books for it through Creech's old clerk, Peter Hill, who now had his own bookshop in Edinburgh and was a close friend of the poet. He ran it well, if not always according to the exact wishes of the members. On 2nd March 1790 he sent Hill an order:

At a late meeting of the Monkland Friendly Society it was resolved to augment their library by the following books which you are to send us as soon as possible – The Mirror – The Lounger – Man of feeling – Man of the world (these for my own sake I wish to have by the first Carrier) Knox's history of the Reformation – Rae's History of the Rebellion 1715 – Any good history of the Rebellion of 1745 – A Display of the Secession Act and Testimony of Mr Gib. – Hervey's Meditations – Beveridge's thoughts – and another copy of Watson's body of Divinity – This last heavy Performance is so much admired by many of our Members that they will not be content with one Copy, so Capt Riddel our President & Patron agreed with me to give you private instructions not to send Watson, but to say that you could not procure a Copy of the book so cheap as the one you sent formerly & therefore you await further orders.

With the order he asked Hill to watch out for a large number of plays by both English and French dramatists. His interest in plays had been stimulated by the success of the prologue he had written for the Dumfries theatre and by that of another he had composed for Mrs Sutherland's benefit night on the following evening. He had discussed with Ramsay of Ochtertyre his intention to write a play based on the traditional story of Rob McQuechan, the cobbler who accidentally pierced Robert the Bruce's foot with an awl while trying to repair one of the King's shoes. But the project never came to anything.

The poet was welcomed by Riddell's friends, among them Joseph Farrington, the painter, and Francis Grose, then in Scotland to collect material for his *Antiquities of Scotland*. Grose was an excellent artist and a good writer, though Burns liked him for himself – he was fat and jovial, and good company. His search inspired Burns to poke fun at the Englishman:

Hear, Land o' Cakes, and brither Scots,
Frae Maidenkirk to Johny Groats! –
If there's a hole in a' your coats,
   I rede you tent it:
A chield's amang you, taking notes,
   And, faith, he'll prent it.

Burns supplied a list of old buildings in Ayrshire, among them Alloway Auld Kirk, for possible inclusion in the book. He must have described the eerie old church well, for Grose agreed to include it provided Robert would supply a "witch story" to be printed with the drawing. The result was his greatest poem, "Tam O' Shanter", which was composed during a single day as he paced a path along the banks of the Nith below Ellisland farmhouse – a path which still looks very much as it did in Burns's time. He sent the poem off to Grose with a covering letter, telling the story:

On a market day in the town of Ayr, a farmer from Carrick, and consequently whose way lay by the very gate of Aloway kirkyard, in order to cross the river Doon at the old bridge which is about two or three hundred yards further on than the said gate, had been detained by his business till by the time he reached Aloway it was the wizard hour, between night and morning.

Though he was terrified with a blaze streaming from the kirk, yet as it is a well-known fact, that to turn back on these occasions is running by far the greatest risk of mischief, he prudently advanced on his road. When he had reached the gate of the kirk-yard, he was surprised and entertained, through the ribs and arches of an old gothic window which still faces the highway, to see a dance of witches merrily footing it round their old sooty blackguard master, who was keeping them all alive with the power of his bagpipe. The farmer stopping his horse to observe them a little, could plainly descry the faces of many old women of his acquaintance and neighbourhood. How the gentleman was dressed, tradition does not say; but the ladies were all in their smocks; and one of them happening unluckily to have a smock which was considerably too short to answer all the purpose of that piece of dress, our farmer was so tickled that he involuntarily burst out, with a loud laugh, "Weel luppen, Maggy wi' the short sark!" and recollecting himself, instantly spurred his horse to the top of his speed. I need not mention the universally known fact, that no diabolical power can pursue you beyond the middle of a running stream. Lucky it was for the poor farmer that the river Doon was so near, for notwithstanding the speed of his horse, which was a good one, against he reached the middle arch of the bridge, and consequently the middle of the stream, the pursuing, vengeful hags were so close at his heels, that one of them actually sprung to seize him; but it was too late; nothing was on her side of the stream but the horse's tail, which immediately gave way to her infernal grip, as if blasted by a stroke of lightning; but the farmer was beyond her reach. – However, the unsightly, tail-less condition of the vigorous steed was to the last hours of the noble creature's life, an awful warning to the Carrick farmers, not to stay too late in Ayr markets.

For the best part of two centuries "Tam O'Shanter" has been taken apart, examined and put together again, none the worse for being meddled with. Its form of eight-syllabled rhyming couplets had been used before, particularly in Ramsay's *Fables* and *Tales*, and individual lines and passages have been disputed, none more so than that beginning "But pleasures are like poppies spread" in which the poet is alleged to switch for Scottish dialect to English – clearly some critics have never heard my father or any other Ayrshire farmer recite the lines. Although the written form may appear to be English, the lines have a resounding Scottishness when spoken by a Scottish tongue.

The characters who were Burns's inspiration have also been

sought: Tam, his drinking friend Souter Johnny, the miller with whom Tam drank as long as he had siller, and Kirkton Jean, whose house was as attractive as the Lord's House. Only Douglas Graham, a Kirkoswald farmer with a scolding wife, has been identified for sure as the prototype of Tam O' Shanter, but other characters were Kirkoswald folk.

The setting of the poem can be more certainly identified, however, for the inn at which Tam spent the roistering market-day evening stands unchanged in Ayr High Street, except that now it is an interesting Burns museum. The Auld Kirk and bridge over the Doon at Alloway are still there and attract thousands of tourists every year.

In "Tam O' Shanter" Burns took a folk tale which he must have heard many times from his mother and turned it into a scintillating, witty, outrageous narrative poem, which starts in a low key with a short philosophical prologue and reaches its peak as Tam is pursued by a hellish legion of witches.

Tam was a sore trial to his wife Kate, who told him often that he was a "blethering, blustering, drunken blellum", but we have some sympathy for him because she is a "sulky sullen dame ... nursing her wrath to keep it warm". Tam quickly forgot his wife on market nights as he lingered in Ayr, enjoying his friends' company, and on this particular evening he forgot also a storm which was gathering outside as he drank with Souter Johnny and enjoyed the landlord's jokes and the landlady's compliments:

As bees flee hame wi' lades o' treasure,
The minutes wing'd their way wi' pleasure:
Kings may be blest, but Tam was glorious,
O'er a' the ills o' life victorious!

At last even Tam realized that he had a long way to ride, across the bents to Alloway, over the Doon bridge into Carrick, and by the moorland path which skirted the hills to Maybole and Kirkoswald. It was midnight and not the kind of night anyone likes to face:

The wind blew as 'twad blawn its last;
The rattling showers rose on the blast;
The speedy gleams the darkness swallow'd

Loud, deep, and lang, the thunder bellow'd:
That night, a child might understand,
The Deil had business on his hand.

Tam defied the storm as he "skelpit on" towards home, although the carefree moments were followed by touches of sobering fear:

Whiles holding fast his gude blue bonnet;
Whiles crooning o'er some auld Scots sonnet;
Whiles glowering round wi' prudent cares,
Lest bogles[1] catch him unawares: [¹ghosts

The road led past eerie places – scenes of death, both natural and unnatural. Here was the spot where the pedlar was smothered and the stone where drunken Charlie broke his neck. He passed the cairn where a murdered child was found and the thorn-tree on which Mungo's mother hanged herself. Now he was approaching Alloway Auld Kirk, well known to be haunted and filled nightly with cries of ghosts and owls. Tonight Tam was fired by the beer and whisky of the Ayr inn, and he would face the devil himself at the old church. Suddenly he arrived at the church and there he saw an "unco sight" – the Auld Kirk was ablaze with light, its altar covered with the most terrible adjuncts to murder, its walls lined with open coffins, and in the body of the Kirk witches and warlocks danced to the skirling bagpipes of Auld Nick himself. His mare, Meg, was transfixed:

As Tammie glow'rd, amaz'd, and curious,
The mirth and fun grew fast and furious:
The piper loud and louder blew;
The dancers quick and quicker flew;
They reel'd, they set, they cross'd, they cleekit,
Till ilka carlin swat and reekit,
And coost her duddies to the wark,
And linket at it in her sark!

One named Nannie bewitched the farmer as she "linket at it" in the most provocative of short shifts, until he roared out:

... 'Weel done, Cutty-sark!'
And in an instant all was dark:
And scarcely had he Maggie rallied,
When out the hellish legion sallied.

As bees bizz out wi' angry fyke,
When plundering herds assail their byke;
As open pussie's mortal foes,
When pop! she starts before their nose;
As eager runs the market-crowd,
When 'Catch the thief!' resounds aloud;
So Maggie runs, the witches follow,
Wi' mony an eldritch skreech and hollow.

Tam fled towards the bridge, where he knew safety lay, since
witches could not cross running water. But Nannie was in
pursuit, far ahead of all the others:

And flew at Tam wi' furious ettle;
But little wist she Maggie's mettle –
Ae spring brought off her master hale,
But left behind her ain gray tail:
The carlin caught her by the rump,
And left poor Maggie scarce a stump.

The reader, limp after the unbearable excitement of the chase,
is then left with a piece of mock moralizing at the end of the
poem:

Now, wha this tale o' truth shall read,
Ilk man and mother's son, take heed:
Whene'er to drink you are inclin'd,
Or cutty-sarks run in your mind,
Think, ye may buy the joys o'er dear,
Remember Tam o' Shanter's mare.

"Tam O'Shanter" is not merely a long, entertaining poem: it is
an experience. The pace suits the narrative brilliantly – at one
moment a fine description of contemporary Ayrshire, at the
next it races ahead with hair-bristling suspense. Characters
and Kirk are drawn with such deftness that they are vividly
real. Four lines give a lifelike character to Tam's shoemaker
friend:

And at his elbow, Souter Johnny,
His ancient, trusty, drouthy crony;
Tam lo'ed him like a vera brither;
They had been fou for weeks thgither.

And you can hear the wailing noise as auld Nick plays for all
he is worth for the ghostly dancers:

He screw'd the pipes and gart them skirl,
Till roof and rafters a' did dirl. –

To balance the suspense there is a kind of moralizing which,
by its very absurdity, only serves to emphasize the action of
the remainder of the poem. So it grips and amuses, frightens
and entertains, gives joy through its word-pictures – when it is
not horrifying by its starkness:

Near the thorn, aboon the well,
Whare Mungo's mither hanged hersel. –

"Tam O' Shanter" is Burns's finest poem, and not
surprisingly it was his own favourite. When Alexander Fraser
Tytler, a law professor in Edinburgh, read the poem he wrote
to Burns: "Go on – write more tales in the same style – You
will eclipse Prior and La Fontaine."

The poet replied. "I am already revolving two or three
stories in my fancy." But he never did produce another long
poem like "Tam O' Shanter".

During that first autumn when he was on his own at
Ellisland, Robert had plenty of time to think and talk politics
and, in spite of his desire to obtain a government post and the
risk of offending his friend Mrs Dunlop, he could not steer
clear of the subject. In April 1789 he sent Mrs Dunlop a copy
of his "Ode on the Departed Regency Bill", together with a
note admitting that he could not resist sending it and adding:
"Politics is dangerous ground for me to tread on, and yet I
cannot for the soul of me resist an impulse of any thing like
Wit."

At the centenary of William of Orange's landing in
England, which was celebrated on 5th November 1788, the
parish minister, Joseph Kirkpatrick, gloated from the pulpit

over the Stuarts and their lost cause, and this stung Robert into sending a long letter to the editor of the *Edinburgh Evening Courant*. It was carefully worded, and many Lowland Scots would have agreed with its sentiments.

In Stuart times, said the poet, there was a different conception of the relationship between a king and his people. The Stuarts sought only what their contemporaries in other countries enjoyed, but that was "inimical to the happiness of a nation and the rights of subjects". He would not hear scorn poured on the former royal house of Scotland: "The Stuarts have been condemned and laughed at for the folly and impracticability of their attempts in 1715 and 1745. That they failed, I bless my God most fervently; but cannot join in the ridicule against them. ..."

He compared the situation with that of the American colonies in the recent revolution. "I dare say," he wrote, "the American Congress, in 1776, will be allowed to have been as able and enlightened, and, a whole Empire will say, as honest, as the English Convention in 1688; and that the fourth of July will be as sacred to their posterity as the fifth of November is to us."

Burns did not hide the fact that he disliked George III and the Tory administration of the day, and, when a service of thanksgiving was announced for the king's recovery from one of his bouts of madness, Burns exploded with a poem on this "solemn farce of pageant mummery", which he sent to *The Morning Star* in London. Late in 1789 he weighed in with a series of election ballads in his own district and, against his usual views, supported the Tory candidate. The Whig candidate was the son of his landlord Patrick Miller, whom Burns might have been expected to support. The Duke of Queensberry backed Miller, however, and Robert so disliked the Duke that he supported the Tory, Sir James Johnstone of Westerhill, producing four poems, "The Fête Champetre", "The Five Carlins", "The Election Ballad for Westerha" and "The Second Epistle to Robert Graham".

In sending the poem "A New Psalm for the Chapel of Kilmarnock on Thanksgiving-day for His Majesty's Recovery" to Peter Stuart, editor of the London *Star*, who was trying to woo Burns south to join his staff, the poet drew attention to his politics and also to his unchanged views on the subject of patronage in the Scottish Kirk, for he could not resist taking the chance to attack that as well. He wrote:

And now thou hast restor'd our State,
  Pity our kirk also,
For she by tribulations
  Is now brought very low! –

Consume that High Place, PATRONAGE,
  From off thine holy hill;
And in they fury burn the book
  Even of that man, McGILL. –

Now hear our Prayer, accept our Song,
  And fight thy Chosen's battle:
We seek but little, L–, from thee,
  Thou kens we get as little. –

The McGill to whom the poem refers was Dr William McGill, an Ayrshire minister who was in trouble with Ayr Presbytery over a theological point which he had made in a book, *An Essay on the Death of Jesus Christ*. In April 1789 the Presbytery appointed a commission to investigate the offending minister's orthodoxy, and Robert could not resist entering the battle once again against his Auld Licht enemies. The resulting "Kirk's Alarm" reintroduced many of the characters of the Mauchline poems of 1786. "Daddy" Auld and "Holy Willie" Fisher were there; so too were the ministers Russell from "The Holy Fair" and Mackinlay from "The Ordination". And Poet Burns was as impudent as ever:

Poet Burns, Poet Burns, wi' your priest-skelping turns,
  Why desert ye your auld native shire?
Tho' your Muse is a gipsey, yet were she even tipsey,
  She could ca' us nae waur than we are, Poet Burns,
  She could ca' us nae waur than we are. –

Although the poem achieved nothing in religious terms, for McGill capitulated and withdrew the offending sentence in his book, it did remind people of Burns's views and of the Kirk's abuses. It did little however for his relations with influential friends such as Mrs Dunlop, who disapproved and lectured him on his behaviour.

At this time Burns needed all the support he could muster, for problems were closing in on him at Ellisland. On 18th August 1789 Jean bore him another son, who was named Francis Wallace in honour of Mrs Dunlop, and this added responsibility served to bring home the fact that he could not continue on the farm for much longer. The harvest was again poor and he told his brother that his nerves were in a damnable state. "I feel that horrid hyperchondria pervading every action of both body & soul. – This Farm has undone my enjoyment of myself. – It is a ruinous affair on all hands. – But let it go to hell! I'll fight it out and be off with it."

As an afterthought he added: "If once I were clear of this accursed farm, I shall respire more at ease."

For a year longer he hung on and it was only on 4th September 1790 that he wrote to Graham of Fintry informing him that he intended to give up Ellisland. "I am going either to give up, or subset my farm directly," wrote Burns. "I have not liberty to subset, but, if my Master will grant it me, I propose giving it just as I have it to myself, to an industrious fellow of a near relation of mine. – Farming this place in which I live, would just be a livelyhood to a man who would be the greatest drudge in his own family, so is no object; & living here hinders me from that knowledge in the business of Excise which it is absolutely necessary for me to attain."

The story is that this industrious near-relation was his brother Gilbert, but that Miller would not accept him as tenant because he was much more anxious to sell the farm than to relet it. The worry during the autumn of 1790 brought on more illness until Burns felt "very near the precincts of the Grave". For a short time he even stopped writing to his friends, but illness could not keep him down for long, and by the beginning of October he was back in Dumfries and writing again.

The new year began badly with the death of his patron, the Earl of Glencairn. Burns wrote to Alex. Dalziel, factor to the Earl, to ask the date of the funeral "that I may cross the country & steal among the crowd, to pay a tear to the last sight of my ever-revered Benefactor". Then a broken arm, sustained when his horse fell, made life so miserable that only occasionally did the real, ranting Robert emerge, as on the day when a poor soldier on his way to Ayr met Robert at an inn. At once the bard sat down and wrote a note to John Ballantine – a letter which bubbled over at the chance to enjoy a crack about Ayr. Then he wrote:

> While here I sit, sad & solitary, by the side of the fire in a little country inn, & drying my wet clothes, in pops a poor fellow of a sodger & tells me he is going to Ayr – By Heavens! say I to myself with a tide of good spirits which the magic of that sound, Auld Toon o' Ayr, conjuring up, I will send my last song to Mr Ballantine. – Here it is.

The song was "Ye Flowery Banks o' Bonie Doon", which is better known in its other version:

> Ye banks and braes o' bonie Doon,
>   How can ye bloom sae fresh and fair;
> How can ye chant, ye little birds,
>   And I sae weary, fu' o' care!
> Thou'll break my heart, thou warbling bird,
>   That wantons thro' the flowering thorn:
> Thou minds me o' departed joys,
>   Departed never to return. –

So even in his troubles, when home and the river of childhood were his only solace, Burns still wrote fine verses. No doubt these memories stayed him in the spring and summer of 1791 until the Ellisland question was resolved. At last John Morin, who owned the neighbouring estate of Laggan, expressed interest in purchasing the farm to increase his holding and to iron out a great bulge in it caused by a loop of the Nith. Miller accepted Morin's offer of £1900, and Robert was free to abandon the farm.

First he took the family to Mauchline, where he wanted to attend Gilbert's wedding; then he left his family at Mossgiel and returned to Ellisland to sort out farm matters and find a home for his family in Dumfries. He sold his standing crops by auction on 25th August at a very good price – "a guinea an acre, on an average, above value," Robert wrote to Thomas

Sloan on 1st September. Then the farm equipment was sold off and on 10th September the poet was free to sign the formal renunciation of the lease. Farm sales, or roups as they are called, were always social occasions, but Robert's surpassed most. "Such a scene of drunkenness was hardly ever seen in this country," he told Sloan. In the farmyard the drunk fought for three hours and in the house they lay on the floor "decanting, untill both my dogs got so drunk by attending them, that they could not stand". It was a scene to cheer Burns's heart, doubly so because it brought him nearer to freedom from the bondage of farming.

As a kind of final fling he paid a visit to Edinburgh to see Clarinda, then returned to Dumfries and rented a cramped half-house in the Stinking Vennel down by the riverside. It was not ideal, but on 15th November he brought his family back from Mossgiel and installed them there. Jean understood: Ellisland had cost her husband most of his capital and three years of unremitting trouble. She gladly endured life in the Stinking Vennel to see him free of the burden of Ellisland.

13

In Song

When Burns came to live in Dumfries it was an attractive town, like Ayr a bustling and prosperous market town and an important seaport. It was large, with more than 5500 inhabitants, and was set in fine countryside from which it drew much of its wealth, its fine red sandstone face turned towards the Nith, which was navigable for sea-going ships. It attracted many incomers who had made fortunes abroad, and they gave it standards of cultural life denied to many a place twice its size. In the Ellisland days, Burns had already sampled this life and he had written prologues for the theatre.

The poet's first house, rented from Captain John Hamilton, stood down near the Whitesands by the Nith. It was not large, but it held Robert, Jean, their children, Robert, Francis Wallace, William Nicol, and soon afterwards, Anna Park's baby. It was not until May 1793 that Hamilton offered them a larger house in Mill Vennel (now Burns Street), a house which still stands and is a museum of Burns relics. The Mill Vennel house is a fine sandstone detached building, two storeys high, and worthy of a well-shod family. Indeed, it was far superior to the houses of many professional men in the town at the time.

Dumfries opened up new avenues of friendship for the poet and at the same time enabled him to cultivate even more the friends he had already made. He continued to enjoy the company of Riddell at Friars Carse and extended this friendship to Glenriddell's sister-in-law, Maria, who had just returned from the West Indies.

Maria Riddell was born Maria Banks Woodley in London on 4th November 1772, the youngest of three daughters of William Woodley, who became Governor and Captain-

General of the Leeward Islands. In April 1788 she sailed to join her father and four years later (with an introduction to the publisher from Burns) she published a book about her experiences. In the West Indies she met and married a widower, Walter Riddell, the feckless younger brother of Robert Riddell of Friars Carse. Maria returned to London in the summer of 1791 to have her first child, and it was during that autumn that she moved to Scotland and first met the poet.

The following May, Maria's husband decided to buy Holm of Dalscirth, near Dumfries; he renamed it Woodley Park in her honour and installed her in it, although he then had to sail for the West Indies to try to raise the balance of the money to pay for it. A second daughter was born there in November 1792.

Maria was young, she was in many ways immature, but she had already done more than many a woman of twice her age. She had beauty, wit and intelligence, qualities which appealed to Burns, and indeed her only fault was capriciousness and an inability to disguise her dislike of certain people.

Burns and Maria enjoyed one another's company: they visited the lead mines at Wanlockhead together, and on this journey she fell under the spell of the poet's conversation. Some weeks after their return they began to correspond, rather after the style of the Clarinda-Sylvander letters, but without the white-hot passion that Nancy Maclehose had generated. Robert was guarded in his references to love, and she responded with protests that her brother-in-law would not approve of such close friendship in the absence of Walter Riddell. None the less, Maria invited the poet to visit her, and they exchanged verses and discussed poetry.

Maria apart, there was much to enjoy in Dumfries, and Robert enjoyed it. He was an important person, known and respected wherever he went, and the rich and influential invited him to their homes, while the gregarious shared his conversation at the Globe Inn. Whatever Burns did in the narrow confines of Dumfries, he was bound to be observed, and there were enemies waiting to make sure that every erring move was widely reported.

During his Dumfries years, Burns gave his critics

ammunition to fire at his character by his choice of friends. He became intimate with Dr William Maxwell, a doctor whose acquaintance furthered the poet's anti-establishment indiscretions, for Maxwell was a fully committed Jacobin. He had trained as a doctor in France and at the Revolution had joined the Republican Army, serving as a guard at the execution of King Louis XVI, when he dipped his handkerchief in the King's blood. Eventually the brutality and excesses of the revolutionaries had cooled his ardour for the cause, but after his return to Dumfries in 1794 he was carefully watched by the authorities, especially since he was connected with the formation of a group known to support unpalatable ideas on constitutional reform. Burns became associated with this group, as did the man who became the poet's best friend in Dumfries, John Syme.

Syme was the son of a Kirkcudbright laird and had intended to help his father to run the family estate after a spell in the army. The failure of the Ayr Bank ruined the father, however, and all his lands had to be sold off. John Syme therefore entered the Excise Service in Dumfries, where he managed to obtain the sinecure post of Collector of Stamps. His office was on the ground floor of the house in which Burns lived in Stinking Vennel, so Robert saw much of him there and also visited the Syme home at Ryedale on the Maxweltown side of the Nith. Although they had known one another in the Ellisland days, their friendship blossomed after Burns moved into the town.

Syme was an intelligent man, vague, disorganized and kindly – not really a revolutionary, rather concerned to reform the unfair social structure. And this, of course, gave him common ground with the poet. More than thirty years later Syme recalled the poet vividly:

The poet's expression varied perpetually, according to the idea that predominated in his mind; and it was beautiful to remark how well the play of the lips indicated the sentiment he was about to utter. His eyes and lips – the first remarkable for fire, and the second for flexibility – formed at all times an index to his mind. ... I cordially concur with what Sir Walter Scott says of the poet's eyes. In animated moments, and particularly when his dander was roused by instances of tergiversation, meanness, or tyranny, they were actually like coals of living fire.

Burns also became friendly with the Reverend James Gray, Latin master and later Rector of Dumfries Academy, and with another teacher, Thomas White, but his closest friends were his colleagues in the Excise Service, John Mitchell, Alexander Findlater and John Lewars.

The poet was immediately responsible to Findlater, who surveyed his work very strictly. In June 1791 he took Burns to task for a faulty entry in one of his books, and Robert's reply shows how seriously the poet took his work. Yet a postscript reveals a warm relationship between the two colleagues:

I am both much surprised & vexed at that accident of Lorimer's Stock – The last survey I made prior to Mr Lorimer's going to Edinr I was very particular in my inspection & the quantity was certainly in his possession as I stated it. – The surveys I have made during his absence might as well have been marked "key absent" as I never found any body but the lady, who I know is not mistress of keys, &c. to know anything of it, and one of the times it would have rejoiced all Hell to have seen her so drunk. I have not surveyed there since his return. – I know the gentleman's ways are, like the grace of G–, past all comprehension; but I shall give the house a severe scrutiny tomorrow morning & send you in the naked facts. –

I know, Sir, & regret deeply that this business glances with a malign aspect on my character as an Officer; but as I am really innocent in the affair, & as the gentleman is known to be an illicit Dealer, & particularly as it is the single instance of the least shadow of carelessness or impropriety in my conduct as an Officer, I shall be peculiarly unfortunate if my character shall fall a sacrifice to the dark manoeuvres of a Smuggler.

I am, Sir, your obliged & obedient humble servant.

                                                          Robt. Burns.

Sunday even

I send you some rhymes I have just finished which tickle my fancy a little. –

Lorimer, father of the girl for whom Burns wrote his song "The Lassie Wi' the Lintwhite Locks", was a known dealer in contraband in the district, so the affair did not reflect too

badly on Burns. In spite of the complaint the poet did well in
the Excise Service and was promoted in February 1792 to the
Dumfries Third or Port Division, a small area which could be
covered on foot. He was progressing well and was earning £70
a year plus another £15 to £20 from "percuisites". He was
happy with his lot too and told Maria Riddell: "So rejoice
with them that do Rejoice."

During his early days in the service at Dumfries Burns
helped to capture a smuggling vessel, the *Rosamond*; this
resulted in another of those accusations against his character
which cannot be proved but which linger and damage Burns's
reputation. It was said that when the ship was auctioned the
poet bought four carronades from her and tried to send them
to France to help the revolutionaries. This information ought
to have been contained in papers which Lewars passed on to
Joseph Train, antiquary and supervisor of Excise at Castle
Douglas, and which Train in turn gave to Sir Walter Scott.
The papers came to light at Abbotsford in 1930 when the
Scott papers were being catalogued by the National Library of
Scotland, but the one document which might have proved or
disproved the story was missing.

Train, normally reliable, claimed that the information was
there, and Lockhart states that Burns paid four pounds for the
guns, so the evidence, although not first hand, is strong.
Perhaps Train might be allowed the last word on the matter.
He said that Scott, in an unsuccessful effort to trace the receipt
of the guns in France, applied to the Custom House authorities
who, "after considerable search, found that they had been
seized at the port of Dover, as stated by Mr Lewars in his
memorandum".

If Train and Scott are right then Burns's action was
particularly foolish. It is true that at that moment France and
Britain were not actually at war, but the peace was uneasy,
and anyone in an official post who showed sympathy towards
revolutionaries on either side of the Channel was asking for
trouble. Trouble came soon, and Burns was to be reminded
sharply and severely of the limitations of his position.

Although information may have been trickling through to
the authorities about Burns's sympathies, he was by no means
thought of as a rebel or enemy of the state. Indeed, at the very

time of the sale of the *Rosamond* he was made an honorary
member of the Royal Company of Archers, a great honour
and one not lightly given. Robert was still held in high esteem.

So too was his literary work. Creech had suggested a new
edition of the poems and two years earlier had actually
announced a new volume, though he had done nothing to
produce it. Now the London publishers Cadell and Davies
pushed him into action and he wrote anxiously to Burns about
getting the book under way. Robert replied, offering about
fifty pages of additional material in return for no more than "a
few Books which I very much want ... together with as many
copies of my own works as Friendship or Gratitude shall
prompt me to present ...".

Creech had the type set quickly, but there followed a long
delay while Alexander Fraser Tytler corrected the proofs (not
very well), and the book did not appear until February 1793.
It was to be the last edition of Burns's poetry published during
his lifetime.

More gratifying to the poet was the appearance of the
fourth volume of the *Scots Musical Museum* in August 1792 and
a letter which arrived a few weeks later from George Thomson
in Edinburgh, inviting him to take part in a new collection of
Scottish song, an invitation which Burns could not resist.

Thomson was the son of a Fife schoolmaster and had
trained as a lawyer's clerk. In 1780 the author John Home
recommended him for a junior clerical appointment with the
Board of Trustees for the Encouragement of Manufactures in
Edinburgh. He spent his entire career with the Board, and
became its chief clerk. Outside this dull career Thomson made
another more interesting one – playing in the orchestra at the
St Cecilia concerts and collecting songs. His musical taste was
not particularly good, but that did not prevent him criticizing
or altering Burns's work. He was also sharp enough to try to
obtain the copyright of a number of Burns's songs for himself,
and after the poet's death he put about malicious and
distorted stories about Burns's way of life. Ironically, but for
Burns, Thomson would be forgotten today.

During the summer of 1792 Thomson interested Andrew
Erskine, brother of the Earl of Kellie, in bringing out a
collection of Scots tunes married to "respectable" words. In

September he asked Alexander Cunningham for a letter of introduction to Burns and, armed with this, he wrote to the poet explaining his plan.

He had engaged Pleyel, "the most agreeable composer living", to write accompaniments and an instrumental prelude to each air, and

> to render this work perfect, we are desirous to have the poetry improved wherever it seems unworthy of the music. ... Some charming melodies are united to mere nonsense and doggerel, while others are accommodated with rhymes so loose and indelicate as cannot be sung in decent company. To remove this reproach would be an easy task to the author of The Cotter's Saturday Night.

Burns's reply was wildly enthusiastic, but part of it must have sounded as indelicate to Thomson's genteel ear as the songs he complained of. Refusing payment, Burns wrote: "To talk of money, wages, fee, hire &c. could be downright Sodomy of the Soul!" When Thomson sent this letter to Burns's first biographer, James Currie, after the poet's death, he suggested that some other word should be substituted. Currie showed a fine sense of moral distinction and altered it to "prostitution".

Fortunately Burns did not live to see that, although it might have amused him enormously: nor did he see the folly of Thomson's idea of setting his fine lyrics to tunes by Pleyel and other German composers. Often the composer did not even understand the words his music was to match, and at times he did not even see the words. As he had done with Johnson, the poet gave Thomson a free hand, but whereas the editor of the *Musical Museum* showed good sense and modesty, Thomson was endowed with neither quality.

By the end of the year Burns had sent Thomson the first half dozen of the twenty-five songs he had promised; among them were "The Lea-Rig", "My Wife's A Winsome Wee Thing", "Auld Rob Morris" and "Duncan Gray". As he said of himself, he was "in song".

Burns patiently listened to Thomson's suggestions, many of which were harmful to his work. Only occasionally was he adamant. "Dainty Davie," he told him, "I have heard sung, nineteen thousand, nine hundred & ninety-nine times, &

always with the chorus to the low part of the tune; & nothing, since a Highland wench in the Cowgate once bore me three bastards at a birth, has surprised me so much as your opinion on this subject."

Thomson winced at the coarse comparison and capitulated.

Thomson's aim was to "clean up" Scottish folksong: Burns wanted to preserve it. Thus, for very different – and apparently conflicting – reasons the clerk and the poet were able to work together. Burns provided 114 songs for Thomson and 160 for Johnson. In terms of sheer volume this was a fantastic achievement, doubly astonishing when one considers the remarkable range and quality of the songs.

Until the end of his life, Burns went everywhere with an ear cocked for a tune. He would listen to some old country person singing, or to a fiddler in an inn, then "south [hum] the tune" over and over until he had caught its inspiration. Some of his finest songs were derived from the chance hearing of an air. In 1794 he gave Thomson a version of "Ca' the Yowes to the Knowes", which he had heard sung seven years earlier by a clergyman, and he gave Johnson his other version of it. On his way through Fife at the end of his Highland tour he picked up a fragment which he turned into "Hey Ca' Thro'", a spirited song which mentions a number of the little seaports on the Fife coast:

Up wi' the carls of Dysart,
  And the lads o' Buckhiven,
And the Kimmers o' Largo,
  And the lasses o' Leven.
    Hey ca' thro' ca' thro'
      For we hae mickle a do,
    Hey ca' thro' ca' thro'
      For we hae mickle a do.

Burns must have had a far better ear than Murdoch realized, for he could adjust the tempo of an air until it was right for his purpose. In his correspondence with Thomson – the main source of information on both the sources of Burns's songs and his method of writing them – he showed deep interest in the origins of folksong. "The Gray Goose and the Gled" he was told was "an old chant of the Romish Church, which corroborates the old tradition that, at the Reformation, the Reformers burlesqued much of the old Church Music with setting them to bawdy verses". By slowing these tunes down Burns unwittingly restored to them much of their original feeling.

Sometimes Burns would use an old chorus or a snatch of lines when he came to write the words. In other cases he would reshape a complete song or even supply an original lyric.

> I consider the poetic Sentiment, correspondent to my idea of the musical expression, [he told Thomson] "then chuse my theme; begin one Stanza; when that is composed, which is generally the most difficult part of the business, I walk out, sit down now & then, look out for objects in Nature around me that are in unison or harmony with the cogitations of my fancy & workings of my bosom; humming every now & then the air with the verses I have framed: when I feel my Muse beginning to jade, I retire to the solitary fireside of my study, & there commit my effusions to paper, swinging at intervals on the hind-legs of my elbow-chair, by way of calling forth my own critical strictures, as my pen goes on.

So much for the working methods of the man who was supposed to spend most of his time in taverns or with women!

Burns's knowledge of folkmusic must have been unrivalled in Scotland. When he asked Thomson for the list of airs to be included in his collection he was able to tell him simply to send the name of the tune and the first line of the verses, "because if they are verses that have appeared in any of our Collections of songs, I know them". That was proof of the thorough apprenticeship he had served.

When there were gaps in his knowledge he did not hesitate to call in help. James Clarke took down the tune of "Ca' the Yowes" for him, and once he kept a fiddler at work for two days until a tune was right. Jean, who had some of his mother's natural gift for music, was called on to sing a song over for him, or he would ride off to Closeburn to ask Kirsty Flint to sing the new piece, stopping her from time to time to make an alteration to the lyric.

With such enthusiasm at work for him in Dumfries Thomson quickly saw his chance to widen the scope of his work from a few select songs to include "every Scotch air and song worth singing". And that was precisely the aim of Burns.

Words or tune alone give no real impression of the quality of Burns's songs: they were made to be sung and they have to be sung to be appreciated. They range over every facet of the life of the plain man in Scotland in the last quarter of the eighteenth century – politics, carousing, patriotism, man's worth and love in all its aspects. It is hard to comprehend how any one man could comment so accurately and so profoundly on such varied subjects.

Naturally there are drinking songs, and they have none of the usual artificial half-hearted theorizing. This is the real stuff, based on personal experience. A joyous meeting with his friend Nicol at Moffat resulted in "Willie Brew'd a Peck o' Maut" with its happy, drunken chorus:

> We are na fou, We're nae that fou,
>   But just a drappie in our e'e;
> The cock may craw, the day may daw,
>   And ay we'll taste the barley bree.

Burns poked fun at himself and his colleagues with "The De'il's Awa' wi' th' Exciseman", he laughed at the henpecked in "Sic a Wife as Willie's Wife" (Willie Wastle dwalt on Tweed), and he never forgot the underdog or the underprivileged. On 1st July 1795 he sent a song to Thomson with the comment: "I do not give you the foregoing song for your book, but merely by way of Vive la bagatelle; for the piece is not really poetry." The "piece" was more than poetry – it was a timeless assertion of the dignity of man:

> Is there, for honest Poverty
>   That hings his head, and a' that;
> The coward-slave, we pass him by,
>   We dare be poor for a' that!
> For a' that, and a' that,
>   Our toils obscure, and a' that,
> The rank is but the guinea's stamp,
>   The Man's the gowd for a' that ...

Then let us pray that come it may,
   As come it will for a' that,
That Sense and Worth, o'er a' the earth
   Shall bear the gree, and a' that,
For a' that, and a' that,
   Its comin yet for a' that,
That Man to Man the warld o'er,
   Shall brothers be for a' that.

He touched on politics in "When Guilford Good Our Pilot
Stood" and delved deeply into patriotism with "Scots Wha
Hae" and "Does Haughty Gaul Invasion Threat" and, of
course, with his Jacobite songs. Burns was one of four song-
writers who tried their hand at "Charlie, He's My Darling",
and he turned it into a song of the common people, a real
folksong. But he did more: to these songs he added a
dimension of patriotism and longing which elevated the Lost
Cause to heights to which Charles Edward Stuart himself had
been unable to lift it. For generations to come, when
thousands were pouring out of Scotland to establish Britain's
dominions overseas, Burns's Jacobite songs such as "It Was
A' For Our Rightfu' King" struck straight to the heart:

It was a' for our rightfu' king
   We left fair Scotland's strand;
It was a' for our rightfu' king,
   We e'er saw Irish land, my dear,
   We e'er saw Irish land. –

Now a' is done that men can do,
   And a' is done in vain:
My Love and Native Land fareweel,
   For I maun cross the main, my dear,
   For I maun cross the main.

He turn'd him right and round about,
   Upon the Irish shore,
And gae his bridle-reins a shake,
   With, Adieu for evermore, my dear,
   And adieu for evermore.

The soger frae the wars returns,
   The sailor frae the main,
But I hae parted frae my Love,
   Never to meet again, my dear,
   Never to meet again.

When day is gane, and night is come,
   And a' folk bound to sleep;
I think on him that's far awa,
   The lee-lang night and weep, my dear,
   The lee-lang night and weep. –

Of course parting came into many of the love songs too "Ae Fond Kiss and Then We Sever" and "Of A' The Airts the Wind Can Blaw" are but two of these. This is just one of the aspects of love on which he touches. His songs run the gamut from immaturity to old age, from deep longing to basic physical passion. These, like the drinking songs, were not derived from or designed for the New Town drawing-room; they are couthy, earthy singing of a countryman who knew what love was about and who was not too inhibited to express it. And yet, how he captured the feelings which he could not have experienced himself, a young girl's fear at first wooing!

I am my mammy's ae bairn,
   Wi' unco folk I weary, Sir,
And lying in a man's bed,
   I'm fley'd[1] it make me irie,[2] Sir.   [¹frightened ²apprehensive
     I'm o'er young, I'm o'er young,
       I'm o'er young to marry yet;
     I'm o'er young, 'twad be a sin
       To tak me frae my mammy yet.

And how could Burns, a recently married man in his thirties, have known the depth of love which can develop over the years between a man and a woman?

John Anderson my jo,[1] John   [¹sweetheart
   When we were first acquent;
Your locks were like the raven,
   Your bony brow was brent;
But now your brow is beld, John,

Your locks are like the snaw;
But blessings on your frosty pow,
    John Anderson, my Jo.

John Anderson my jo, John,
    We clamb the hill the gither;
And mony a canty day, John,
    We've had wi' ane anither:
Now we maun totter down, John,
    And hand in hand we'll go;
And sleep the gither at the foot,
    John Anderson my Jo.

Between these extremes Burns wrote on a number of themes –
on constancy in "A Red, Red Rose":

And fare thee weel, my only Luve!
    And fare the weel, a while!
And I will come again, my Luve,
    Tho' it were ten thousand mile!

on sexual triumph among the corn rigs:

Corn rigs, an' barley rigs,
    An' corn rigs are bonie:
I'll ne'er forget that happy night,
    Amang the rigs wi' Annie.

and on a warmly remembered friendship, the kind that defeats
time and distance, in "Auld Lang Syne":

Should auld acquaintance be forgot
    And never brought to mind?
Should auld acquaintance be forgot,
    And auld lang syne!

This is the best known of all Burns's songs, one which has
become not merely a national but an international song of
parting. It is sung in many languages; it is sung on every
occasion; but to the Scot it has the deepest meaning, for every
man has his own vision of the braes and burn of the song. Yet it
is not mere nostalgia, mourning for something that is gone.

"Auld Lang Syne" ends on a high note, offering a hand of friendship and promising future conviviality. It is a song of parting, but of parting with high hopes for future meetings:

> And there's a hand, my trusty fiere![1]   [1companion
>   And gie's a hand o' thine!
> And we'll tak a right gude willie waught,[2]   [2drink
>   For auld lang syne.

Songs were the one thing that sustained Burns in the difficult last years of his life: he was like a song-thrush which returns to his branch to sing no matter how bad the day may be. No matter how ill Burns felt, how busy he was kept, how his heart was torn after some new tragedy in his life, he was not silent for long. Soon he returned to full song.

And as 1792 closed he needed to sing loudly and clearly as fate struck him mercilessly once again.

14

Liberty in Every Blow

The trouble this time was not so much because of Burns's own actions as the political situation in Scotland. The whole period between the fall of the Bastille and the Reform Bill of 1832 saw deep political division throughout the country, but no time was more unsettled than the early 1790s. Many respectable, peaceable Scotsmen supported the cause of the revolution in France until it degenerated into bloody tyranny which threatened to spread to Britain.

Thomas Paine's *Rights of Man* was the radicals' charter for freedom, and in Scotland those who followed it banded themselves together as the Friends of the People to agitate openly for political reform. These Friends were by no means the lowest section of the community: on the contrary they were the élite — scholars, intellectuals and a fair number of aristocrats. Their first convention, held at Edinburgh in December 1792, was attended by Thomas Muir, the advocate, William Skirving, Colonel Dalrymple of Fordel, the Reverend Thomas Fysshe Palmer and Lord Daer. They also had support from Henry Erskine, Dean of the Faculty of Advocates, Maurice Margarot, Joseph Gerald and William Johnstone, publisher and editor of the *Edinburgh Gazetteer*, an outspoken liberal newspaper.

Opposing the Friends was the establishment, led by "King" Dundas, who ruled Scotland in the name of William Pitt and his government in London. Dundas held every county and burgh in his pocket, and his spies were everywhere to report to him any anti-government act or remark. We do not know who these spies were in Dumfries, but they were there, watching Burns among others.

So far as we know Burns never belonged to the Friends of

the People, but he certainly sympathized with their aims, and, as the Edinburgh convention approached, let this sympathy be known. The government spies had two pieces of information to report to their masters: first, Burns wrote to the editor of the *Gazetteer* in November, subscribing to the paper and exhorting Johnstone to further attacks on the establishment: "Go on, Sir! Lay bare, with undaunted heart and steady hand, the horrid mass of corruption called Politics and State-Craft! Dare to draw in their native colours these 'Calm, thinking Villains, whom no faith can fix' – whatever be the Shibboleth of their pretended Party." A fortnight later he wrote to Johnstone again, enclosing a letter from Robert Riddell under the pen name Cato.

The second piece of information from the spies was more trivial, yet it was more widely known in Dumfries. After the Caledonian Hunt's annual meeting at Dumfries that autumn, members attended a gala performance of *As You Like It* at the Theatre Royal, and at the end of the performance, just before the National Anthem was played, a cry arose from the pit for "Ça Ira", the militant song of the French revolutionaries. Robert Burns was in the pit that night and, although no one has ever said that he joined in the cry, to be there was enough. He sent an aggrieved letter to Mrs Dunlop: "For me, I am a *Placeman*, you know, a very humble one indeed, Heaven knows, but still so much so as to gag me from joining in the cry. – What my private sentiments are, you will find out without an Interpreter, so, alas, could less friendly folk!"

The political situation was steadily growing more tense and dangerous; and though Burns tried to work on as if nothing untoward were happening, even enjoying a brief moment of joy when Jean presented him with a daughter, Elizabeth, it was only a matter of time before he was caught up in the political warfare. There was more gossip about the poet's views and finally an informer denounced him to the Board of Excise.

For a time he was in danger of summary dismissal, but Graham of Fintry managed to stave that off, and instead Mitchell was instructed to inform Burns that an enquiry would be made into his political conduct.

In consternation Burns wrote at once to Graham:

I have been surprised, confounded & distracted by Mr Mitchel, the Collector, telling me just now, that he had received an order from your Honble Board to enquire into my political conduct, & blaming me as a person disaffected to Government. Sir, you are a Husband – & a father – you know what you would feel, to see the much-loved wife of your bosom, & your helpless, prattling little ones, turned adrift into the world, degraded & disgraced from a situation in which they have been respectable & respected, and left almost without the necessary support of a miserable existence. – Alas, Sir! must I think that such, soon, will be my lot! And from the damned, dark insinuations of hellish, vile, groundless Envy too! ... I say, that the allegation, whatever villain has made it, is a LIE! To the British Constitution, on Revolution principles next after my God, I am most devoutly attached!

Graham replied on 15th January 1793 with a soothing letter listing the charges against Burns, which brought a long, almost hysterical reply refuting everything. Burns denied participating in the "Ça Ira" incident, he offered to keep silent in future on his reform opinions, he was willing to cancel his subscription to the *Edinburgh Gazetteer*, and, while he admitted supporting the revolutionaries in France to begin with, he had now changed his opinions. But he would not abandon his principles. "At the same time," he told Graham, "I think, & you know what High and distinguished Characters have for some time thought so, that we have a good deal deviated from the original principles of that Constitution; particularly, that an alarming System of Corruption has pervaded the connection between the Executive Power and the House of Commons."

Graham laid the poet's first letter before his Board, and he probably had to talk persuasively to make them accept Burns's innocence. In the end they decided to send the General Supervisor of Excise, William Corbet, to Dumfries to enquire there about Burns's conduct. They were obviously expecting nothing more serious to emerge, for they told Corbet to tell the poet that his business was to act and not to think and (as Robert put it) "that whatever might be Men and Measures, it was for me to be silent and obedient".

Robert fought back by continuing to use Graham's

influence – boldly (almost cheekily) suggesting once again that another man's job might be given to him. The Galloway Supervisor was ill and Burns was angling for the post. As Mitchell was unwilling to propose the sick man's replacement, the poet wrote to Graham suggesting that his own "hardy constitution and inexperience (*sic*) in that line of life" fitted him for the post. Later he proposed to Graham that the number of Excise divisions in Dumfries be reduced by one and the work divided among the other officers. Not surprisingly, he asked Graham to say nothing to Corbet or Findlater about this plan.

In many ways Burns was lucky to keep his job, for by February war had broken out with France and the British government was on the point of taking hysterical action against the Friends of the People.

Clearly the poet's friends were worried about the possible consequences for him, and in fact a rumour went around that he had been dismissed. Mrs Dunlop wrote anxiously for news, and Nicol sent him a letter with fatherly advice disguised as light comment on the matter. "Dear Christless Bobby," he wrote, "What concerns it thee whether the lousy Dumfriesian fiddlers play 'ça ira' or 'God save the King'? Suppose you *had* an aversion to the King, you could not as a gentleman use him worse than He has done. The infliction of idiocy is no sign of Friendship or Love. ..."

John Erskine of Mar heard the rumour too and wrote tactfully to Robert Riddell suggesting that if it were true a fund might be started for Burns. On seeing the letter Burns was deeply touched and wrote to Erskine:

Does any man tell me, that my feeble efforts can be of no service; & that it does not belong to my humble station to meddle with the concerns of a People? – I tell him, that it is on such individuals as I, that for the hand of support, & the eye of intelligence, a Nation has to rest. – The uninformed mob may swell a nation's bulk; & the titled, tinsel Courtly throng may be its feathered ornament, but the number of those who are elevated enough in life, to reason & reflect; & yet low enough to keep clear of the venal contagion of a Court; these are a Nation's strength.

In Dumfries the affair cost Burns none of the respect he

enjoyed in the town, for publication of the second Edinburgh Edition had brought new honours. The local subscription library elected him a free member, and the following month, on the strength of a suggestion he had made for closing a loophole in the burgh's tax-gathering system, he petitioned as a freeman of the burgh that his children might be educated at the High School free of charge.

In June of that year the first volume of Thomson's *Select Collection of Original Scottish Airs* appeared, including the twenty-five songs which Burns had promised. Thomson was so delighted with the book that he sent Robert a copy and enclosed a five pound note, explaining:

> I cannot express to you how much I am obliged to you for the exquisite new songs you are sending me; but thanks, my friend, are a poor return for what you have done. As I shall benefit by the publication, you must suffer me to enclose a small mark of my gratitude, and to repeat it afterwards when I find it convenient. Do not return it, for by Heaven if you do, our correspondence is at an end.

Burns reacted sharply, for the money degraded him in his own eyes, and warned Thomson never again to send him payment for songs. Thomson respected this and offered no more money until a few days before the poet's death when, in desperation, Burns begged another five pounds.

Delighted with Thomson's book, Burns was in high spirits when he set out on 27th July 1793 to make a journey through Galloway, accompanied by his friend Syme. Alas, his mood soon changed, and on the journey he displayed every facet of his mercurial temperament, from irritation and rage over small incidents to sweet gentleness as a house guest at St Mary's Isle.

The tour was a leisurely one and, for once, the poet appreciated the scenery, a sign perhaps that he had managed to purge farming from his soul. On the road from Parton to Kenmore he just stopped his grey Highland shelty pony and forgot time as he drank in the beauty of the scenery, until Syme had to hurry him on so that they might reach Kenmore in time to dine with their hosts. After three days with the Gordons of Kenmore, during which the poet was set the painful task of writing an epitaph for his hostess's lapdog which had just died, they moved on to Gatehouse-of-Fleet. The sky grew darker as they rode along, the wind sighed, then thunder and lightning tore the clouds apart, and floods of rain poured down on them. For a time Robert enjoyed the storm, then he lost himself in his own thoughts as he used to do in wild weather at Mossgiel until they came to Gatehouse-of-Fleet. Here Burns insisted on getting utterly drunk to revenge himself on the elements. However, the storm won the contest, for next morning the poet found his boots had been dried so badly that he could not put them on. He tried force and tore them to shreds, then rode off towards Kirkcudbright bemoaning the loss of the boots, a sick stomach and a headache. Syme carried the "torn ruins" of the boots across his saddle, and eventually they were sent back to Dumfries, because the poet insisted that they were worth mending.

Burns continued to fume until Syme pointed across the Solway to the home of a nobleman whom the poet hated and, "having expectorated his spleen", Robert reached St Mary's Isle in good humour again. Political thoughts rankled, and Burns comforted himself with the thought that the Earl of Selkirk, whose guest he was to be, was not an aristocrat – at least not as he understood the word. So the pair spent a happy evening, Robert reciting poetry and another guest, the musician Urbani, singing.

Burns rode silently back to Dumfries and Syme wisely did not interrupt his thoughts. He was contemplating the political situation and fretting over the trials of the Friends of the People. These thoughts soon matured as a letter, written to Thomson on 30th August, showed:

I am delighted with many little melodies, which the learned Musician despises as silly & insipid. I do not know whether the old air, *Hey, Tutti Taitie* may rank among this number; but well I know that … it has often filled my eyes with tears. – There is a tradition, which I have met with in many places of Scotland, that it was Robert The Bruce's March at the battle of Bannockburn. – This thought, in my yesternight's evening walk, warmed me to a pitch of enthusiasm on the theme of Liberty and Independence

which I threw into a kind of Scots Ode, fitted to the Air, that one
might suppose to be the gallant ROYAL SCOT'S address to his
heroic followers on that eventful morning.

The song was "Scots, wha hae wi' Wallace bled", and,
although its first verses clearly refer to the long-gone war of
independence, the last two were inspired by the recently
ended treason trials in Edinburgh and the fight for freedom
and reform then being waged in the country.

> By Oppression's woes and pains!
> By your Sons in servile chains!
> We will drain our dearest veins,
>   But they *shall* be free!
>
> Lay the proud Usurpers low!
> Tyrants fall in every foe!
> LIBERTY's in every blow!
>   Let us DO – OR DIE!!!

And at the end of the song Burns added the comment: "So
may God defend the cause of Truth and Liberty, as he did
that day! – Amen!"

Thomson liked the words but not the tune and suggested
that instead they should be matched to the tune *Lewie Gordon*.
This ruined the last line which had to be lengthened, so that,
in the powerful penultimate verse, it ran "But they shall be,
they shall be free." Robert disagreed with the suggestion, but
Thomson won the support of his Edinburgh advisers and the
poet at last permitted the change. And that was how "Robert
Bruce's March to Bannockburn" was first published. It was
only after Burns's death that Thomson realized his mistake
and, in the 1802 edition, corrected the words and set them to
Hey Tutti Taitie.

With this song Robert Burns once again found his voice as a
political commentator and, although he was never again as
outspoken as he had been before the Excise Board's
reprimand, he continued to let his views be known. But at the
same time he was never disloyal to his country.

15

My Spirits Fled! Fled!

The year which had begun with the inquisition by the Excise Board ended with another great tragedy. Throughout the autumn Walter Riddell had been in the West Indies trying to raise money to complete the purchase of Woodley Park. He did not return until the following spring, empty-handed, and had to hand back the estate, losing not only £1000 he had already paid but another £2000 he had spent on alterations.

In the absence of her husband Maria Riddell could not receive Burns in her own home, but they met frequently at other people's houses, and a warm and close relationship developed. This was carried forward by letters which, on the poet's part at any rate, became fuller and franker. He sent her a love song, "The Last Time I Came O'er the Moor", accompanied by a note claiming that it did not refer to their relationship. It was the poem of a man frustrated in his desire for someone beyond his reach:

> Love's veriest wretch, despairing, I,
>   Fain, fain my crime would cover:
> The unweeting groan, the bursting sigh,
>   Betray thy guilty lover.
> I know my doom must be despair:
>   Thou wilt nor canst relieve me;
> But, O Maria, hear my prayer,
>   For pity's sake forgive me.

This was an irksome situation for Burns, especially at a time when he felt insecure and at odds with the establishment, although Maria gave him no cause to feel inferior to or unwelcome in her circle. Once when he saw her at the theatre he turned away abruptly because some officers were there and told her afterwards: "I meant to have called on you yesternight, but as I edged up [to] your Box-door, the first object which greeted my view was one of these lobster-coated Puppies, sitting, like another dragon, guarding the hesperian fruit."

The friendship with the Riddells came to a stormy and unexpected end during Christmas week, when Robert was dining at Friars Carse one evening. The detail of the incident is not absolutely certain, but it appears that both Riddell and his male guests had drunk considerably more than usual and, after the ladies retired, the conversation turned to the rape of the Sabine women. Someone suggested that they should stage a mock Sabine rape as they returned to the drawing-room. Robert Burns's "victim" was to be Riddell's prim wife, Elizabeth, and the poet carried the joke too far, and a dreadful scene ensued. Riddell naturally took his wife's part and, although some of those present tried to make light of the whole thing, Burns was ordered out of the house.

In the morning Robert was desperately sorry and sent an apology to his hostess, a strange letter beginning with a high-flown justification of his action and ending with an abject apology:

I daresay that this is the first epistle you ever received from this nether world. I write you from the regions of Hell, amid the horrors of the damned. The time and manner of my leaving your earth I do not exactly know, as I took my departure in the heat of a fever of intoxication, contracted at your hospitable mansion; but, on my arrival here, I was fairly tried, and sentenced to endure the purgatorial tortures of this infernal confine for the space of ninety-nine years, eleven months, and twenty-nine days, and all on account of the impropriety of my conduct yesternight under your roof. Here am I, laid on a bed of pityless furze, with my aching head reclined on a pillow of ever-piercing thorn, while an infernal tormentor, wrinkled, and old, and cruel, his name I think is *Recollection*, with a whip of scorpions, forbids peace or rest to approach me, and keeps anguish eternally awake. Still, Madam, if I could in any measure be reinstated in the good opinion of the fair circle whom my conduct last night so much injured, I think it would be an alleviation of my torments. For this reason I trouble you with this letter. To the men of the company I will make no apology. – Your husband, who insisted on my drinking more than I chose, has no right to blame me; and the other gentlemen were partakers of my guilt. But to you, Madam, I have much to apologise. Your good opinion I valued as one of the greatest acquisitions I had made on earth, and I was truly a beast to forfeit it. There was a Miss I– too, a woman of fine sense, gentle and unassuming manners – do make, on my part, a miserable d-mned wretch's best apology to her. A Mrs G, a charming woman, did me the honour to be prejudiced in my favor; this makes me hope that I have not outraged her beyond all forgiveness. – To all the other ladies please present my humblest contrition for my conduct, and my petition for their gracious pardon. O all ye powers of decency and decorum! whisper to them that my errors, though great, were involuntary – that an intoxicated man is the vilest of beasts – that it was not in my nature to be brutal to any one – that to be rude to a woman, when in my senses, was impossible with me – but –

* * *

Regret! Remorse! Shame! ye three hellhounds that ever dog my steps and bay at my heels, spare me! spare me!
Forgive the offences, and pity the perdition of, Madam,
        Your humble Slave ...
        Robt Burns.

The apology failed to reach Elizabeth Riddell's heart, although it might have been accepted by Maria. Perhaps abject regret unaccompanied by defence or justification were needed in the circumstances, but that was not Robert Burns's way. Nor was his case helped by pointing out that her husband was partly to blame for forcing drink on his guests and by suggesting that at least one of the female guests did not consider the crime too outrageous.

Maria was in a difficult position. In the absence of her husband she had to take the part of her sister-in-law, and when she met Burns a few days later she gave him a look which "froze the very life-blood" of his heart. On 12th January a bitterly upset Burns returned Maria's Commonplace Book which she had lent him, with the explanation that it seemed "the Critic has forfeited your esteem." The loss of the Riddells was a terrible blow as this note, added to his song "The Day Returns", shows. "At their fireside I have enjoyed more pleasant evenings than at all the houses of fashionable people in this country put together; and to their kindness and hospitality I am indebted for many of the happiest hours in my life."

The whole sorry affair of Friars Carse ignited all the fires of hatred that smouldered in Burns, and, just as he would have done in the insecure days before he made his name and reputation, he turned viciously on poor Maria. The "Epistle from Esopus to Maria", a spiteful piece of rubbish, can only be excused by the fact that the author was on the verge of nervous collapse when he wrote it, for in truth he missed her dreadfully. One of the people to whom he now turned for comfort was Clarinda, intellectually a pale imitation of Maria Riddell. He sent her copies of the lampoons of his former friend.

> Here lies, now a prey to insulting Neglect,
>   What once was a butterfly gay in life's beam:
> Want only of wisdom denied her respect,
>   Want only of goodness denied her esteem.

When he wrote these verses he must have realized how untruthful they were and how much they might hurt the innocent Maria. Yet he seemed unable to stop himself. When he saw her carriage pass he wrote:

> If you rattle along like your Mistress's tongue,
>   Your speed will outrival the dart:
> But, a fly for your load, you'll break down on the road,
>   If your stuff be as rotten's her heart. –

Later correspondence between Maria and Dr Currie indicates that she did not see this cruel rubbish until after Burns's death, although there must have been many in Dumfries who would have taken pleasure in pointing it out to her. It is perfectly possible that she knew of the poems' existence, although not perhaps of their exact wording, and chose to ignore them.

Of course, Burns missed the Riddells, but other troubles were pressing down on him. His money worries were growing because of the reduction in trade as a result of the French wars, and at home the health of his dear little Elizabeth was giving him terrible anxiety. On 15th December he told Mrs Dunlop:

> These four months a sweet little girl, my youngest child, has been so ill, that every day, a week or less threatened to terminate her existence. ... I cannot describe to you, the anxious, sleepless hours these ties frequently give me. I see a train of helpless little folks: me & my exertions all their stay; & in what a brittle thread does the life of man hang! If I am nipt off at the command of Fate; even in all the vigour of manhood as I am, such things happen every day – gracious God! what would become of my little flock. ... But, my God, I shall run distracted if I think any longer on the subject!

His hypochondria returned and he told Cunningham in February that for two months he had been unable to lift a pen. Then on 21st April Robert Riddell died suddenly without being reconciled to Burns. Burns felt the loss of his former friend keenly, and on the day he heard the news he wrote a sad little sonnet which ended:

> Thee, Spring, again with joy shall others greet,
> Me, mem'ry of my loss will only meet.

At the time of the estrangement the poet had been copying out some of his poems into books for Glenriddell, and he now wrote and asked that they should be returned or destroyed by Elizabeth. Fortunately, she did neither, and the Glenriddell Manuscripts, as they are now called, survived. Burns very nearly lost Maria at the same time, for her husband, returned from the West Indies empty-handed, could have inherited Friars Carse under his brother's will. But, out of spite it was said, the executors and Elizabeth insisted on selling the estate and sharing the proceeds. Maria settled at Hallheaths, on the east side of Lochmaben, where she lived until she left Scotland for ever in 1797.

During this period Burns's Excise work was going well. Despite his financial difficulties, he did resist the lure of a writing career in London once again when the Editor of the *Morning Chronicle* invited him to become an "occasional correspondent" for five guineas a week. Burns felt wary of trying to live solely by his pen, but he did offer to send occasional writings to the paper. This decision was confirmed as right by the addition of another son to his growing family – James Glencairn, born on the 12th August 1794 and named after his former patron. The birth of this son heralded another productive period of song-writing, and, shortage of money and poor health notwithstanding, Robert was contented.

By and large he managed to avoid serious political trouble, despite another incident when the Caledonian Hunt was again in the town in the autumn of 1794. Burns was infuriated over a prank in which a servant had his hair plastered with mustard and spiked with toothpicks, and at the house of a lawyer, Samuel Clark, he gave an ambiguous toast in front of some of the hunt members: "May our success in the present war be equal to the justice of our cause." There followed a great row in which one of the members used the kind of language which often "ends in a brace of pistols", Robert explained in a letter of apology to his host.

The poet's nerves were on edge that autumn, and sometimes he blurted out far more than he intended. It is quite likely, too, that he was less and less able to stand drink, a small amount of alcohol having a devastating effect. At Ryedale one evening Syme rebuked Burns, and the poet flew into a rage – his face turned black with anger as he fumbled with his sword cane. Syme, half laughing and half serious, said, "What! And in my own house too." Burns threw away the cane, burst into tears and grovelled in contrition.

At last, keyed up to breaking-point, Robert wrote a stupid letter which cost him his friendship with Mrs Dunlop. Throughout the correspondence there had been complaints from Mrs Dunlop, often followed by huffy little silences. In 1790, for example, Jenny Little, a milkmaid at Dunlop House and a burgeoning poetess, had come to Ellisland (with Mrs Dunlop's blessing no doubt) not to learn from the master but to show off her work to him. She went home rebuffed. Two years later Jenny's poems were published with the help of her mistress, and on Burns's next visit they were thrust before him with a request for his opinion of them. Where as anyone else would have read them out of respect for his friend, Burns glanced at them and asked, "Do I have to read all these?" The comment was a rebuff for Mrs Dunlop, who no doubt thought she was merely asking one peasant poet's opinion of the work of another, and it resulted in a lengthy silence. The incident of January 1795 was much more serious, however. In a letter he referred to Louis XVI as a perjured blockhead and to Marie Antoinette as an unprincipled prostitute, who had both met the fate they deserved. The letter must have seemed a deliberate insult to Mrs. Dunlop, two of whose daughters had married French refugees and whose sons were in the army which daily awaited a French invasion. She refused to reply to the poet and maintained silence until the end of his life, when he sent her a sad farewell letter and she wrote in return the letter which was the last to reach him before he died. Burns did not mean his letter to hurt his friend – it was a mere statement of his opinion.

Perhaps the poet's judgment was clouded at this time. A few weeks earlier Findlater had taken ill and Burns was doing his work as Acting Supervisor – a hard, demanding job which meant checking the gaugers' work and their records. He filled the post for four months and the only criticism that was made of his work during the entire period was one small matter in his final report, and that was the fault of one of his subordinates. Robert now was well on the way to the promotion he sought and which he would certainly have received if his health had held out.

He was now desperately short of money and had to send a "painful, disagreeable letter" to William Stewart, factor at Closeburn estate, asking for a loan of three or four guineas. The money was sent to him by return and was handed on to his landlord Captain Hamilton with an apology:

It is needless to attempt an apology for my remissness to you in money-matters: my conduct is beyond all excuse. – Literally, Sir, I had it not. – The distressful state of Commerce at this town, has this year taken from my otherwise scanty income no less than 20£. – That part of my Salary depended upon the Imports, & they are no more, for one year. – I enclose you three guineas and shall soon settle all with you.

Hamilton made light of the arrears of rent and sent the poet a card asking why he was avoiding him. Robert replied that he would pay a call on his "first leisure evening". Even the smallest debt was embarrassing to the poet.

Others showed sympathy too. Burns sent Maria Riddell a poem on her birthday, "Canst Thou Leave me Thus, my Katy?" – a hint that he would welcome a reconciliation; she responded with some verses of her own and an assurance that her feelings towards him were friendly. In January 1795 she lent him a book, which he acknowledged formally, as if waiting for her to make the first substantial move.

He returned the book in due course and took up the old correspondence just as it had been before the Friars Carse breach. He gave her his news: how Thomson was finding it difficult to communicate with Pleyel because of the wars; he sent her three indifferent songs which he had set to three of Thomson's Irish airs; and he told her he had just been sitting to "Reid in this town for a miniature" in which "I think he has hit by far the best likeness of me ever was taken." Later on he told Maria he thought Reid had spoilt the picture.

How lucky that Maria returned to him just as he cut himself off from Mrs Dunlop. Had she not, he would have been left without a confidante to whom he could pour out his troubles – and he needed someone to listen to him. Twice during the first half of 1795 he was ill, yet he made difficult journeys in connection with his work. From Ecclefechan he wrote on 7th February:

In the course of my duty ... I came yesternight to this unfortunate, wicked, little village. ... I have gone forward – but snows of ten feet deep have impeded my progress: I have tried to "gae back the gate I cam again," but the same obstacle has shut me up within insuperable ban. – To add to my misfortune, since dinner, a Scraper has been torturing Catgut, in sounds that would have insulted the dying agonies of a Sow under the hands of a Butcher – and thinks himself, *on that very account*, exceeding good company. – In fact, I have been in a dilemma, either to get drunk, to forget these miseries; or to hang myself, to get rid of these miseries: like a prudent man. ... I, of the two evils have chosen the least & am very drunk – at your service!

This was a flash of the old Robert Burns which showed that

even in the most difficult circumstances his sense of humour did not desert him.

As if he had not enough to cope with, patriotism now laid hold of him. A French invasion was a real threat, so he decided to join the volunteer force being raised in Dumfries. Under Colonel Arent Schuyler de Peyster, an American veteran, Burns drilled twice a week, though perhaps his greatest contribution to the regiment was his patriotic verse.

Does haughty Gaul invasion threat,
    Then let the louns bewaure, Sir,
There's WOODEN WALLS upon our seas,
    And VOLUNTEERS on shore, Sir:
The *Nith* shall run to *Corsincon*,
    And *Criffell* sink in *Solway*,
E'er we permit a Foreign Foe
    On British ground to rally.

It was all too much for his brave heart. In the spring of 1795 he told Maria Riddell that he was "so ill as to be scarce able to hold this miserable pen to this miserable paper". Then his daughter Elizabeth's health began to decline frighteningly and she had to be taken to Mossgiel, where he hoped that the healthy country air might help her. But in September she died, and Robert was so busy with Excise duties that he could not even attend her funeral. He was heartbroken: literature was abandoned, though after a few weeks he began to return to life, a note to Maria ending: "That you, my friend, may never experience such a loss as mine, sincerely prays, R.B."

Fortunately he had sent packets of songs off to both Thomson and Johnson just before this tragedy struck, for he was too ill for a time to go on writing songs. He drove himself to carry out his Excise duties and to support the Volunteers, but the toll was enormous. He knew his health was deteriorating, for he wrote to Cleghorn that after his daughter's death he had fallen victim to rheumatic fever "which brought me to the borders of the grave".

On the last day of January 1796 he made another effort to be reconciled with Mrs Dunlop. He sent her a copy of "Does Haughty Gaul Invasion Threat?", a sure sign of his loyalty, and a painful, touching letter which should have won over any reasonable person:

These many months you have been two packets in my debt. – What sin of ignorance I have committed against so highly a valued friend I am utterly at a loss to guess. ... Will you be so obliging, dear Madam, as to condescend on that my offence which you seem determined to punish with a deprivation of that friendship which once was source of my highest enjoyments? – Alas, Madam, ill can I afford, at this time, to be deprived of any of the small remnant of my pleasures. – I have lately drank deep of the cup of affliction. – The Autumn robbed me of my only daughter & darling child, & that at a distance too & so rapidly as to put it out of my power to pay the last duties to her. – I had scarcely begun to recover from that shock, when [I] Became myself the victim of a most severe Rheumatic fever, & long the die spun doubtful; until after many weeks of a sick-bed it seems to have turned up more life, & I am beginning to crawl across my room, & once indeed have been before my own door in the street. ... I know not how you are in Ayr-shire, but here, we have actually famine, & that too in the midst of plenty. – Many days my family, and hundreds of other families, are absolutely without one grain of meal; as money cannot purchase it. – How long the *Swinish Multitude* will be quiet, I cannot tell; they threaten daily.

But Mrs Dunlop was not moved to reply.

The "Swinish Multitude" did not remain quiet for long. In Dumfries there were alarming food riots from 12th to 14th March, and things became more worrying than ever for Burns.

Robert was constantly ill. His temples and his eyeballs ached and the irregular movements of his heart worsened. He became more irritable and gloomy and fled from himself into society. Currie claims that in January 1796, after a heavy night in a tavern, he came home one bitter morning numb and intoxicated. An attack of rheumatism followed, and his appetite began to fail. From then on his limbs shook, and his voice faltered when emotion welled up in him. Now his pulse became weaker and more rapid, and pains in his joints kept him awake. His friends looked forward to spring, hoping that the returning warmth would bring back health with it. But it did not.

He wrote a few songs again, but in April even that activity faltered. He told Thomson:

Alas! my dear Thomson, I fear it will be sometime ere I tune my

lyre again! "By Babel streams" &c. – Almost ever since I wrote
you last, I have only known Existence by the pressure of the heavy
head of Sickness; & have counted time by the repercussions of
PAIN! Rheumatism, Cold, & Fever have formed, to me, a
terrible Trinity in Unity, which makes me close my eyes in
misery, and open them without hope.

His letters were short, but he struggled on, and in May he
actually told Thomson that he hoped that the approaching
summer might set him to rights. He now believed he suffered
from "a flying gout".

He was cheered when Thomson sent him a seal set in a
Scottish pebble bearing his unregistered arms design, which
the poet and Maria Riddell had worked out between them.
Round the top of the crest was the motto: "Woodnotes wild",
and at the bottom ran the words: "Better a wee bush than nae
bield*". In a way this was a defiant gesture against the
Heralds' Office, which had told him when he was in
Edinburgh that not a single Burns was registered there.
"Gules, Purpure, Argent &c. quite disowned me," he told Dr
Moore:

   My ancient but ignoble blood
Has crept thro' scoundrels ever since the flood.

Whether Thomson sent the seal to Burns merely by way of
thanks for all the songs or whether it was a sweetener to
persuade him to assign the copyright of his songs to him we do
not know, but certainly Burns refused to give the songs away
to his collaborator. In fact he altered the agreement which
Thomson's lawyer drew up, limiting it to the present work
alone. Burns made it clear that he intended to publish his
songs "on a cheap plan" after publication of the *Select Airs* was
completed.

Time was now running desperately short for the poet, and
he knew it. Jean, now expecting yet another child, could not
cope, so Jessie Lewars, sister of Burns's Excise colleague, came
in to help in the house. She told Robert Chambers, an early
biographer of the poet, that one day Burns, fancying himself in
love with her, hobbled into her brother's house and told Jessy
that if she would play her favourite air he would write a song for

* Shelter.

it. She played a seventeenth-century tune *Lennox Love to Blantyre*
several times until the poet was familiar with it. Very soon
afterwards he produced the song:

> Oh wert thou in the cauld blast,
>   On yonder lea, on yonder lea:
> My plaidie to the angry airt,
>   I'd shelter thee, I'd shelter thee:
> Or did misfortune's bitter storms
>   Around thee blaw, around thee blaw,
> Thy bield should be my bosom,
>   To share it a', to share it a'.

> Or were I in the wildest waste,
>   Sae black and bare, sae black and bare,
> The desert were a paradise,
>   If thou wert there, if thou wert there.
> Or were I monarch o' the globe,
>   Wi' thee to reign, wi' thee to reign;
> The brightest jewel in my crown,
>   Wad be my queen, wad be my queen.

This was one of the tenderest expressions of love that ever
came from Burns's pen and was the last great lyric he ever
wrote.

By June a sense of urgency had come into Burns's writings,
almost as if he now was certain that the end was near. He
wrote to Johnson for a copy of the *Musical Museum* for Jessy
Lewars, and in his letter he took farewell of Johnson:

> How are you, my dear Friend? & how comes on yr fifth volume? —
> You may probably think that for some time past I have neglected
> you & your work; but, alas, the hand of pain, & sorrow, & care
> has these many months lain heavy on me! — Personal and
> domestic afflictions have almost entirely banished that alacrity
> and life with which I used to woo the rural Muse of Scotia. — In
> the meantime, let us finish what we have so well begun. — The
> gentleman, Mr Lewars, a particular friend of mine, will bring
> out any proofs (if they are ready) or any message you may have. —
>   farewell!
>   R. Burns.

Maria Riddell had been away and was quite unaware of how ill her friend was. She wrote and invited him to accompany her in uniform to the King's birthday ball in Dumfries, but he declined in a most depressed letter:

> I am in such miserable health as to be utterly incapable of shewing my loyalty in any way. – Rackt as I am with rheumatism, I meet every face with a greeting like that of Balak to Balaam – "Come, curse me Jacob; and come, defy me Israel. ... I may perhaps see you on Saturday night, but I will not be at the ball. – Why should I? – Man delights not, nor woman either!" ...

Dr Maxwell, too, was alarmed by the poet's condition and prescribed sea-bathing and horse-riding in the country for the rest of the summer. So, on 3rd July, so weak that he could scarcely stand, Robert went to Brow-on-Solway, nine miles east of Dumfries, which in those days had a reputation as a spa. He could not afford a horse but waded out every day over the shallow Solway sands until he stood up to the armpits in the sea. It must have been bitterly cold, and the effect was devastating. The day after his arrival at Brow he told Thomson:

> I recd your songs: but my health being so precarious nay dangerously situated, that as a last effort I am here at sea-bathing quarters. – Besides my inveterate rheumatism, my appetite is quite gone, & I am so emaciated as to be scarce able to support myself on my own legs. – Alas! is this a time for me to woo the Muses? However, I am still anxiously willing to serve your work; & if possible shall try: – I would not like to see another employed, unless you could lay your hand upon a poet whose productions would be equal to the rest. ...

Poetry was gone: money too. Now Burns began to be haunted by nightmares of bankruptcy and starvation. Normally an Exciseman who was unable to carry out his duties would be put on half pay, and Burns simply could not live on that. On 7th July he wrote to Cunningham in Edinburgh:

> Alas! my friend, I fear the voice of the Bard will soon be heard among you no more! For these eight or ten months I have been

ailing, sometimes bedfast & sometimes not; but these last three months I have been tortured with an excruciating rheumatism, which has reduced me to nearly the last stage. – You actually would not know [me] if you saw me. – Pale, emaciated, & so feeble as occasionally to need help from my chair. – my spirits fled! fled! – but I can no more on the subject – only the Medical folks tell me that my last & only chance is bathing & country quarters & riding. – The deuce of the matter is this; when an Excise-man is off duty, his salary is reduced to 32£ instead of 50£. – What way, in the name of thrift, shall I maintain myself & keep a horse in Country-quarters – with a wife & five children at home, on 32£. I mention this, because I had intended to beg your utmost interest & all friends you can muster, to move our Commissrs of Excise to grant me the full salary. – I dare say you know them all personally. – If they do not grant it me, I must lay my account with an exit truly en poëte, if I die not of disease I must perish with hunger.

He was becoming more and more agitated. Five days later he wrote to Cunningham because he had received no reply, enclosing the song "Here's a Health to Ane I Lo'e Dear", "the last I made or probably will make for some time." He now told his friend that he intended to petition the Excise Commissioners, but so far as we know he never did.

Yet Burns managed. Currie suggests that a young expectant, Adam Scobie, did Robert's work for no payment, so that the poet could continue to draw his full salary. Another story from Findlater was that Graham of Fintry, unable to restore the poet's full salary, sent him a private gift of five pounds. But by this time it hardly mattered, for Robert's health was worsening.

Maria Riddell, who had also been ill and was convalescing, wanted to see Burns. On the afternoon of 7th July she sent her carriage for the poet. When he arrived she was horrified at his appearance, which bore the stamp of death, and must have shown her feelings. Before she could say a word Burns greeted her: "Well, Madam, have you any commands for the other world?"

Robert Burns knew he was dying, and he faced the fact squarely and honestly as he had faced every unpleasant fact in life. According to Maria they talked of his approaching end.

He ate little and spoke anxiously about his family and about his reputation, fearing that his many indiscretions would enable people to attack him by using "every scrap of his writing" against him. They met again the following day, and as they said farewell and Robert lifted himself into the carriage both must have known that this was their final parting.

Having taken leave of Maria, Burns sat down and wrote his farewell to Mrs Dunlop:

> Madam,
> I have written you so often without rec.g any answer, that I would not trouble you again but for the circumstances in which I am. – An illness which has long hung about me in all probability will speedily send me beyond that bourne whence no traveller returns. – Your friendship with which for many years you honoured me was a friendship dearest to my soul. – Your conversation & especially your correspondence were at once highly entertaining & instructive. – With what pleasure did I use to break up the seal! The remembrance yet adds one pulse more to my poor pulsating heart.
> Farewell!!!!

On the same day he posted a desperate letter to Mauchline, begging his father-in-law to send Mrs Armour to Jean's side as her time was near and he could not be with her. He also told Armour the seriousness of his own condition: "I have now been a week at salt-water, & though I think I have got some good by it, yet I have some secret fears that this business will be dangerous if not fatal."

The letters were painful to write, but they had to be sent. To Gilbert he poured out his fears:

> Dear Brother,
> It will be no very pleasing news to you to be told that I am dangerously ill, & not likely to get better. – An inveterate rheumatism has reduced me to such a state of debility, & my appetite is totally gone, so that I can scarcely stand on my legs. – I have been a week at sea-bathing, & I will continue there all the summer. – God help my wife & children, if I am taken from their head! – They will be poor indeed. – I have contracted one or two serious debts, partly from my illness these many months & partly

from too much thoughtlessness as to expense when I came to town that will cut in too much on the little I leave them in your hands. – Remember me to my Mother.

Two days later another bill struck new fear into him. The tailor from whom he had bought his volunteer uniform was apparently dissolving his partnership and wanted to collect all outstanding debts. Burns owed him seven pounds, four shillings, and in his disordered mind the tailor's letter conjured up visions of death in a debtor's prison. The humiliation was more than he could bear: in agony he wrote to his cousin James Burnes in Montrose and to Thomson in Edinburgh, asking for five pounds.

For a short time the seabathing seemed to help; then a new attack of fever came on, worse than ever, and he was taken home to Dumfries on 18th July. By now he was unable to stand up, his frame shook, his tongue was parched and from time to time he became delirious. He now wrote his last letter – to Jean's father in Mauchline:

Do, for Heaven's sake, send Mrs Armour here immediately. My wife is hourly expecting to be put to bed. Good God! what a situation for her to be in, poor girl, without a friend! I returned from sea-bathing quarters today, and my medical friends would almost persuade me that I am better; but I think and feel that my strength is so gone that the disorder will prove fatal to me.

The four young children were sent off to the Lewars' house opposite, and Jessy Lewars spent much time nursing Burns and tending Jean. Even in these last days, when he rallied, the poet teased Jessy and talked about her future. He told her that she would marry James Thomson, a writer in the town – and she did, on 3rd June 1799.

On 19th July Syme was called to the house and afterwards he wrote to Cunningham in Edinburgh:

I cannot dwell on the scene. It overpowers me – yet gracious God were it they will recover him! He had life enough to acknowledge me, and Mrs Burnes said he had been calling on you and me continually. He made a wonderful exertion when I took him by the hand. With a strong voice he said, "I am much better today – I shall soon be well again, for I command my spirits and my mind. But yesterday I resigned myself to death." Alas, it will not do.

Soon his strength left him again, the fever increased and delirium returned. In the streets little knots of people passed on every scrap of information about his condition, gradually becoming more anxious as the news worsened. At last, on 22nd July, word went round – Robert Burns's brave heart had given out. There was nothing to wait for; and they dispersed.

16

Immortal Mortal

It was a fine funeral.

In their hearts the people of Dumfries knew the real worth of Robert Burns, and John Syme, his closest friend in the town, determined to give him the best funeral possible. He rallied civic leaders, Excise colleagues, Volunteer comrades and friends at every social level to honour their most distinguished citizen. For four days, while all was arranged, Burns lay in the shadowed house on the brow of the hill in Mill Vennel where he had died.

For his widow it must have been a trying time: sorrow for a loved husband, worry over the future, the need for composure as condolences were received and details of the funeral discussed, all seemed to be given an added dimension of tragedy by the fact that she was large with Burns's child – her ninth – and that the first spasm of labour was expected at any moment. It was right that her husband should be given a grand funeral, but Jean knew that she could not be present at it.

On 25th July the funeral took place from the Town Hall. The Volunteers owed the poet a debt which they now repaid by leading the procession and flanking the poet's coffin, on which were set his Volunteer uniform hat and sword. Comrades from the Angus Fencibles and the Regiment of the Cinque Ports, then stationed in the town, lined the undulating pathway from the Town Hall to the top of the hill on which stood St Michael's Church – the Kirk in which Burns and his family had worshipped Sunday by Sunday. Slowly the cortège passed, the Dead March from Handel's *Saul* echoing over the quays on the Nith where much of the poet's Excise work had been done and up the hill to the tall, well-set house in which

Jean lay in labour. Three volleys fired over the open grave in St Michael's kirkyard saluted the departure of Robert Burns and the arrival of another son, whom Jean named after Dr Maxwell, the doctor who had prescribed the treatment which had probably hastened her husband's death.

As summer gave way to autumn Burns's family and friends faced two main problems. They had to preserve his good character and literary reputation and to ensure that Jean and the children did not starve. Maria Riddell, with the acute intuition of an intelligent woman, was disturbed about the first of these; John Syme tackled the second. And in time the two needs merged so that one helped the other. The strange thing is that Jean remained completely passive throughout, maintaining a stolid silence which suggested that she cared neither about her husband's reputation nor about her own future. She just let events happen.

Maria Riddell remembered her last conversation with the poet in which he had talked of those who would not hesitate to attack his character. Thus she at once wrote a *Memoir* which was published a few days later in the Dumfries paper. It was a character-study full of warmth which yet recognized (and accepted) faults of character. "It is only on the gem we are disturbed to see the dust," she wrote. "The pebble may be soiled, and we do not regard it."

Maria's instinct proved right: exaggerated and inaccurate anecdotes about the poet's way of life soon circulated freely, and many men who should have known better added to the mass of half-truths and untruths which spread over the poet's reputation like weeds in an untended garden. As far away as Liverpool Dr James Currie, a Dumfriesshire man deeply interested in Burns, heard the rumours and wrote to Syme: "By what I have heard, he was not very correct in his conduct; and a report goes about that he died of the effects of habitual drinking." Syme did not deny this.

The first blow was struck in cold print only two days after the poet's death, when the *Edinburgh Evening Courant* published an obituary, written by George Thomson, to whom Burns had generously supplied over a hundred songs. Said Thomson:

The public, to whose amusement he has so largely contributed, will learn with regret that his extraordinary endowments were accompanied with frailties which rendered them useless to himself and his family. The last months of his short life were spent in indulgence; and his widow, with five infant children and in the hourly expectation of a sixth, is now left without any resource but what a hope from the regard due to the memory of her husband.

It was an impertinence from a man who had never met Burns and to whom the poet had given superb songs almost to the end of his life. And unfortunately it set the pattern for other biographers and encouraged enemies such as James Maxwell, a poetaster from Paisley, and the Reverend William Peebles (Poet Willie of "The Kirk's Alarm") to attack Burns's poetry as immoral.

Robert Heron, a minister turned writer, was jealous of Burns's success and bore a grudge against the poet for a bitter jibe Burns had made against him six years earlier when he had failed to deliver a letter from Ellisland to Dr Blacklock in Edinburgh. Burns had said:

The Ill-thief blaw the Heron south!
And never drink be near his drouth!
He tald mysel, by word o' mouth,
　He'd tak my letter:
I lippen'd to the chiel in truth,
　And bade nae better. –

But aiblins[1] honest master Heron　　　　　　　　[1perhaps
Had at the time some dainty Fair One,
To ware his theologic care on,
　And holy study:
And tired o' Saul to waste his lear[2] on,　　　　　[2learning
　E'en tried the Body. –

Heron had his revenge. His *Memoir*, published early in 1797, contained a shrewd assessment of the poet's work, but it also told the world without restraint or delicacy that Burns was a drunkard, a fornicator, a boor; that he had contempt for the rich and great; and that his preference was for company found in taverns, or brothels. It accused him of neglecting his farm and spoke belittlingly of his work as an Exciseman.

Against this tide of exaggeration and lies John Syme worked tirelessly in Dumfries and Alexander Cunningham struggled in Edinburgh to ensure that Jean and her children should not go in need.

They had begun before the poet's death, Syme writing to Cunningham on 19th July: "We must think on what can be done for his [Burns's] family. I fear they are in a pitiable condition." Before that letter arrived, however, Cunningham had given thought to the matter and suggested a subscription followed by "the Sale of his posthumous works, Letters, Songs, &c., to a respectable London bookseller".

Within a week of Burns's death seventy guineas had been subscribed around Dumfries, and plans were afoot for a wider appeal. Alas, in Scotland there was apathy and in Edinburgh even bitterness, for the great men of the capital had a long memory: all they offered Cunningham was "cold civility and humiliating advice". Cunningham concluded that "the poor Bard's frailties – excuse this vile word – were not only so well known here, but often, I believe, exaggerated". An edition of Burns's poems was subscribed, but in hard cash less than £180 was received.

Even in Ayrshire there was little enthusiasm, to Syme's intense annoyance: "Col. Fullarton etc, in Ayrshire have as yet done nothing – nay, those friends in Ayr etc. whom the Bard has immortalized have not contributed a sous!!! By heavens, they should be immortally d—d, and a list of the d—d should be made out."

In England the response was rather better, mainly thanks to men such as Currie in Liverpool and James Shaw in London, but even so by spring 1797 Syme had only £500 and promises of a few hundred pounds more. Eventually Shaw collected £400 in London, so Jean was able to live out her life in comfort. Gilbert was his brother's biggest debtor, and it now became clear just how generous Robert had been to his family. Unfortunately, Mossgiel could not repay his debt, and over the next year he came in for some rough handling from his brother's executors. Year by year Gilbert kept his account book with all the care he had taken in the Lochlie days, but to no avail – it took him more than twenty years to clear the account.

With the prospect of a publication to help the family, Syme
and Cunningham asked friends and correspondents to pass
over to them any poems or letters in their possession. A
committee was set up in Dumfries, with Syme as the prime
mover, but as time dragged on enthusiasm flagged, and Syme
was left virtually alone to keep interest alive. Although Syme
had plenty of enthusiasm he had neither literary knowledge
nor flair to edit the work. He was not clear exactly what kind
of book would help the family; instinct told him that it had to
be something more than a book of poems, and Dr Currie
confirmed this. In fact the doctor showed such lively
enthusiasm for the project that he volunteered his own services
as editor. Almost immediately he withdrew the offer in the
hope that Professor Dugald Stewart, an Ayrshire man, or
Syme himself might be persuaded to write it. But the
committee in Dumfries, having found a volunteer, would not
let him go. Reluctantly the Liverpool doctor agreed.

Currie's suggestion was that, with the help of William
Roscoe, a sympathetic Liverpool writer, he would edit the
poems and add a life of the poet. His object was to raise money
for the Burns family; there was no question of attempting a
definitive biography. In fact, Currie said: "Everything that is
now printed should be as free of exceptions as may be, but that
a future volume may contain such things as are now too
vehement, but which yet may stand the test of time."

Currie reserved his final decision on the work until he
received the poet's papers, but when these arrived the poor
doctor was appalled at the size of his task. He wrote:

I viewed the huge and shapeless mass with astonishment! Instead
of finding, as I expected, a selection of his papers, with such
annotations as might clear up any obscurities – of papers perused
and approved by his friends as fit for publication – I received the
complete sweepings of his drawers and of his desk (as it appeared
to me), even to the copy-book on which his little boy had been
practising writing. No one had given these papers a perusal, or
even an inspection; the sheep were not separated from the goats;
and – what has, perhaps, not happened before since the
beginning to the world – the manuscripts of a man of genius,
unarranged by himself and unexamined by his family or friends,
were sent, with all their sins on their head, to meet the eye of an
entire stranger!

An entire stranger! That unfortunate phrase has been used to poison Currie's memory and reputation. It is true that the Liverpool doctor had met the poet only once – and briefly at that – but he had a high regard for Burns and, through his many friends in Dumfries, knew much about the poet's life. He was no stranger to Burns, and he was moved by the finest of motives – desire to help the family. Currie was a Scot, deeply interested in things Scottish, politically in sympathy with Burns, and trusted and respected by many key people in the poet's life. He had one other advantage: he was willing to edit the work, which was more than any man in Scotland could be persuaded to do.

The mass of material on his desk was not the only problem Dr Currie had to face, for an equal amount important for his work remained in the hands of dozens of correspondents and friends who were coy about making public their association with the poet. Maria Riddell was the worst culprit: she went to great lengths to suppress her letters, and her diaries were so mutilated (presumably by herself) that they contain no reference to the poet. Yet Maria worked hard to try to persuade Clarinda to part with Sylvander's letters from that passionate winter in Edinburgh. Mrs Dunlop, who had in her possession more of Burns's letters than anyone else, made only the most carefully-edited excerpts available, and the letters of lesser people such as Peggy Chalmers and Robert Ainslie were destroyed. Indeed, Ainslie spent the rest of his life denying his association with his former friend, though that would not have surprised Burns, who had discovered in his lifetime how unreliable that friendship was.

Currie had no idea how accurate the documents were, and at the doctor's request Syme and Gilbert travelled to Liverpool and spent a hard-working fortnight answering questions and helping with editorial problems. Maria Riddell broke her journey at Liverpool on the way south in November 1796 to discuss plans and leave a number of manuscripts from which Currie could work. But all that was hardly enough. Syme's memory was unreliable, Gilbert had seen little of his brother during the last years of his life, and Maria still maintained that no "shining correspondence" had passed between her and the poet – a remarkable claim in the light of their literary affinity.

All this took so much time that it was almost the middle of 1798 before Dr Currie was in a position even to assess the material. He was now a sick man, but he worked diligently and without payment to produce a four-volume edition of Burns's poems with a biography. It was not intended to be a "warts and all" portrait, although Currie repeated, but without substantiation, many of the criticisms made of the poet's character – the criticisms of which even Maria Riddell had written in her *Memoir* and which none of the poet's friends denied in the years after his death. Indeed, it is the silence of these friends which hurt Burns much more than Currie's strictures.

Currie's mistake was to point a moral:

> Hitherto Burns, though addicted to excess in social parties, had abstained from the habitual use of strong liquors, and his constitution had not suffered any permanent injury from the irregularities of his conduct. In Dumfries, temptations to the sin that so easily beset him, continually presented themselves; and his irregularities grew by degrees into habits. These temptations unhappily occurred during his engagements in the business of his office, as well as during his hours of relaxation; and though he clearly foresaw the consequences of yielding to them, his appetites and sensations, which could not pervert the dictates of his judgment, finally triumphed over the powers of his will.

What a pity Alexander Findlater, Burns's Excise colleague, took fifteen years to come forward with the statement that Burns was exemplary in his attention to his duties and even jealous of his reputation as a good officer. There are, of course, indications that the poet-excise officer enjoyed a drink in the course of his duties, but even when he was denounced to his employers because of his political views there was no suggestion that his work was unsatisfactory. Currie would have learnt this by visiting Dumfries instead of letting Syme, Gilbert and Maria Riddell come to him.

Worse still was an innuendo which invites the worst possible interpretation and which is the hardest to answer: "He who suffers the pollution of inebriation, how shall he escape other pollutions? But let us refrain from the mention of errors over which delicacy and humanity draw the veil."

In the long term Currie's strictures may have done the poet

little harm, but unfortunately, after he had produced his biography, Currie did not return the papers to their owners, and after the doctor's death they were lost, destroyed or scattered to the four winds. A number have reappeared, but many have been lost, and gaps exist in our knowledge of Burns's life. Because the papers were not available to others Currie's account set the pattern for writers for over a century, and too much that was mere gossip passed on by Currie was accepted as fact by others.

Currie achieved his purpose: the publication raised nearly £2000 for Burns's family, but most people have thought the price too high.

In spite of the early biographers, there were enough men prepared to make their own judgment of Burns the man and Burns the poet. From these enthusiasts there grew up a movement which has raised Robert Burns to the status of a demi-god and his poetry to a cult against which no ill word must be said. Many of his followers insist that the poet and all his works be accepted uncritically and condemn any who dare to question either. Robert Louis Stevenson, for one, has never been forgiven for his criticism of the poet.

The Burns cult began quite suddenly and spontaneously. Within five years of the poet's death the cottage at Alloway, taken over by the Incorporation of Shoemakers in Ayr and let as an inn, became a place of pilgrimage. On the poet's birthday in 1801 "a number of non-commissioned officers and privates of the Argyll Militia went out from Ayr to visit the cottage, attended by the band of the Regiment, who played a number of appropriate airs". The landlord welcomed such visitors with enthusiasm for their bar custom but showed so little knowledge of Burns that when the poet Keats visited Alloway in 1822 he complained that "The dull dog made me write a dull sonnet."

The first Burns Club was set up at Greenock in 1801 and, although we have few details of it, the first Burns Supper appeared to have been held in that same year. At Alloway on 29th January 1802 nine people (including "Orator Bob" Aiken, John Ballantine and Dr Patrick Douglas) sat down to "a comfortable dinner, of which sheep's head and haggis formed an interesting part". Accepting the date given by

Currie as Burns's birthday (and who did not believe Currie implicitly in 1802?) they agreed to meet on 29th January each year. Thus began the tradition of a supper of haggis washed down with whisky and eulogies of Burns.

Soon Alexander Boswell, son of Dr Johnson's biographer, and the Reverend Hamilton Paul instituted a movement to erect a memorial at Alloway. Financial support was slow at first, but eventually £3000 was subscribed for the monument of nine Corinthian pillars, one for each of the muses, crowned by a cupola, overlooking Tam O'Shanter's Auld Brig O' Doon. In St Michael's churchyard in Dumfries a grand white mausoleum was erected to take the place of the simple grave in which the poet was first interred. Scotland was now making up for her tardiness in helping Jean and her children in 1796.

In August 1844 thousands, Burns's sons and sister among them, marched to Alloway and at the cottage doffed their hats in the pouring rain. The Earl of Eglinton, a showman in the grand manner, had organized a luncheon for a thousand people – paying himself for those who could not afford the fifteen shillings for the meal which *Punch*'s Editor described as "a piece of cold tongue, a plate of gooseberries almost ripe, and a pint of some mystery calling itself sherry". With some justification he entitled his article "Repentant Scotland". Burns was already being taken with dour seriousness by his countrymen, *Punch* noted: "Scotland is tremendously earnest in all that relates to Burns: in earnest alike her gratitude and her penitence."

Today attitudes have changed hardly at all.

The centenary of the poet's birth in 1859 brought a great resurgence of interest not merely in Scotland but throughout the English-speaking world and even in Europe, where he was now being discovered. Every town of size in England held its own celebration, but the centrepiece was a gathering of 15,000 people at the Crystal Palace in London to hear speeches, music and the winning poem in a competition which had attracted over six hundred entries. In Scotland there were processions, dinners and concerts by the score. A triumphal arch was erected in Dumfries and at Ayr a long procession marched to the Auld Kirk for divine service and then on to Alloway. Shops closed for the day in many towns, although in

Aberdeen, where the people are cannier, they shut only for the afternoon. The poet's son told his audience that his father had once said to his mother: "Jean, one hundred years hence they'll think mair o' me than they do now." He was right: by 1859 Burns's enemies were all dead, and the new generation of Scots would not hear a word against him.

Gradually the Burns movement became more organized. The Burns Federation was formed in 1885, and an annual *Burns Chronicle*, devoted to its activities and to articles about the poet, started in 1891. The Federation now has a membership of over three hundred clubs.

The centenary of Burns's death in 1896 gave enormous impetus to the Burns cult, with celebrations around the world. In addition, the Henley-Henderson edition of Burns's poetry, published that year, brought a new degree of scholarship to his work. Of course there remained much adulation of the legend rather than the poet and, as William Wallace, who had revised Robert Chambers's edition of the life and works of Burns, said at the unveiling of a statue to Highland Mary in Dunoon, it was strange that no statue had been erected to Jean in Dumfries.

Another half century passed and was duly celebrated, but during those years more scholarship had been applied to the poet's life and writings, so that Burns the man could then be seen more clearly. Perhaps this concentration of research into the poet's life endangers the overall view of Burns, however. We are in danger of studying the individual events of his life in such detail that we no longer see the full portrait.

Attitudes to Burns have changed, and there is no longer any need to talk in whispers about him. His life is not a matter for dark mutterings, sniggers and nudges, which it was for so long among the ignorant; it fails to shock now that we understand the man better. Even "The Merry Muses", which shocked Lord Byron so deeply, have now been published and revealed as moderately amusing, mediocre verse, far less capable of horrifying than the chilling letter Burns wrote about his treatment of Jean just before her second confinement.

Robert Burns was what he was because of environment as much as because of inherited gifts. Both parents gave him intelligence, and in addition each gave him complimentary qualities which can be clearly traced. His mother endowed him with the rich heritage of song and legend from Carrick; a treasure of book-learning was his father's contribution. These raw materials were fashioned by an upbringing in a changing countryside at a time of national upheaval.

The second half of the eighteenth century was an age in which men had little to which to cling as the way of life they and their forbears had known was swept away by a new order. Farming had become a science and industry a treadmill for the mass of townsmen. The timid were moulded by machines, while the brilliant often rebelled.

The little farming world in Ayrshire was as insecure as elsewhere. Ambition, even that dour Mearns quality which fired William Burnes, was not enough. Time, money and good fortune were needed to sweeten the sour earth which only a decade earlier had been untilled bog or heath. William Burnes had none of these advantages – he was ageing, poor and short of good luck – and so, from his earliest days, Robert saw worry-lined faces around him and heard the factor's snash as background conversation. To a sensitive youngster it was frightening and infuriating by turns, and Robert grew up to be suspicious of, though not opposed to or jealous of, those who were better off. He was prepared to use privilege to his advantage – to obtain books as a boy, to promote his poems and to win preferment at the expense of others if necessary. He would strike out wildly with an epigram or a sharp remark when he was crossed. This fiery bluster was a sure reflection of the man and the age.

Burns never forgot that he belonged to the tenant farming community: he knew who was below him and who was above, and he got on well with the best of both. Indeed, he had that remarkable Scottish quality of accepting or rejecting a man for his worth rather than for his rank. In Edinburgh Burns tried the intellectuals, found them wanting and rejected them just as surely as they rejected him. It was not a desire for the gay life or bawdy company that drove him into taverns when he might have held court in a New Town drawing-room: it was the fact that he recognized people outside the magic literary circle as more open and genuine than those within it.

From youth Burns was classed as a rebel and consequently

had many enemies. He was a misfit in the hypocritical, narrow-minded village community, an outcast in the Auld Licht Kirk, but he had one great weapon of retaliation – his pen. Soon his enemies came to fear him, but they fought back implacably. Robert was able to react in only one way – by boldly brazening it out, defying individual and organization alike. This shocked Mauchline, made Edinburgh society turn its back on him, and cost him friends in Dumfries.

Burns's natural reaction was bravado – the tied hair and proud mien of youth, the bold retaliatory verse when he was called to the cutty stool alongside Lizzie Paton, and in maturity the spirited letter to the Riddells after the Sabine Rape incident, when they wanted a piece of humble pie.

And yet, Thomson, Heron and Currie were wrong when they said or insinuated that he had lost respect through drunkenness and whoring in those last years in Dumfries. People who saw him day by day knew better: they were well aware that Burns was a sick man doing an exacting job well, that excesses were only occasional, that he found time in addition to his Excise work and writing to be an active member of the community, helping to found a library and to organize the Volunteers. That is why, at his death, they did not leave him to be buried in a pauper's grave but gave him a civic funeral.

It was among those who knew him least that the worst stories spread, the tales of decadence.

For a man with such a reputation for ruining women Robert Burns was singularly well loved by the opposite sex. His heart quickened at the sight of a pretty face, from those early harvest evenings when he removed thistles from Nelly Kilpatrick's hands to the twilight days of 1796 when he chaffed his nurse, Jessy Lewars. His heart was tinder, he readily admitted, and it caught fire time and time again.

Burns wooed passionately and deeply, with a love which was basic – so elemental it frightened off the finer ladies more than once and marred his chances with them. He was from the country, and there full sexual intimacy was natural in a relationship between man and woman, and bastard children were accepted and loved as deeply as those blessed by marriage.

Burns's relationship with women was on four levels. Those such as Meg Cameron and Jenny Clow meant nothing to him the morning after and we would have heard nothing of them but for the man's damned fertility! They were a flash, quickly extinguished. Next came those with whom Burns had a short, sharp (and often wounding) affair – Lizzie Paton, Anna Park and Jean Lorimer. None of these made any call on Burns's intellect but offered only earthy passion which made the poet's pulse beat "a furious ratann".

It must have pained Burns to realize that every woman capable of sharing his passion for literature was beyond his reach socially and sexually. Worse still, Clarinda and Maria Riddell were already married. In the civilized, cultured atmosphere of Harvieston, the more innocent Peggy Chalmers was quickly frightened off by Burns's hot-blooded love-making which, in her social circle, must have appeared coarse and artless. She had known him in Edinburgh the previous winter and must have heard something of his reputation, so when he came to woo her she quickly called a halt. However, even if his wooing had been gentler or more artful, one must doubt whether she would have accepted him instead of the stability – albeit dull stability – of Lewis Hay.

Mrs Dunlop and the wives of such intellectual friends as Dugald Stewart and the Reverend George Lawrie represent the fourth aspect of the poet's relationship with women. They were mother figures, ready to advise, comfort and guide. He could talk to them without love intervening, and to Mrs Dunlop he wrote pages and received in return reams of barely legible advice, which she accused him from time to time (probably quite rightly) of not reading. Even to staid old Mrs Dunlop Robert could not resist a sexual boast. In a letter telling her that Jean was pregnant and that they proposed to name the baby Frances or Francis in her honour he said: "Perhaps in the case of a boy, you would rather wish to wait for one of your own Sex, that might take the exact name; and as I have not the smallest doubt of being very soon able to accommodate you in that way too, I shall expect your commands sometime before the important period."

Two people stand outside these classifications, unwilling to be pushed into any category, yet demanding a place in the scale of Burns's love. They are Highland Mary Campbell and Jean Armour.

Mary, "the White Rose" of Victorian legend, nowadays tends to be banished to the casual bed with Jenny Clow, but that is hardly fair. It is reasonable to assume, since the poet did not mention Mary during the summer of 1786 and kept silent about her for so long after her death, that he never intended to marry her. In fact, the Highland Mary affair was probably as painful as others; but he had to keep quiet that summer because most of his friends knew of his vows to Jean Armour, and to marry Mary Campbell would have been bigamy. Furthermore, if she were pregnant by him, he could not let the Kirk know. So Burns kept silent, bottled up his remorse for nearly three years after her death, until, on the verge of a nervous breakdown, he poured it all out to Mrs Dunlop.

Jean is shown to us as the faithful girl who bided her time until Robert was ready to marry her, but there is also a suggestion that she was a second best. There can be no doubt that she was such in as much as Robert Burns hankered after an intellectual woman and married Jean Armour when he realized that intellectual women were beyond his reach socially. She was second best, too, in that, apart from singing over occasional songs, she could do nothing to further his literary career. On the other hand she made a home for him, she helped to run his farm, she reared his children well, and she made no great demands in return. Jean waited patiently at Ellisland or the Mill Vennel house while her husband dined with the great, but she did not hector him if he returned home in his cups. She had no literary views to foist on to him but was simply a good wife, who left him to get on with his main interest in life and understood when he went astray. Of course Jean appeared a dull drudge to smart Edinburgh people such as Bob Ainslie, but she suited Robert Burns very well, and he never said a word against her.

To dismiss Burns's love-making as a kind of nasty, ribald joke, as the ignorant sometimes do, is just as wrong as to build him into a saintly wooer. Burns's passion was hot, it was basic – he wanted everything a woman could give him and he was seldom satisfied sexually. "Oh, what a fool I am in love!" he said to Clarinda. "What an extravagant prodigal of affection! Why are your sex called the tender sex, when I never have met with one who can repay me in passion? They are either not so rich in love as I am, or they are niggards where I am lavish."

He probably sinned no more than many of his contemporaries, but he was unlucky in being found out and pursued in youth by the "unco guid" who bore him a grudge and, after success came, by those who thought he could well support his offspring. He was not a man to hide his sins, and the fact that he was Robert Burns the poet made these sins more noteworthy.

Today we salute Burns, not as a great lover but as the man who helped Scotland preserve her language and her traditions. During his life Scotland was fast becoming a mere appendage of England, and her language and lore were in grave danger of dying out. Poets aped their southern neighbours, with grand heroic couplets full of artificiality. Burns tried this but soon took up where Allan Ramsay and Robert Fergusson left off and carried to the people the great tradition of Scottish vernacular poetry. The fact that he was taken up by the literati in Edinburgh helped his work, but in the long term what really counted was that servant men and women remote from the capital eagerly paid away the whole of their wages for a copy of the Kilmarnock Edition. Burns had reached the core of the Scottish soul and has continued to do so ever since.

For Burns, poetry was not something to sit down and compose – it was a way of life. He had no writing pattern but rhymed as he ploughed, or harvested or walked the countryside. There is thus a constant vibrant movement in his verse, which has the rhythm of life. It is not surprising therefore that he took up song-writing and that his songs always started from the music. He worked through emotion towards words which caught the mood of the air exactly, and the resulting songs are a perfect match of lyric and music. Nearly four hundred, many of them the most exquisite in the language, are an incredible output for a man who was working against such great odds and against time.

A language and tradition cannot be preserved merely because a poet is using them: what he says is important too, and one commentator, writing of the 1859 centenary celebrations, reached the heart of the matter when he said: "It is ... partly because he represents his countrymen more thoroughly both in their virtues and their failings than any other man of equal note among them."

Burns says clearly what every Scot feels; he says it beautifully and with a dash of that sentimentality to which the nation is so partial. His truths come to mind so easily that many have become clichés. It is deep truth to say that

> The best laid schemes o' mice and Men,
>   Gang aft agley,
> An' lea'e us nought but grief an' pain,
>   For promised joy

or is it an obvious cliché?
   Of course we are aware that

> The heart's aye, the part aye,
> That makes us right or wrang,

but has it ever been so perfectly expressed?

Perhaps this ability to put on paper the feelings of all men, to remind them of their best qualities and of the importance of the brotherhood of man is the reason why the Burns cult remains so strong from generation to generation. Scotland still reaps a fine harvest from that genius who spent a mere thirty-seven summers on her soil. The gatherings on 25th January may seem to some to be little more than an opportunity to drink whisky and eat haggis and to tell the world how Scottish we all are. To the Scot, however, it is a time to take stock of himself, of his life and of his fellow-men. The Burns Supper is good therapy for any man and any nation – in its best aspects it does immense good.

What better gift could any man give to his country, and how many nations will go on year by year expressing their gratitude?

Bibliography

Since Maria Riddell wrote her *Memoir* in the dying days of July 1796, innumerable books, pamphlets and articles have been published about Robert Burns and the Ayrshire of his time. This bibliography lists only a small selection, but among them are the most important.

Agriculture, Reports of Board of. *General View of Agriculture in the County of Ayr*; 1793, Col. William Fullarton; 1811, William Aiton.

Angus-Butterworth, L.M. *Robert Burns and the Eighteenth-Century Revival of Scottish Vernacular Poetry*. Aberdeen, 1969.

Brown, Hilton. *There Was a Lad*. London, 1949.

Brown, R.L. *Clarinda. The Intimate Story of Robert Burns and Agnes Maclehose*. Desbury, 1968.

——. *Robert Burns's Tours of the Highlands and Stirlingshire*. Ipswich, 1973.

——. *Robert Burns's Tour of the Borders*. Ipswich, 1972.

Burns, Robert. *The Book of Robert Burns*. Ed. Charles Rogers (vols 1 and 2) and J.C. Higgins (vol 3). Edinburgh, 1889-91.

——. *Commonplace Book*. Facsimile Edition. Ed. J.C. Ewing and Davidson Cook. 1838.

——. *Letters of Robert Burns*; Ed. J. De Lancey Ferguson. Oxford, 1931.

——. *The Merry Muses of Caledonia*. Ed. James Barke and Sydney Goodsir Smith. London, 1965.

——. *The Merry Muses of Caledonia*. Edinburgh, 1800.

——. *Poems and songs of Robert Burns*; Ed. James Kinsley. London, 1968.

——. *Poetry of Robert Burns*; Ed. W.E. Henley and T.F. Henderson. Edinburgh, 1896.

——. *Poems Chiefly in the Scottish Dialect*. (Kilmarnock Edition). Kilmarnock, 1786.

——. *Poems Chiefly in the Scottish Dialect*. (1st Edinburgh Edition) Edinburgh, 1787.

——. *Poems Chiefly in the Scottish Dialect*. (2nd Edinburgh Edition) Edinburgh, 1794.

Burns, Robert. *Songs of Robert Burns*; Ed. J.C. Dick. 1903
——. *Works of Robert Burns*; Ed. James Currie. London, 1800.
——. *Works of Robert Burns*; Ed. Allan Cunningham. London, 1834.
——. *Life and Works of Robert Burns*; Ed. Robert Chambers. London 1850.
——. *Life and Works of Robert Burns*; Ed. W. Scott Douglas. London, 1871.
Burns Chronicle Published annually since 1892.
Carswell, Catherine. *Life of Robert Burns*. London, 1930.
Crichton-Browne, Sir James. *Burns From a New Point of View*. London, 1926.
Currie, William Wallace. *Memoir of the Life, Writings and Correspondence of James Currie*. London 1831.
Daiches, David. *Robert Burns*. London, 1952.
Dent, Alan. *Burns in his Time*. London, 1966.
Douglas, Hugh. *Portrait of the Burns Country*. London, 1968.
Egrerer, J.W. *A Bibliography of Robert Burns*. London, 1964.
Ferguson, J. De Laney. *Pride and Passion*. New York, 1939.
Fitzhugh, R.T. *Robert Burns. The Man and the Poet*. London, 1971.
Ford, Robert. *The Heroines of Burns*. Paisley, 1906.
Gladstone, Hugh S. *Maria Riddell, The Friend of Burns*. Dumfries, 1915.
Henderson, T.F. *The Auld Ayrshire of Robert Burns*. London, 1906.
Hecht, Hans, *Robert Burns. The Man and His Work*. Edinburgh, 1936/50.
Hill, John C. *Life and Work of Robert Burns in Irvine*. London, 1933.
——. *Love Songs and Heroines of Robert Burns*. London, 1961.
Johnson, James. *Scots Musical Museum*. Edinburgh, 1787-1803.
Keith, Christina. *The Russet Coat*. London, 1956.
Kinnear, George H. *History of Glenbervie*. 1910.
Letham, E.H. *Burns and Tarbolton*. Kilmarnock, 1900.
Lindsay, Maurice. *Robert Burns. The Man, His Work, The Legend*. London, 1954.
——. *The Burns Encyclopaedia*. London, 1959.
Lockhart, J.G. *Life of Robert Burns*. Edinburgh, 1828.
M'Bain, James. *Burns's Cottage*. Glasgow, 1904.
M'Dowall, William. *Robert Burns in Dumfriesshire*. Edinburgh, 1870.
M'Lehose, W.E. (Ed.) *Correspondence between Burns and Clarinda*. Edinburgh, 1843.
M'Naught, Duncan. *The Truth About Burns*. Glasgow, 1921.
M'Vie, John. *Burns and Stair*. Kilmarnock, 1927.
——. *Robert Burns and Edinburgh*. Kilmarnock, 1969.
Mitchell, John. *Memories of Ayrshire about 1780* (Printed: Miscellany, Scottish Hist. Soc. 1939).

Montgomerie, William (Ed.). *Essays on Robert Burns* by six contemporary writers.

Muir, J. *Robert Burns till his Seventeenth Year*. Kilmarnock, 1929.

Rae, Elsie S. *Poet's Pilgrimage*. Glasgow, 1960.

Robertson, William. *Old Ayrshire Days*. Ayr, 1905.

Shairp, Principal *Robert Burns*. London, 1879.

Shaw, James Edward. *Ayrshire 1745-1950*. Edinburgh, 1953.

Skinner, Basil C. *Robert Burns. Authentic Likenesses*. Edinburgh, 1963.

Snyder, Franklin Bliss. *Life of Robert Burns*. New York, 1932.

———. *Robert Burns. His Personality, His Reputation & His Art*. Toronto, 1936.

Strawhorn, John. *Ayrshire at the Time of Burns*. (Collection of Ayrshire Archaeological and Natural History Soc.) Ayr, 1959.

Thomson, George (Ed.) *Select Collection of Original Scottish Airs*. Edinburgh, 1793-1818.

Thornton, R.B. James Currie. *The Entire Stranger and Robert Burns*. Edinburgh, 1963.

Wallace, William (Ed.) Robert Burns and Mrs Dunlop. London, 1898.

Will, William. *Robert Burns as a Volunteer*. Glasgow, 1919.

———. *John Murdoch. Tutor of Robert Burns*. Glasgow, 1929.

Ward, J. Maxwell. *Robert Burns and the Riddell Family*. Dumfries, 1922.

Wright, Andrew. *Present State of Husbandry in Scotland*.

Index

Poems and songs with + against the title are quoted